Introduction to Police Science

John L. Sullivan

ASSISTANT PROFESSOR AND
COORDINATOR OF POLICE SCIENCE
PASADENA CITY COLLEGE

McGRAW-HILL
BOOK COMPANY

Edward J Steenberg

Introduction to Police Science

New York
St. Louis
San Francisco
London
Toronto
Sydney

Dedicated to all police science students who are seeking a career in law enforcement and to their instructors for their specialized guidance.

Preface

This book opens the door of law enforcement by providing students with a realistic preview of police work. It was written for the many thousands of police officers-to-be who are now attending our schools and junior colleges and who are considering, or have already decided on, a career in law enforcement.

Introduction to Police Science focuses on three important fields that are of great concern to the potential law enforcement officer: (1) a career in law enforcement: what it demands, what the student needs to bring to it, and how the student may begin such a career, (2) crime: criminal law and how law enforcement actually works, and (3) police organization: how it developed, how it functions, and how it solves the problems of public relations and police ethics.

The early chapters of the book explore specific job qualifications and the numerous career opportunities that now exist in police work on local, state, Federal, and private levels. This career information helps a student to analyze his own mental, physical, and moral qualifications and to match these traits with the specific job requirements of many jobs typical of police work. Thus, the student is helped to make his own decision about whether or not he qualifies for police work in interest, aptitude, and ability.

The second important area of police science with which the book deals is the history and development of police organization, traced from its early English beginnings to the present. Criminal behavior is also discussed, as is criminal law and the role of the police in modern law enforcement. Here the student can develop a working knowledge of the history, the responsibilities, the purposes, and the scope of today's police profession. Here, too, the student gets a revealing look into criminal behavior and criminal types and sees how the police actually carry out their primary mission of enforcing the law.

A third major portion of the book shows the student how the police are organized, supervised, and trained, how the police organization handles public relations, and how police ethics are important to everyday police work.

All told, this introduction to police science will help the interested student gain important and necessary background knowledge. This knowledge will help him not only to make an intelligent choice of a career in law enforcement, but also to do so with clear understanding and lasting dedication. Even those who may not consider themselves qualified for the demands of police work—every citizen in fact— can get from this book a better comprehension and appreciation of the dedicated service that the law enforcement officer renders to the local, state, and national community.

ACKNOWLEDGMENTS

I little realized, when I began this book, how much help I would need to finish it. The steady encouragement of my wife, Jean, our two sons, Jay and Greg, and our daughter, Laurie Jean, were motivating factors for which I am exceedingly grateful. The excellent typing of Norma Bird and her consistent contribution of time and energy are sincerely appreciated and will long be remembered.

In order to obtain the thinking of police science instructors and co-ordinators, I consulted the following highly regarded police science specialists whose suggestions and ideas greatly assisted in the selection of the subject matter and organization of this book:

Vincent Alfaro, *Grossmont College, El Cajon, California*
Dr. James Carnahan, *California State College at Los Angeles*
Paul Howard, *Bakersfield College, Bakersfield, California*
Robert Crosby, *San Diego City College, San Diego, California*
Charles E. Grant, *Diablo Valley College, Concord, California*
John J. Horgan, *San Bernardino Valley College, San Bernardino, California*
Richard McGrath, *Cerritos College, Norwalk, California*
Gilbert B. Stuckey, *Mt. San Antonio College, Walnut, California*

Since this book is intended to open the doors of law enforcement, the following members of that great calling reviewed and constructively corrected various chapters to make certain that I was opening the right doors factually:

Carl R. Bell, Sergeant, Monrovia Police Department
Wilbur R. Brantley, Sergeant, Los Angeles Police Department
William Bute, Lieutenant, Pasadena Police Department
John C. Elliott, Lieutenant, Pasadena Police Department
John Gillette, Sergeant, South Pasadena Police Department
Evelyn D. Purkapile, Policewoman, Alhambra Police Department
W. Cleon Skousen, former FBI Agent and former Chief of Police,
    Salt Lake City, Utah
Frank Slocum, Special Agent, U.S. Secret Service, Los Angeles
Claud T. Smith, Chief, Civil Division, Los Angeles Sheriff's Office
Martin P. Stornie, Lieutenant, Pasadena Police Department

One section of this book is devoted to security forces. The wise counsel from the following three experts in this field generously and significantly assisted in the compilation of this material:

John J. Canny, Retired Special Agent, FBI, and Special Agent,
                Richfield Corporation, Los Angeles, California
Fred T. McIntyre, Retired Special Agent, FBI, and retired Chief
                Special Agent, May Company, Los Angeles,
                California
Robert Warner, Chief Special Agent, General Telephone Company,
                Santa Monica, California

In conclusion, I would be remiss if I did not publicly acknowledge the splendid cooperation received from the outstanding faculty, employees, and dedicated police science students of Pasadena City College, in general, and those of the engineering and technology department, in particular.

John L. Sullivan

Contents

I would sooner trust the smallest slip of paper for truth, than the strongest and most retentive memory ever bestowed on mortal man.
J. LUMPKIN
Miller v. Cotton, 5 Ga. 341, 349 (1848)

1. Note-taking in police work

DEVELOPING AN IMPORTANT SKILL

The ability to take notes and organize them effectively is essential to success in both police training and police work. Since note-taking is such an important tool in law enforcement, any serious student of police science must learn to take notes. The sooner he acquires this not too difficult skill, the more effectively the student can master police science and the faster he can progress in his law enforcement career.

WHY TAKE NOTES?

The fact is that almost everybody has a frail memory. We too often depend upon our faulty memories and then wonder why we forget vital information. Of course, we cannot all be exceptional like James Farley, former United States Postmaster General, or General George C. Marshall, former Secretary of State and General of the Armies, who were noted for their extraordinary memories. But we can all learn to take notes to assist our fleeting but needed faculty of memory.

1

Experiments in hypnosis reveal that the subconscious mind absorbs and retains nearly 100 percent of all that it receives through the five senses of touch, taste, smell, sound, and sight. However, we cannot take advantage of this ability of our subconscious mind. We must rely on our conscious mind, which does not have sharp recall powers. Even immediately after a given event, the conscious mind can recall only about 10 to 30 percent of the sense impressions received from this event. On a more permanent basis, the mind will retain only 2 to 5 percent of the impressions received from this event. It is obvious that our memories are not very reliable.

Fortunately, the memory can be refreshed by a review of some happening—such as an accident. Recalling an event with the aid of a report or a tape recording or written notes, the conscious mind will remember about 75 percent of the happening. Hence, note-taking is a very convenient and necessary way of refreshing the memory.

The case for good note-taking. The value of taking notes was emphatically brought home to a young police officer in an actual case. This officer had been involved in a large number of cases, including traffic violations. One morning he was handed several subpoenas to appear in court as a witness for the prosecution. As he read the subpoenas, there was one about which he was unable to recall anything regarding the accident or the parties involved. So he took this particular subpoena to his commanding officer and told him that there was some mistake. The commanding officer checked the records and verified that this officer had investigated this case. He casually reminded the officer to check his notebook. When the officer checked his notebook for the day in question, he found that he had an excellent set of notes on the case. By refreshing his memory, he was then able to serve as an excellent witness. This officer later confided that because he had made a habit of taking copious notes, he was spared embarrassment and his testimony helped the jury to render a just decision in this case.

On the other hand, an officer who investigated a drunk-driving case did not fare so well. On the witness stand, he was asked this simple question: "What was the name of the officer who was also assigned to the case?" Since months had elapsed and the officer had worked with many other officers, he was unable to recall the name of his partner on that particular occasion. Worse yet, he had no notes to refresh his memory. Of course, the jury felt that if the officer was unable to remember the name of his brother officer, his memory would also be faulty regarding the defendant in this case. A verdict of acquittal resulted.

During police training, it must be remembered that the student may be tested at some later date on the material presented in class. So, also, when an investigation is made, the investigating officer may subsequently have to testify to the facts of that investigation in a court of law. Unless the student takes notes in class and the officer takes notes in the field, each will have to depend on the 2 to 5 percent memory recall—and this is not sufficient to enable a police student to pass an exam or to allow an officer to testify truthfully and reliably in court. Obviously, it is better to have pale ink than a poor memory.

Eventually, as they accumulate, the daily classroom notes can develop into a valuable source of information for police students. In addition to serving as review material for examinations, this personal library of information may be used as a permanent reference, a guide for handling unfamiliar assignments, and a record of investigative techniques.

Note-taking will also keep alert the student who has a tendency to daydream in class. It will help sustain interest, focus attention, and force concentration. These traits should be developed early in police training because they are so essential to an officer.

How to take notes. The student who takes the best notes is the one who is properly equipped. He must have good note-taking materials and some clear ideas about the best way to write down his notes. A large, three-ring, loose-leaf notebook, using 8½ by 11-inch paper, is best for note-taking in class. This is the most convenient size because insert and handout materials are usually printed on 8½ by 11-inch paper and are often punched to fit this kind of notebook. Paper with wide lines is best because the space allows the person taking notes to make inserts and to write down afterthoughts. A pen is best for writing. If he uses a pencil, the student is plagued by lead breakage, the problem of sharpening, and the problem of smudging. Besides, the pen is less tiring, and when ink is used, the final results are more legible and longer lasting.

The student will achieve good results in recording notes if he follows these helpful hints:

1. Listen to the instructor with undivided attention; especially note key topics and areas emphasized.
2. Be brief but accurate in recording notes.
3. Use the key words used by the instructor.
4. Use abbreviations to speed note-taking.
5. Record all diagrams and illustrations, especially those drawn on the blackboard.
6. Ask questions to clarify a hazy point.
7. If necessary, ask the instructor to repeat questions, quotations, statistics, definitions, numbers, and lists of items.
8. Do not try to write down everything the instructor says; get down the key points.

Outlining classroom notes. A well-planned classroom presentation or lecture is always made according to a logical plan, not left to chance. This means that the instructor has organized his instruction in some orderly fashion. It is important for the police student to be able to follow his instructor's plan when taking notes during class. The instructor will very likely take up one or two major topics in each class session. As he takes up each topic, he will usually give many supporting facts and figures. These topics and their supporting statements are all related to each other in some way. Since they are related, a student's notes should reflect this relationship. The student must keep the flow of facts sorted out in his own mind. There is an easy way of keeping this information sorted out when taking notes. It is done by means of an outline which follows the pattern of the instructor's plan. Keeping the instructor's outline or plan in mind as the instructor takes up each topic provides a basic framework. The student can use this framework to fill in any amount of information presented and still keep everything sorted out.

The following is a typical suggested format for outlining notes in class. The name of the instructor, the date, and the subject are recorded on the right side of the first page. Each page should be numbered consecutively, beginning with page 1.

OUTLINE

I. The first important topic heading
  A. First meaningful statement related to I
    1. Significant statement supporting A
      a. Logical data relating to 1
      b. Next point supporting 1
      c. Next point supporting 1
    2. Second fact related to main point A
      a. Logical information supporting 2
      b. Additional facts related to 2
II. Second important topic heading
  A. First significant statement relating to II
    1. Significant statement supporting A under II
      a. Logical data relating to 1 above
      b. Next point supporting 1 above
    2. Second fact related to main point A
    3. Third fact related to main point A

SAMPLE OUTLINE
FOR
CLASSROOM NOTE-TAKING

Date   12-12-6—

Course   Criminal Law

Class Topic(s)   Penal Code

Instructor   J. L. Sullivan

PENAL CODE

I. Specific crimes
  A. Homicide
    1. Felonious homicides
      a. Murder
        (1) Degrees
        (2) Examples
      b. Manslaughter

2. Nonfelonious homicides
  B. Robbery
II. Preliminary Provisions

This somewhat mechanical method of note-taking according to plan tells a student when he is or is not following the presentation. It also helps him to keep the major and minor points of the discussion straightened out in his own mind. If the outline and notes appear to be hanging together logically, the student knows he is "on the track" of the discussion. If he gets lost, he can always ask his instructor to fill in the gaps. Note-taking outlines such as this are like bins for sorting out facts, figures, and information presented in class. Moreover, notes arranged according to plan are easier to review and refer to later.

Speeding up note-taking. In order to keep up with the lecturer and avoid illegible notes, an acceptable system of abbreviation should be used. Samples of timesaving abbreviations, found in dictionaries, are given below, although any system of abbreviations is actually all right for class note-taking just so long as the student is able to figure out his own notes later on when his ability to recall the points is weak.

Bk	book	P.C.	Penal Code
Info	Information	V.C.	Vehicle Code
Feb	February	Ref	reference
#	number	Gov't	government
etc.	and so forth		

Organizing notes. A review of all notes taken each day will help fix in the mind any material presented that day. Typing classroom notes will also help make a lasting imprint on the mind. The notes should also be reviewed as often as possible to refresh the memory of the conscious mind. An index and a table of contents will add to the notebook's use as a ready reference in the future.

By cultivating the habit of taking notes, the police science student will develop a talent that will prove to be a great asset to him when he becomes a peace officer. The expert notetaker is often an excellent report writer—and a reliable report writer quickly attracts the attention of the police executive, who always is looking for promising future administrators. To add further to his qualifications, the conscientious notetaker has one of the prime qualities of becoming a fair and impartial witness. The notetaker can refresh his memory from his notes and so assist materially and effectively in the administration of justice in our courts.

QUESTIONS

1. Describe the psychological necessity for taking notes.
2. Outline the purpose for taking notes.
3. Name the techniques for recording notes.
4. Describe the recommended type of notebook for classroom use.
5. Why is size of notebook important?
6. Why is a pen better than a pencil for taking notes?
7. Make an outline for a suggested format for taking notes.
8. Give several examples of accepted abbreviations, and explain why abbreviations are permitted.
9. When should notes be reviewed and why?
10. Should a person with a good memory be excused from taking notes? If not, why not?

2. Career orientation

The selection process

Sooner or later every young man and woman arrives at a time in life when it becomes necessary to choose an employment career. When this time comes, all must answer the question, "What do I want to do to make a decent and rewarding living for the rest of my life?"

The capable, conscientious young person seeks an answer to this query. When he researches this question, he will find the word "career" emphasized as the medium to the full life and contentment. He will also observe that there are many varied careers (professions and occupations) in the world. Many different avenues of choice are open for the person seeking a career, and he must consider many things in order to make a wise and lasting choice. He must explore and weigh such factors as sincere personal interest, worthwhile objectives, sensible ambitions, natural talent, and expert counseling.

The matter of counseling is particularly crucial to the person seeking a career. Students are urged to search out the expert and secure his valuable guidance. Many people, because they do not plan their career program, fall haphazardly and aimlessly into employment for which they have no special talents or motivation. By seeking the assistance of a counselor, the fortunate few are safely guided to avoid the pitfalls awaiting those who do not know where they are going or what they want.

Fame, fortune, power, and adventure are the usual goals of young men and women in the prime of life. However, there is one greater objective, and that is service to mankind. Law enforcement offers this. Besides many excellent opportunities, Federal, state, county, and city law enforcement careers provide the additional challenge of dedicated service to community and to country.

Although police service will not bring great material wealth, it will give the kind of fame and fortune worth possessing. It will give a person the knowledge that he is daily rendering an indispensable service to his fellow man. It will give him the knowledge that his work offers the kind of life that conscience approves, that duty inspires, and that is dedicated to the preservation of the health, safety, and welfare of society.

UNDERSTANDING JOBS AND SELF

How can an individual remove the element of chance from his selection of a career? There are three basic kinds of understanding which can greatly assist in planning the right career.

1. *Understanding of self.* The person who understands himself knows his abilities, skills, and aptitudes; he is aware of his strengths and weaknesses; he recognizes what he can do and what he cannot do.

2. *Understanding of jobs.* This is knowing the duties they involve, what requirements have to be met to be successful, what opportunities they provide to get ahead, and what their disadvantages are.

3. *Correlating understanding of self and of jobs.* To do this, it is necessary for the individual to compare his personal pattern (interests, abilities, etc.) with the job pattern (mental, physical, and emotional requirements). When the personal pattern and the job pattern match closely, the right individual has very likely found the right job.

Need for police personnel

Retirements, promotions, transfers, and the population explosion have created a continuing and constant demand for police personnel in all levels of government. With 315,000 men and women employed in more than 49,000 law enforcement agencies in the United States, new personnel, relief personnel, and replacement personnel are always in short supply. In the words of the Director of the Federal Bureau of Investigation, J. Edgar Hoover, "Never before has there been such an urgent need for dedicated young men and women to enlist in the war against the crime colossus in America." The present law enforcement organizations in the various government agencies constitute a large force, but, as Mr. Hoover emphasizes, it is not nearly large enough.

Most police departments are undermanned and understaffed. Chief William H. Parker of the Los Angeles Police Department advertises currently in the Los Angeles newspapers that he has funds to hire needed patrolmen, but he is unable to locate willing and qualified applicants to fill his quotas.

Meanwhile, as dedicated law enforcement officers patrol conscientiously and administrators work unceasingly with undermanned staffs, crime moves continuously and ruthlessly along. As the second and minute hands sweep around the clock, countless crimes are committed throughout the length and breadth of our land. Crime statistics published today are out-of-date tomorrow. Time and time again FBI uniform crime statistics show that crime is increasing even faster than our population growth. This is a threat to our civilization, especially when the demand for law enforcement personnel cannot be met. Hence, law enforcement executives face a most difficult challenge to secure desirable applicants. Some departments even advertise and solicit applicants in nationwide recruiting programs through the press, radio, and television and through personal contact. Even residence requirements for police candidates, strictly observed in the past, are no longer invoked today. Although attractive offers are made, there is still a shortage of applicants. Hence, interested, qualified applicants need not stand in line for careers in law enforcement.

The rest of this chapter will discuss in detail the many job opportunities for police work—locally, nationally, and privately— that are open to interested and qualified applicants.

The total process of selecting a police applicant is an expensive one. In order to reduce the cost, some departments have inaugurated a prescreening selectivity test. This examination takes about 20 minutes and is composed of questions to ascertain if the applicant has the basic intelligence and the emotional stability to be worthy of consideration. If the candidate passes this initial hurdle, he then receives further consideration, and is requested to fill out an application. So far, the departments that have adopted this procedure report that considerable savings in time, money, and energy have been accomplished by weeding out those applicants who can readily be identified as not qualified.

APPLICATION — PERSONAL HISTORY

When seeking employment in law enforcement, the successful applicant presents all his qualifications in the best possible manner. This may be accomplished by preparing beforehand a neat folder containing typewritten data reflecting all pertinent information concerning his qualifications. In this application folder, the candidate should include the following information:

Personal-history résumé
1. Name in full
2. Address and phone number
3. Age, date and place of birth
4. Marital status
5. Name of wife (if he has one)
6. Names of children (if he has children)
7. Personal description (optional)
8. Race and nationality (optional)

Educational record
1. High school (name; date of graduation; copy of transcript, if possible)
2. College (name; date of graduation; copy of transcript, if possible)

3. Technical courses (name; date of completion; copy of transcript of specialized courses, if possible)

Employment record (past five years)
Name of employer, address, date of employment

Organization membership
1. Clubs, societies, etc.
2. Church affiliation (optional)

Hobbies

Character references
Names of five persons who are not relatives

Recent photograph

Letter of introduction
This should be addressed to the employer, explaining why you want to become a law enforcement officer.

When compiling this personal-history data, the applicant should prepare an original with several copies for future use and reference. Obviously, the personal-history résumé is also most helpful to review for the oral interview.

PERSONAL APPEARANCE

Another important factor that should not be overlooked is the applicant's personal appearance at the time he presents his personal folder or meets with the employing authority. His appearance should be absolutely above reproach. Before the initial and all oral interviews, the applicant is well advised to follow these suggestions:

1. Bathe and shave carefully.
2. Make sure shoes are shined.
3. Have a recent haircut.
4. Wear a conservative, dark, pressed suit.
5. Wear a clean white shirt.
6. Wear a conservative tie.
7. Do not wear pins or other emblems.
8. Be polite.
9. Relax, but do not be too casual.
10. Speak clearly and distinctly; avoid slang.
11. Be natural; do not put on an act.

12. Be attentive and alert.
13. Do not be witty or sarcastic.
14. Maintain your equilibrium at all times.
15. Do not become annoyed or belligerent.
16. Be honest and factual.
17. Follow orders and directions explicitly.
18. Try above all to make a favorable impression.

BACKGROUND INVESTIGATION OF APPLICANT

One of the most important and revealing investigations utilized by law enforcement agencies is the use of background inquiries. No investigation would be complete unless the employment, scholastic, and credit records of the candidate were obtained. Traffic and criminal records can be most revealing. No department will accept an applicant who has a criminal conviction or has been a party to any morals crime. Many law enforcement agencies, moreover, are likely to eliminate a candidate who is accident-prone and has an unfavorable traffic record. In discussing an applicant's employability, the investigator trys to determine if the applicant has the ability to get along with other people. While employment experts rate the ability to get along with others as one of the finest qualities for any type of employment, this ability is especially necessary for law enforcement personnel.

PROCESSING AN APPLICATION

An application is usually processed by the personnel division or by the civil service department connected with the police agency. The training officer usually conducts the entire investigation. This is done carefully and is never routine, for much is at stake. Failure to inquire into all of a candidate's past may result in the employment of a person who may bring discredit and embarrassment to a department. Employment investigators believe that it is much better to be thorough than sorry. Occasionally, a chief or sheriff has regretted the fact that he did not carefully investigate a candidate. Several good reasons why police departments make a total applicant investigation are demonstrated in the following cases.

REVIEWED BY	**APPLICATION FOR EMPLOYMENT**	DATE OF EXAM
ACCEPTED_____REJECTED_____	PERSONNEL DEPARTMENT ROOM 118, CITY HALL PASADENA, CALIF. 91101 We Are An Equal Opportunity Employer	ELIGIBLE NO.
REASON		EXAMINATION SCORE

POSITION FOR WHICH YOU ARE APPLYING:_____ (Print exact title)

HEIGHT: _____FT. _____IN. WEIGHT: _____LBS.

NAME (Please Print)_____ Last _____ First _____ Middle

MALE: ☐   FEMALE: ☐

ADDRESS_____ Street _____ City _____ PHONE_____

ARE YOU A U. S. CITIZEN?	YES ☐ NO ☐	DATE BORN: MO.____ DAY____ YR.____	ARE YOU NOW, OR HAVE YOU EVER RECEIVED ANY FORM OF COMPENSATION INSURANCE FOR DISABILITY? If yes, please explain on reverse side.	YES ☐	NO ☐
MARRIED ☐ WIDOWED ☐ SINGLE ☐ DIV. OR SEP. ☐		NO. OF DEPENDENTS, INCLUDING YOURSELF____ MAIDEN NAME____	HAVE YOU EVER BEEN DISCHARGED OR FORCED TO RESIGN FROM ANY EMPLOYMENT? If yes, please explain on reverse side?	YES ☐	NO ☐
SOCIAL SECURITY NO.____ DO YOU DRIVE AN AUTOMOBILE: YES ☐ NO ☐ IF YES, CALIF. OPR'S. LIC. NO.____			DO YOU HAVE ANY PHYSICAL OR MENTAL DISABILITIES? If yes, please explain on reverse side.	YES ☐	NO ☐
IF RELATED TO ANY CITY EMPLOYEE, GIVE NAME:____ RELATIONSHIP____DEPT.____			HAVE YOU EVER BEEN CONVICTED OF A CRIMINAL OFFENSE OTHER THAN MINOR TRAFFIC VIOLATION? If yes, please explain on reverse side.	YES ☐	NO ☐

ARE YOU NOW, OR HAVE YOU EVER BEEN EMPLOYED BY THE CITY OF PASADENA?   YES ☐   NO ☐

IF YES, GIVE DATES EMPLOYED: FROM____ TO____

HOW DID YOU LEARN OF THIS POSITION? STAR NEWS____ L.A. TIMES____ CITY BULLETIN____ FRIEND____ CITY EMPLOYEE____ ADVERTISEMENT (Specify)____

EDUCATION

CIRCLE HIGHEST GRADE YOU COMPLETED

	1 2 3 4 5 6 7 8 9 10 11 12	DATES COMPLETED
GRAMMAR AND HIGH SCHOOL	1 2 3 4 5 MAJOR AND DEGREES:	
COLLEGE OR UNIVERSITY: (NAME AND LOCATION OF SCHOOLS)	PERTINENT COURSES:	
CERTIFICATES OF PROFESSIONAL OR VOCATIONAL COMPETENCE:		

EMPLOYMENT RECORD (LIST WORK RECORD, INCLUDING MILITARY SERVICE, BEGINNING WITH PRESENT TIME)

EMPLOYMENT DATES	EMPLOYER'S NAME AND ADDRESS	OCCUPATION AND DESCRIPTION OF DUTIES	SALARY RECEIVED	REASON FOR LEAVING
FROM				
TO				
TOTAL TIME				
FROM				
TO				
TOTAL TIME				
FROM				
TO				
TOTAL TIME				
FROM				
TO				
TOTAL TIME				
FROM				
TO				
AL TIME				
FROM				
TO				
TOTAL TIME				

NAME (Please Print) Last First Middle

10.4 1m 10-27-64 T8

(OVER)

City of Pasadena
PERSONNEL DEPARTMENT
City Hall
100 N. Garfield
Pasadena, California
Phone: 449-1886 Ext. 294

Print Name____

Address____

City and State____

Telephone No.____

APPLICATION ACCEPTANCE AND NOTICE OF TEST
(Personnel Department use only. Do not fill in)

☐ Your application has been rejected because it was felt the qualifications indicated were not as acceptable as those of other candidates, therefore you were not selected to take the examination.

☐ Your application has been accepted. This card is your admission slip; bring it when you report for:

☐ Written test ☐ Interview

☐ Performance test

Time____ Date____

Place____

The examination will take approximately ____hours.

Figure 1. Application form (front).

INDICATE SPECIAL SKILLS THAT YOU HAVE ACQUIRED AND THE DEGREE TO WHICH YOU ARE QUALIFIED:
(* indicates familiarity with use of equipment; and ** indicates that you are fully qualified)

OFFICE AND CLERICAL		OUTSIDE AND TRADE	TRACTOR
☐ SHORTHAND	☐ KEY PUNCH	☐ JACK HAMMER	☐ UNDER 35 H.P.
☐ TYPING	☐ TAB EQUIPMENT		☐ 35 H.P. OR OVER
	☐ TEN KEY ADDING MACHINE		
	☐ BURROUGHS BILLING MACHINE	WELDING	ROLLER
OFFICE MACHINES	☐ DATA PROCESSING (LIST EQPT.)	☐ ELECTRIC	☐ UNDER 5 TONS
☐ CALCULATORS (INDICATE TYPE)		☐ ACETYLENE	☐ 5 TONS OR OVER
			CRANE
_____	_____	TRUCK DRIVING	☐ UNDER 5 TONS
_____	_____	☐ UNDER 5 TONS	☐ 5 TONS OR OVER
_____		☐ 5 TONS OR OVER	SHOVEL
	☐ BURROUGHS ACCOUNTING MACHINE 7200	☐ DITCHING MACHINE	☐ BACK HOE
☐ SENSIMATIC	☐ BURROUGHS ACCOUNTING MACHINE 7800	☐ FORK LIFT	☐ OVER ½ YD. SHOVEL
☐ COMPTOMETER	☐ P B X	☐ SKIP LOADER	☐ MOTOR PATROL GRADER

MILITARY SERVICE: HAVE YOU HAD ANY MILITARY SERVICE IN ARMED FORCES OF THE UNITED STATES?

YES_____ NO_____ IF "YES," BRANCH_____ DATE ENTERED_____ DATE DISCHARGED_____

TYPE OF DISCHARGE_____ MONTHS OF SERVICE_____ HIGHEST RANK OR RATE ATTAINED_____

RANK OR RATE AT TIME OF DISCHARGE:_____ SERIAL NO._____

ARE YOU RECEIVING ANY SERVICE-INCURRED DISABILITY COMPENSATION? YES_____ NO_____ IF "YES," DESCRIBE_____

ARE YOU NOW A MEMBER OF ANY RESERVE ORGANIZATION?_____ ACTIVE_____ INACTIVE_____ NAME OF RESERVE ORGANIZATION_____

USE THIS SPACE TO MAKE ANY NECESSARY EXPLANATIONS OR TO FURNISH ADDITIONAL INFORMATION

_____

CERTIFICATE OF APPLICANT. (READ CAREFULLY BEFORE SIGNING)
I hereby certify that all statements made in this application are true and I agree and understand that any misstatements or omissions of material facts herein will cause forfeiture on my part of all eligibility to any employment in the service of the City of Pasadena.

SIGNATURE_____ DATE_____

LEAVE THIS SPACE BLANK — CITY USE ONLY	LEAVE THIS SPACE BLANK — DEPARTMENT USE ONLY
MEDICAL EXAM. NO._____ DATE_____ 19_____	
(Signature of Physician)	
FINGERPRINT & PHOTOGRAPH RECORD_____	

Figure 1. (*back*)

TYPICAL EXAMPLES OF INVESTIGATIONS

The immoral applicant. A certain department, thoroughly professional in its approach to screening procedure, was considering a young, single man who was outstanding in all of the tests given as well as in appearance and in ability to express himself. This department had a rule that all candidates must be interviewed in their homes. After many failures to find this applicant at home, he was called into the office for an interview and subsequently hired on the strength of this office interview. Sometime later, it was discovered that this man had used his apartment as a studio in which he took pornographic pictures of female juveniles. This department no longer hires prior to the home interview.

The mentally unsound applicant. In another case, a police department developed a procedure for employing regulars from the reserve forces. A recent arrival in this particular city made application and was accepted for the police reserve. Then, about one year later, he applied for a job on the regular police force and was accepted. Later, while driving a police car, armed, and in uniform, he went berserk. Fortunately, no one was injured. A departmental inquiry later revealed that the man had spent some time in two mental institutions. This department now does a careful background investigation on every applicant.

In still another case, a man was hired in an official but auxiliary position to work with the police department. His duties required him to bear arms and wear a uniform. A background investigation found that this man was classified as a homicidal maniac by two different psychiatrists, but when not under stress, he was a likable, personable individual. If this applicant had been hired by a less professional department, he could very well have triggered a tragedy.

The physically unfit applicant. One city that does a meticulous job of background investigation routinely checks the military service of an applicant even though he has an honorable discharge. Their standards are such that they would not accept any other type of discharge. In one case, a man was hired pending the outcome of the investigation. It was later learned, however, that this applicant had been a malingerer while in service and had spent a good portion of his service in the hospital complaining of "lower back pains." After a medical analysis of the reports, the man was terminated. A potential liability to the city was eliminated.

The married applicant. Two cities had a man apply from a distant state. The applicant stated that he was married and that his wife lived with him. Both cities investigated and found that the applicant had deserted a family in his home state and that legal process had been started against him. Good screening thus avoided embarrassment and inconvenience to the two cities involved.

Another applicant stated that he was married and had four children. No marriage license, however, was requested by the hiring authority. Two years after hire it was discovered that this man was not married. The incident caused considerable embarrassment to the city and to the department. This department now checks marriage licenses.

The credit risk. One agency hired a man without making a credit check. After hire, the department was deluged with demands from former places of residence for payments of judgments and overdue bills, and the man had to be terminated.

The criminal applicant. Some departments are under the impression that any kind of conviction will be revealed by a state bureau of identification and FBI check. In one case, a man hired had committed statutory rape and pleaded guilty. This fact did not show up at the state bureau of identification or FBI because the man, having learned that a warrant had been issued, got his attorney, went to court, and pleaded guilty. He was given a suspended sentence and a year's probation. But he had never been booked or fingerprinted until he was hired as a police officer. Had the police department checked with the other departments and the district attorneys in cities and counties of former residence, the applicant's record would have been made known.

The slovenly applicant. Another department, very professional and businesslike in its selection process, routinely checks the home of each applicant. One such applicant had passed all the tests and was considered employable until the investigator went to the man's home in a different county. All homes in the neighborhood were neat and well kept except that of the applicant. The lawn was a mass of tall weeds into which beer cans and bottles had been casually tossed. The house was so filthy that the investigator did not even go in. Imagine the reaction of neighbors to hiring a man like that as a police officer!

Obviously, a police department cannot be too careful in screening and investigating job applicants. The serious candidate for employment will present all of his qualifications. Any questionable past activity will appear in the best possible light if put forth by

STATE OF CALIFORNIA
DEPARTMENT OF JUSTICE

BUREAU OF CRIMINAL IDENTIFICATION AND INVESTIGATION

P. O. BOX 1859, SACRAMENTO 9, CALIFORNIA

CURRENT ARREST OR RECEIPT

DATE ARRESTED OR RECEIVED	CHARGE OR OFFENSE (If code citation is used it should be accompanied by charge)	DISPOSITION OR SENTENCE (Include ONLY FINAL dispositions)
		FOR INSTITUTIONS USE ONLY
		Sentence expires_____

Nearest relative or friend_____
Name_____
Address_____
Crime and/or arrest report number_____
Social Security number_____
Drivers license number_____

INSTRUCTIONS

1. TYPE OR PRINT all information.
2. Note amputations in proper finger squares.
3. REPLY WILL QUOTE ONLY NUMBER APPEARING IN THE BLOCK MARKED "CONTRIBUTOR'S NO."
4. Indicate any additional copies for other agencies in space below—include their complete mailing address.
5. Do not withhold submission of fingerprints waiting for development of photograph.

SEND COPY TO:

FORM CII-6

Figure 2. Fingerprint card (front).

the applicant himself. Regardless, the investigation will uncover any off-color activity and disqualify the candidate. Candidates should remember that an investigator will make the most capable background check possible. Otherwise, he would be remiss in his administrative responsibility.

SUBMISSION OF FINGERPRINTS AND OATH

Today all law enforcement agencies of any consequence fingerprint every applicant. One copy of the applicant's fingerprint card (Figure 2) is sent to the Identification Division of the Fed-

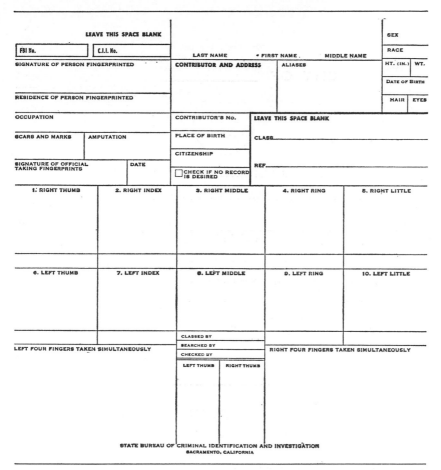

LEAVE THIS SPACE BLANK				SEX

The form shown contains the following fields:

LEAVE THIS SPACE BLANK

FBI No.   C.I.I. No.

LAST NAME   • FIRST NAME .   MIDDLE NAME

SEX

RACE

SIGNATURE OF PERSON FINGERPRINTED   CONTRIBUTOR AND ADDRESS   ALIASES

HT. (IN.)   WT.

DATE OF BIRTH

RESIDENCE OF PERSON FINGERPRINTED

HAIR   EYES

OCCUPATION   CONTRIBUTOR'S No.   LEAVE THIS SPACE BLANK

SCARS AND MARKS   AMPUTATION   PLACE OF BIRTH   CLASS

CITIZENSHIP

SIGNATURE OF OFFICIAL TAKING FINGERPRINTS   DATE   ☐ CHECK IF NO RECORD IS DESIRED   REF

1. RIGHT THUMB	2. RIGHT INDEX	3. RIGHT MIDDLE	4. RIGHT RING	5. RIGHT LITTLE
6. LEFT THUMB	7. LEFT INDEX	8. LEFT MIDDLE	9. LEFT RING	10. LEFT LITTLE

LEFT FOUR FINGERS TAKEN SIMULTANEOUSLY

CLASSED BY
SEARCHED BY
CHECKED BY
LEFT THUMB   RIGHT THUMB

RIGHT FOUR FINGERS TAKEN SIMULTANEOUSLY

STATE BUREAU OF CRIMINAL IDENTIFICATION AND INVESTIGATION
SACRAMENTO, CALIFORNIA

Figure 2.   (back)

eral Bureau of Investigation at Washington, D.C., another copy is sent to the state bureau of identification, and one copy is kept in the employing department's identification files. Some departments also require the applicant to sign a non-Communist oath. A typical example of this oath is shown in Figure 3.

MATTERS RESULTING IN DISQUALIFICATION

If you are planning a career as a police officer, the following requirements must be met:

CITY OF _____

OATH OF AFFIRMATION OF ALLEGIANCE

FOR CIVIL DEFENSE WORKERS AND PUBLIC EMPLOYEES

I, _____, do solemnly swear (or affirm) that I will support and defend the Constitution of the United States and the Constitution of the State of California against all enemies, foreign and domestic; that I will bear true faith and allegiance to the Constitution of the United States and the Constitution of the State of California; that I take this obligation freely, without any mental reservation or purpose of evasion; and that I will well and faithfully discharge the duties upon which I am about to enter.

And I do further swear (or affirm) that I do not advocate, nor am I a member of any party or organization, political or otherwise, that now advocates the overthrow of the Government of the United States or of the State of California by force or violence or other unlawful means; that within the five years immediately preceding the taking of this oath (or affirmation) I have not been a member of any party or organization, political or otherwise, that advocated the overthrow of the Government of the United States or of the State of California by force or violence or

other unlawful means except as follows:_____

_____

(If no affiliations, write in the words "No Exceptions")

and that during such time as I am a member or employee of the City of _____ I will not advocate nor become a member of any party or organization, political or otherwise, that advocates the overthrow of the Government of the United States or of the State of California by force or violence or other unlawful means.

_____

Signature

_____

Title or Department

The above oath was taken and subscribed to before me this ____ day of _____, 19____.

_____

City Clerk (Notary or other person authorized to administer oaths)

FORM 78B

Figure 3.   Oath of allegiance.

1. Criminal record—none.
2. Traffic record—no recklessness or indication of accident proneness.
3. Height—men, 5 ft 8 in. minimum to 6 ft 6 in. maximum; some departments have no maximum;
   women, 5 ft 3 in. minimum to 6 ft maximum.
4. Weight—men, 145 pounds minimum to 225 pounds maximum, according to height;
   women, 115 pounds minimum to 192 pounds maximum, according to height.
5. Age—21 minimum to 30 maximum; some departments have age 35 as maximum.
6. Eyes—20/20 in one eye and at least 20/30 in the other (uncorrected); free from color blindness and astigmatism.
7. Teeth—teeth in good condition, free from decay and infection; some departments require 20 natural teeth, no bridges or dentures.
8. Hearing—normal.
9. Health—no physical defects, such as flat feet or back injuries.
10. Education—high school graduate or acceptable equivalent minimum.
11. Citizenship—United States of America.

EDUCATIONAL REQUIREMENTS

Although most police departments and sheriffs' offices encourage and accept applications from high school graduates or those with equivalent education received in the armed services, recent surveys reflect that law enforcement executives are highly in favor of preservice training programs that prepare young men and women for careers in law enforcement. Candidates with previous college or university educational background are encouraged to apply. Moreover, preferential attention and consideration may be expected from law enforcement agencies toward those candidates who have had the good fortune and foresight to complete police science courses. It is generally agreed that these law enforcement courses in our colleges and universities greatly assist in elevating the standards and the quality of law enforcement in the United States.

Not everyone is qualified to be a peace officer. Before enrolling in a police science course at a college or university, the prospective peace officer should visit the local police department, sheriff's office, highway patrol, or Federal building and talk to the personnel officer. While there, he should obtain all the written data and check the qualifications required. After thoughtfully perusing the material, he may select the kind of law enforcement agency for which he is qualified and in which he desires to serve.

If a candidate chooses the position of a police officer, deputy sheriff, or highway patrolman, the qualifications are specific and the requirements are rigid. Gone are the days when police positions were for sale and police officers were appointed by politicians and ward heelers. Instead, definite standards are established that are applicable to all candidates without favoritism or waivers.

STATE STANDARDS

As an example, the state of California created the Peace Officers' Standards and Training (POST) Commission by legislative action that became effective September 19, 1959. Immediately, the commission conducted studies and surveys in cooperation with all law enforcement agencies in the state to establish uniform standards to guide law enforcement in the selection, recruitment, and training of qualified applicants. This objective was realized when the POST Commission under Section 1002 in its Rules and Regulations set forth the following minimum standards for the acceptance of a peace officer for employment in California, effective October 23, 1960:

1. Citizen of the United States.
2. Minimum age of 21 years.
3. Fingerprinting of applicant with a search of local, state, and national fingerprint files to disclose any criminal record.
4. No conviction by any state or by the Federal government of a crime, the punishment for which could have been imprisonment in a Federal penitentiary or a state prison.
5. Good moral character as determined by a thorough background investigation according to specifications entitled "The Personal-history Investigation" published by the commission.

6. Graduation from high school or a passing of the General Education Development test indicating high school graduation level or a score on a written test of mental ability approved by the commission and equivalent to that attained by the average high school student.
7. Examination by a licensed physician and surgeon. Only those applicants who are found to be free from any physical, emotional, or mental condition which might adversely affect performance of their duty as a peace officer shall be eligible for appointment. The applicant's declaration of medical history and the physician's findings upon the examination shall be recorded on forms which shall include but are not limited to all the items set forth in the specifications entitled "Physical Examination" published by the commission.
8. An oral interview shall be held by the hiring authority or his representative or representatives to determine such things as the recruit's appearance, background, and ability to communicate.

It is emphasized that these are minimum entrance standards. Higher standards are recommended whenever the availability of qualified applicants meets the demand.

In addition to the minimum standards for selecting police employees, the state of California also requires that the recruits receive a minimum of 200 hours of police training within 18 months of the date of employment with the department. The prescribed basic course specifications are described in detail in the chapter in this book entitled *Police Training;* thus only a brief outline of the 200-hour course is set forth here to indicate the general topic area.

Introduction to Law Enforcement
Criminal Law
Criminal Evidence
Administration of Justice
Criminal Investigation
Patrol Procedures
Traffic Control
Juvenile Procedure
Firearms

Defensive Tactics
Public Relations and Human Relations
Ethics
First Aid
Examinations
Interviewing
Testifying

Meeting education and training requirements

Degree course. High school graduates who plan a career in law enforcement have several alternatives. They may enroll in a certified junior college police science course and graduate with an Associate in Arts degree with a police science major after two years of concentrated study. Thereafter, they may transfer to a state college for two more years of police science study and acquire a Bachelor's degree. With this educational background, they will be well versed in the problems, advantages, and demands of their chosen profession. Besides, by then they most likely will have reached the age of 21, the minimum age necessary to file an application for police employment.

Junior college course. On the other hand, the police aspirant may desire to enroll in an approved junior college police science course on a terminal basis and to seek employment with a law enforcement agency immediately upon graduation with an Associate in Arts degree, provided, of course, he has reached the age of 21. Preservice college training of at least 60 semester college units instead of a basic state-required police course of 200 hours is acceptable in California.

Police department courses. Some police candidates may elect not to attend college. Instead, they may seek employment in another field of endeavor and, upon reaching age 21, apply for police employment. In California, upon the recruit's appointment, the department will provide him with at least 200 hours of approved training in the police academy. If the police agency does not have a police academy, the recruit will be enrolled in an approved junior college police academy and will receive a minimum of 200 hours of police training.

Purpose of the programs. For those students who are financially unable to attend college there is still another possibility. Various progressive police departments throughout the United States have adopted the cadet method of maintaining high school graduates' interest in law enforcement during the age period 18 to 21. Many high school students consider a career in law enforcement upon graduation from high school, but during the interim, between 18 and 21, other influences may intervene and they may be lost to law enforcement. But as cadets, they have the opportunity to study and actually serve in a law enforcement agency. In this way, police cadets are able to absorb the fundamentals of law enforcement during their period of duty. Consequently, when they reach the age of 21 and are eligible to take the police examination, they have an excellent chance to pass it, for they have been "through the mill." Besides, under the cadet-system law enforcement supervisors and cadets both have a splendid opportunity to judge and determine whether the individual cadet has the qualifications to pursue a career in law enforcement.

Cadet status. When discussing the cadet program, it is necessary to stress a very important point: a police cadet is not a police officer or a peace officer in any sense of the word. A police cadet is a clerical police trainee whose duties are very similar to that of secretary, civilian communications operator, or attendant. If this point is kept in mind, the cadet program may be accurately brought into focus for an objective discussion.

History of police cadet program. The concept of a police cadet program originated in England about 1935 but did not find acceptance in the United States until the early 1950s (Seares). The first cadet programs in North America were started in Hamilton, Ontario, in 1951 and in Milwaukee, Wisconsin, in 1952. Pasadena, California, opened a cadet program in January, 1954, and has the distinction of maintaining one of the oldest established cadet programs in southern California. Other departments that have experimented with or are conducting successful cadet programs are those in Baltimore, Maryland; Burbank, California; Baldwin Park, California; Chicago, Illinois; Cincinnati, Ohio; Detroit, Michigan; Fresno, California; Hermosa Beach, California; Honolulu, Hawaii; Lincoln, Nebraska; Los Angeles, California; Philadelphia, Pennsylvania; Riverside, California; Rockford, Illinois; San Diego, California; and Seattle, Washington.

Objectives. The primary aim of a cadet program is to attract to police work young men physically, mentally, and morally qualified for such service. The goal is to expose the potential officers to police work and its many operations. This, it is hoped, will stimulate a desire for a permanent career in law enforcement.

Regarded from an economic standpoint, the police cadet program is an excellent opportunity to release trained policemen from clerical duties and to assign them to the field where the need is more critical. A police cadet can perform for less money clerical duties normally done by an experienced, trained police officer, thus releasing a needed police officer to law enforcement work. Besides, the cadet gains valuable experience that can assist him in learning the overall police operation.

The police cadet program presents another golden opportunity to improve and professionalize law enforcement personnel by requiring cadets to attend police science courses and work toward a college degree. Thus, a cadet can easily earn sufficient college credits for a junior college Associate in Arts degree or he can be well on his way to a degree by the time he is 21 years of age and becomes eligible for acceptance as a qualified peace officer candidate.

With the rapid growth of population in many cities, more and more police personnel will be employed to provide the needed protection for our communities. A cadet program can ensure a constant supply of capable, trained recruits to fill law enforcement openings as they arise.

Duties of the police cadet. The duties of a police cadet are generally clerical in nature. The cadet is usually assigned to work on records; operate the various radio, telephone, teletype, and other means of public communication; do typing as required; and perform other duties as needed. Some departments are toying with the idea of assigning the cadet to ride on patrol with a veteran officer under strict supervision. However, most departments are apprehensive of the obvious dangers involved in exposing a young cadet to police patrol operations. The cadet's position within the department, therefore, is usually classified as that of miscellaneous civilian employee.

Cadet salaries. The police cadet may be a full-time employee or a part-time cadet of the municipality. If he is a full-time employee, the eight hours of employment are usually 8:00 A.M. to 5:00 P.M., daily, five days per week. A survey of salary schedules for cadets shows that most departments have entrance salary scales ranging from $350 to $380 per month for police cadets employed eight hours per day. Salaries for cadets are about $200 less per month than the starting pay for regular officers. Since the cadet program is normally two years, there is a three-step raise schedule during the two years of cadet service which brings the maximum pay to about $450 per month. Of course, all salary schedules, whether high or low, depend upon the policy of the department and the duties of the cadet. Also, each department has its own unique fringe benefits for its cadets. Cadet candidates should check pay scales and fringe benefits during the processing of their applications.

INTERNSHIP

In order to maintain interest among high school students who are potential law enforcement candidates, another administrative procedure has been devised. This method is called "internship." An internship program becomes possible when a police agency and a local junior college or state college agree to collaborate in a student-intern program. The law enforcement agency appraises and screens all police science majors before the college accepts them and recommends assignment of selected interns.

How the program works. The intern is required to carry a certain number of college courses in law enforcement administration and operation. He also spends a designated number of hours each week during the semester at the police agency observing, typing, filing, sorting, reporting, surveying, acting as messenger, and doing other related work. All work is supervised and recorded. Pay, if any, for services rendered by the intern is agreed upon beforehand. Any special clothing or equipment is furnished by the police agency. Police chiefs who have internship programs point to the obvious advantages of the program to both the police agency and the student intern.

Police service qualifying examinations

Purpose of examinations. The applicant for police service can expect to take a number of examinations designed to check out his qualifications for law enforcement work. Since certain standards for acceptance into police work have been established, some objective methods of determining how well an applicant can meet these standards is necessary. A simple yardstick can measure height, and an ordinary scale can measure an applicant's weight. But how does one measure educational achievement, physical ability, or emotional stability? Police entrance examinations vary with each law enforcement agency. However, the police candidate can expect to be exposed to all or most of the following types of police entrance examinations: written, medical, physical, agility, psychiatric, polygraph, and oral interview. Each of these examinations is a step toward an appointment as a police officer; hence, these examinations should be understood and taken seriously.

To examine applicants, most police departments use standardized tests which every applicant must take. How well the applicant does on these tests is compared with how well other applicants have done. Thus, in competitive tests, police officials have an excellent tool with which they can measure the qualifications of each applicant. Some of these tests are written, some are oral, and some, like the medical examination, involve a thorough checkup made by a competent examiner. The principal tests, examinations, and other screening devices used with police service applicants are discussed in this section.

Written examination. If an application reveals that the applicant meets minimum job requirements, the applicant is requested to take a written examination on a certain date with a group of other hopeful candidates. The written examination is a general, comprehensive test which includes basic mathematics, vocabulary, spelling, grammar, and other factors necessary to determine the general intelligence and aptitude for police work of the applicant. Many departments, including the Los Angeles Police Department, require the police candidate to have a minimum IQ of approximately 110. This minimum IQ was based on the premise that the policeman of today and of the future will have to deal with many complex problems which require rapid, accurate thinking. Men in other professions, such as medicine and law, may take time to consider a case carefully, but frequently the police officer has to decide a course of action with almost split-second timing. Often lives may be at stake. Wrong decisions may subject him to false arrest suits or other legal embarrassments.

Those applicants who have taken police written examinations have described them as primarily typical civil service intelligence tests. The examination questions are usually multiple-choice with some true-false. Occasionally, an essay question may be asked.

Some examinations are time tests, in which the applicant is asked to complete a certain number of questions in a given time. In timed tests, attention should be given to answering, first, all questions that the candidate positively knows and, next, those about which he is not sure. Some tests provide a penalty for guessing or for every question missed.

Medical examination. Usually, a medical examiner designated by the law enforcement agency conducts the preemployment medical examination. Typical standards the applicant must meet are:

1. Vision: At least 20/30 vision in each eye without glasses or contact lenses. This standard may vary slightly with each department. Thus, the applicant should determine the vision requirement at the very beginning of his application inquiry.
2. Normal color vision: A candidate should be able to pass the regulation color vision examination. Color-blind persons are eliminated because it is usually impossible for them to distinguish between red and green colors. Since traffic lights, descriptions of people, and other police activities involve these two colors, such a color-blind applicant could not be accepted.
3. Hearing: No applicant with hearing loss in either ear of more than 10 percent will be considered.
4. Teeth: All teeth must be in good condition and free from decay

and infection. Some departments require that the candidate must possess a given number of teeth.

5. Varicosities: No person with marked varicose veins will be accepted.
6. Flat Feet: Anyone with flat feet is (usually) disqualified.
7. Other required examinations may include testing of the lungs, chest, nose, throat, thyroid, neck, head, extremities, heart, blood pressure, abdomen, and nervous system. Blood tests and urinalysis are necessary without exception. Also, any disabling injuries of any kind are disqualifying.

Physical-agility tests. Every candidate must pass the physical-agility tests. These tests include a series of physical exercises that serve to measure the physical ability of applicants. They include tests of strength, endurance, coordination, and the completion of an obstacle course. The obstacle course consists of climbing over a barricade, crawling under and over obstacles, jumping over hurdles, and running a specified distance in 35 to 45 seconds, depending upon the length of the course.

Besides the obstacle course, each applicant is required to do a specified number of pull-ups and push-ups. Even weight lifting is required in some physical tests. Unquestionably, the candidate must be in good physical condition in order to pass these rigorous tests. A passing score must be achieved in all phases of this examination. There are no loopholes or excuses for candidates who have allowed themselves to get out of good physical condition and are unable to perform the required feats of strength and endurance. For those who are contemplating taking such physical tests in the future, now is the time to start training.

Psychiatric examination. A growing number of law enforcement agencies are not satisfied with the usual tests and measurements of a candidate and will not employ an applicant until he has been examined by a psychiatrist. Some departments retain a staff psychiatrist to interview all prospective officers and to conduct a searching examination with appropriate tests.

These tests are designed primarily to eliminate applicants who are emotionally unstable. If the psychiatrist finds that the applicant is a potential risk, the applicant is rarely, if ever, hired. Thus, the psychiatric examination is a crucial one.

Polygraph test. In recent years, many departments have included in their battery of tests the services of an expert polygraph operator in order that every facet of a candidate's background, strengths, or weaknesses may be probed.

The polygraph is simply a collection of recording apparatus brought together to form one unit. The whole instrument is designed to detect disturbances from emotional causes and, in particular, those disturbances which are caused by lying (Cuthbert).

All dependable polygraph instruments used for lie detection are

Figure 4. Applicant exposed to polygraph test.

essentially pneumatically operated. They record changes in blood pressure, pulse, and respiration, as well as skin reflexes. The blood pressure, pulse, respiration, and skin reflexes are recorded simultaneously and continuously on the surface of moving graph paper driven by a small electric motor. An additional unit in the Reid polygraph permits a recording of certain muscular activity, particularly muscular pressure exerted from the examinee's forearms, thighs, or feet (Inbau and Reid).

The polygraph examiner frequently uses as a basis for his examination the information furnished by the applicant in his own application. Since this form contains a considerable amount of information concerning the applicant's personal history, medical data, and other pertinent information, the examiner has an adequate source from which to test the truth of any statements originally made by the applicant. Obviously, an applicant should honestly and accurately answer all questions on his original application for employment.

It should be remembered that the polygraph is only as good as its operator. The operator is the true lie detector because the machine can detect neither lies nor truth. It merely records responses which are interpreted by the operator. Courts of law have not fully accepted its findings. However, it is considered by many to be a valuable investigative aid and is widely used by law enforcement organizations and industry to narrow fields of investigation and to test applicants for various jobs within an organization.

Interview. When an applicant passes the written examination, he is requested subsequently to appear before a board for an oral evaluation and appraisal. This board is composed largely of police executives and sometimes has citizen representatives. During the interview, the members of the board observe the applicant's attitude, appearance, demeanor, clothing, habits of cleanliness, and ability to express thoughts and answer pertinent questions under the pressure of an interview.

Typical oral board questions. Police science students are always anxious to know what questions are usually asked by members of the oral board during the interview. As those who have experienced such an appraisal interview can testify, this may be the most important, crucial part of the entire application process. Here are some typical questions an applicant may be asked at an oral interview and which he should be prepared to answer adequately.

1. Why do you want to become a police officer?
2. How did you happen to select this department?
3. Why do you think that you are capable of performing police work?
4. Are there any members of this police department who are related to you in any way?
5. Do you have any friends in this department?

6. What do your friends think of your choice of a career as a police officer?
7. Have you any hobbies? If so, what are they?
8. Have you submitted any applications to other law enforcement agencies for employment?
9. Have you ever been fired from a job, and if so, why?
10. If you are selected for employment, do you intend to make police work a permanent career or a temporary job?
11. Do you realize that police work is or may be dangerous and hazardous?
12. What do your parents think of your choice of law enforcement as a career?
13. If you are married, does your wife know that you would be on call for duty 24 hours per day?
14. Do you think that this department is doing a good job in law enforcement?
15. What experiences or employment have you had that will assist you in the field of law enforcement?
16. What are your ideas about a police officer's having a college degree?
17. Do you intend to obtain a college degree?
18. What courses in college have you taken already, if any?
19. Are you attending any police science classes at the present time?
20. Have you ever been in trouble with any law enforcement agency either as a juvenile or as an adult?
21. If a known criminal tried to cultivate your friendship, what would you do?
22. Suppose the owner of a liquor store or a merchant on your beat offered you merchandise free. What would you do?
23. If one of your department superiors gave you an order which you believed to be wrong, what would you do?
24. If you observed your wife, mother, or brother violate a traffic law such as exceeding the speed limit, what action would you take, if any?
25. If you found a superior officer from your department drunk in an auto on your tour of duty, what action would you take?
26. If you had reasonable grounds for believing that your police

partner may be committing thefts while off duty, what would you do?

27. Do you have any racial or religious prejudices? If so, explain fully.
28. Are there any laws that you could not, in good conscience, enforce?
29. Do you belong to any organizations? If so, what are they?
30. What do you believe is the most important function of law enforcement?
31. Do you intend to seek promotion in this department?
32. Do you believe that the police handle juveniles unfairly and without understanding?
33. Suppose a friend of yours asked you to obtain some information for him from the official police files. What course of action would you follow?

Preparation for interview. As immediate preparation for the interview, the police candidate should review the personal history he submitted so that he can answer all questions concerning his application intelligently, accurately, and spontaneously.

He should also familiarize himself with the qualifications, duties, and requirements of the police position he seeks by studying the police department's announcements and brochures.

Moreover, he should realize that the interview may last from 15 to 45 minutes. Hence, it is recommended that the candidate be patient rather than exhibit anxiety and a desire to get the whole matter over as quickly as possible.

Lastly, the candidate should try to be natural and to exert every effort to make a favorable impression, particularly in his appearance, attitude, emotional stability, alertness, sincerity, and honesty. He must convince board members that he has the necessary qualications for law enforcement work.

QUESTIONS

1. What is meant by career orientation?
2. What inquiries should be made by an interested police applicant? How and where should they be made?

3. Explain the need for personnel in law enforcement and enumerate the authorities with their observations.
4. Describe the general qualifications required for position as a peace officer.
5. Relate and explain the various examinations that must be passed before appointment.
6. Explain the meaning of preservice college training and describe the procedure for becoming eligible for this training.
7. Enumerate and explain the physical requirements that must be met in order to qualify as a peace officer.
8. What is the recommended IQ for a police candidate, and why is this desired?
9. Describe and explain the values of the cadet programs now flourishing in some police departments.
10. Why are the credit, criminal, and traffic records of a police candidate important?

3. Employment opportunities

City, county, and state police jobs

GETTING JOB INFORMATION

Employment opportunities for both men and women in local and city police departments, county sheriff's departments, and state highway patrols have never been better. The need is critical. Law enforcement is actually calling for help. Surveys reflect that the present need for law enforcement officers, particularly on the local level, will not diminish but will continue to be urgent. In the states experiencing great population growth, the local and state personnel offices mail notices, announcements, and brochures to all interested agencies advertising for applicants. The minimum qualifications, salary schedule, and description of duties are included in these materials. A student who checks the bulletin boards of his respective police science department will find the latest announcements of job opportunities in local law enforcement.

In large cities, current information concerning examinations for police officer may be obtained by writing or phoning the city civil service commission. If inquiry is desired pertaining to the possibilities of employment in a smaller city police department, a personal letter or phone call to the chief of police, mayor, city clerk, or city manager will elicit a prompt reply.

When a police science student is interested in obtaining information relating to opportunities for employment in a large sheriff's department, a letter or a phone call to the county civil

Figure 5.   Law enforcement calling you.

service commission will meet with cordial reception and a prompt response.

Periodically, the state highway patrol departments schedule examinations for the position of state traffic officer or state highway patrolman. Information concerning careers in the highway patrol should be directed to the commissioner of the highway patrol at the capital city of the state in which the student of police science is interested.

Education. The minimum educational requirement for police work is graduation from high school. Some departments accept an equivalent high school certificate awarded by the United States Armed Forces and by many states. More and more departments require at least 30 units of college work. Others request two years of college leading to an Associate in Arts degree. Still others have already stipulated that all applicants must have a four-year college degree. The trend is toward requiring an increase in college education as an entrance qualification.

Physical. All candidates must pass a rigid physical examination which includes a back and chest X-ray. The minimum height required is 5 ft 8 in. Some departments insist on a height of 5 ft 9 in. as the minimum. Weight limitations are dependent upon size and body structure. However, most departments follow the standard insurance company height and weight charts. The minimum height requirement for female applicants varies from 5 ft 3 in. to 5 ft 5 in., but the minimum weight is 115 pounds.

Age. Minimum age requirements for both male and female applicants range from 21 to 25. Some departments permit men 19 or 20 years of age to take the examination but postpone employment until age 21. The maximum entry age varies from 30 to 40, depending upon the department and the type of police work involved.

Other requirements. All departments insist on United States citizenship and the possession of a valid driver's license. Any candidate with a convicted felony record or chronic reckless driving record is automatically disqualified.

Pay and hours. The pay for policeman, deputy sheriff, and state highway patrolman varies throughout the United States. However, the trend is definitely toward better and higher salaries. Usually, the larger cities pay their law enforcement officers more than do the smaller communities. Nevertheless, the average salaries range from about $400 per month to over $600 per month for beginning pay. There may be as many as five periodic salary increases to maximums of $575 to over $700 per month. Most police departments pay policewomen the same rate as regular male officers. It is customary for motorcycle officers to receive a hazardous duty differential which adds $20 to $71 per month to their salary. Marksmanship bonus pay may also be available to those who qualify. Full or part payment of tuition is sometimes available for those officers who enroll in police science or other academic courses. Even allowances for college books for courses taken at state and junior colleges is provided by some departments.

The basic workweek is 40 hours. In case of emergencies, the needs of the service may require that the officer complete his assignment before ending his shift as per schedule. During the first few years, the new officer should not expect to work any shift that he pleases or that is convenient to him and his family. Instead, he must be willing to work any day or any shift. With seniority and proven ability will come greater responsibilities and more choice regarding assignments.

SPECIALIST JOBS

In addition to the traditional and well-known local law enforcement positions of police officer, deputy sheriff, and highway patrolman, there are other desirable law enforcement positions which are open to competitive examinations. Such jobs include those of fingerprint examiner, deputy marshal (county), corrections officer (county and state), district attorney investigator, and criminalist.

Fingerprint examiner. An individual wishing to disguise his identity may falsify his name, color his hair, grow a beard or moustache, or change his residence, but he cannot escape from his own fingerprints. The skin ridge patterns of the fingers remain constant throughout life. The job of examining and classifying fingerprints is a very responsible one. Those who are so employed are known as fingerprint technicians, identification technicians, and frequently by the public as fingerprint experts.

Law enforcement agencies invariably check the fingerprints of arrested persons. Applicants for jobs in civil service and defense work as well as persons entering the Armed Forces are also fingerprinted. Fingerprints are taken in order to determine if a person has a past police record and to establish a record for possible future identification. Fingerprints have been used not only to convict the guilty but also to free the innocent. Amnesia victims and bodies found at disasters have been identified by fingerprints.

The fingerprint examiner, who is usually employed by a police agency, obtains an individual's fingerprints on an 8 by 8-inch card. Each fingertip is inked and rolled to make an impression on a designated space on the card. Prints of four fingers taken simultaneously are also usually included on the bottom of the card. Name, age, sex, height, weight, eye and hair color, occupation, marital status, identifying marks, and other pertinent information are recorded on the fingerprint card.

Fingerprints are presently classified according to a system de-

Figure 6. Fingerprint examiner.

vised by Sir Edward R. Henry. His system was first used by Scotland Yard in 1901. Classification may be resolved into three large general groups of patterns, each group bearing the same characteristics or family resemblance. These patterns may be further divided into subgroups by means of smaller differences existing between the patterns in the same general group.

A major duty of the fingerprint examiner is searching the fingerprint files. He may examine hundreds or perhaps thousands of fingerprint cards to determine if there are fingerprints identical with the ones on the card he is searching. If not, the new set of fingerprints is filed alphabetically under the name of the person.

If the file search reveals a prior record, this fact is reported to the agency where the fingerprints were taken.

The examination and classification of fingerprint patterns is exacting work and is usually done with the aid of a magnifying glass. Good eyesight is essential. The fingerprint examiner either sits at a table or stands at a file drawer as he works. In the field, a fingerprint examiner searches premises to locate latent fingerprints. These latent prints, or hidden prints as they are known in police terminology, are dusted with contrasting powder, photographed, and then lifted with special tape. On occasion, the examiner may be called upon to take the fingerprints of a dead body. Invariably, he can expect to be called as an expert witness in court.

Employment in criminal identification work is reasonably stable and without seasonal change. Applications for employment may be made directly to the Federal, state, county, and city law enforcement agencies for the position of fingerprint technician or examiner. Most fingerprint examiners are men. However, more and more women are being employed as fingerprint examiners by the various bureaus of criminal identification and investigation in the United States.

The salary entry level of the fingerprint examiner under state civil service ranges from $350 to $450 per month. An experienced fingerprint examiner earns from $450 to $550 per month. The salary for a fingerprint technician with a city police department ranges from about $380 to $460 per month.

Deputy marshal (county). The position of deputy marshal was created in certain California counties to relieve the sheriff's office of the tremendous work load of civil responsibilities. The deputy marshal serves in the judicial branch of the county government to enforce court orders. Marshals serve civil processes such as subpoenas, summonses, small-claims declarations; and they act as bailiffs in the municipal courts. This is a full-time peace officer position which entitles the officer to wear a uniform and carry a weapon. He drives a radio-equipped, marked official car in the pursuance of his duties.

The employment requirements are similar to those of most sheriff's departments, and the salary range is comparable. Marshal Leslie R. Keays, Los Angeles County, states in his brochure, "Young men with vision, and a keen desire to fortify our American way of life are urgently needed. . . . The Los Angeles County Marshal's Office affords the opportunity for civic-minded adults to become an integral part of the judicial system which preserves our civil rights and liberties."

Corrections officer (county). An emerging concept in counties with large penal programs is that of sheriff's minimum detention facilities. The need for such facilities has given rise to the position of corrections officer. These officers maintain order and supervise the work and conduct of the sentenced inmates. These positions and facilities are unique to California, but indications are that they will develop elsewhere because they efficiently and economically distribute manpower. The minimum age requirement is only 19, and the height minimum is 5 ft 7 in. This is an opportunity for police science students who cannot meet regular police employment age or height requirements.

Corrections officer (state). The state, as well as the county, has the position of corrections officer. Corrections officers are key personnel in the rehabilitation programs of correctional institutions, reception centers, and forestry camps. Their job consists of supervising inmates at work, at play, and in living units. Applicants must be between 21 and 45 years of age. High school education or its equivalent is required for this job, which starts at a salary of $463 per month.

For complete details, the California State Personnel Board at Sacramento may be contacted. The shortage of women in this occupation is acute, and efforts to stimulate interest and recruit additional employees have only been partially successful. An intensive recruitment program aimed at recent junior college graduates is being jointly developed by the Department of Corrections and the State Personnel Board in California in an attempt to attract trained applicants.

District attorney investigator. The position of investigator for the county district attorney in large counties has attracted applicants who are interested primarily in basic investigation and detective work for a public agency. There are several investigator levels. The salary, qualifications, and requirements increase with each level. Besides a high school education, two years of experience as a law enforcement officer in a civilian governmental agency is required. Two years of education at a recognized college majoring in police science or criminology may be substituted for one year of the required experience. Entrance salaries are comparable to those of deputy sheriff of large sheriff's departments.

Criminalist. Police executives report that the demand for criminalists in police work is increasing and will continue to do so. The incumbent in this position employs highly specialized scientific techniques in the collection, preservation, and examination of physical evidence. His work includes laboratory analyses of samples of soil, glass, blood, hair, paint, poison, wood, alcohol, narcotics, and related dangerous drugs. He evaluates and interprets his findings, serves as a consultant, assists in training, and testifies in court as an expert witness.

The qualifications for criminalist specify such educational requirements as graduation from a recognized college or university with a major in the field of criminalistics, chemistry, or biochemistry. Salaries start at about $650 and range to $800 per month.

Federal law enforcement jobs

OPPORTUNITIES

There are many interesting, challenging, exciting, and well-paying careers in the field of Federal law enforcement. By selecting the United States government as an employer, the careerist chooses the nation's largest employer, easily the wealthiest, and, doubtless, one of the very best. From dawn to dusk and around the clock, Federal agencies are working endlessly for the American public. Hence, prospects for rewarding careers in the Federal agencies were never better. Many opportunities await those who demonstrate that they are able to meet qualifications and perform duties efficiently in Federal career service.

QUALIFICATIONS AND DUTIES (GENERAL)

In order to qualify for any position in Federal law enforcement, the applicant should have at least a four-year college degree, in which 18 hours of police science, as follows, are recommended: Criminology, or law enforcement subjects such as police administration, criminal law, criminal investigation, interrogation, criminal psychology, case preparation, and police science laboratory. Law degrees and accounting degrees are given special recognition by some Federal agencies. Experience in police work and knowledge of foreign languages, especially Russian and Chinese dialects, entitle applicants to special consideration for jobs.

The duties of the Federal officers include investigating crimes, evaluating evidence, reporting findings, and testifying in court. In the course of their work they may have to participate in raids, arrests, searches, and surveillances.

HOW APPOINTMENTS ARE MADE

To get the best possible employees, the United States government conducts open competitive examinations for qualified applicants. These competitive examinations are conducted or supervised by the United States Civil Service Commission, which is the central recruiting agency of the executive branch of our government. All competitors who pass the exams are ranked according to their scores in the examination. Government agencies select employees from those who rank highest on the eligibility list regardless of race, politics, religion, or nationality.

The examinations are designed to measure the ability of the applicant to perform specific types of employment. Hence, they are practical. How difficult the examination is depends upon the kind of job to be filled. There are examinations that measure aptitude, those that ascertain achievement, and those that test skills. At times, no written tests are given and the applicant is rated on the previous training or experience reflected in his application file.

Announcements for examinations are posted in Federal buildings, United States post offices, and United States civil service regional offices located in major cities throughout the United States. For specific information, a letter directed to the agency in which the applicant is interested or to the United States Civil Service Commission, Washington 25, D.C., will bring immediate response.

WORKING CONDITIONS

Benefits—pay. In order to secure and keep well-qualified employees, the Federal government has geared its career plan for employees so that it meets the competition of private employers. As an example, the Federal Salary Reform Act of 1962 raised pay rates and provided that government employees be paid salaries comparable to those paid by nongovernment employers in the same category of work. Each year salaries are reviewed and adjustments recommended to Congress. Hence, those choosing government careers can expect salaries comparable to those in private employment.

The following additional benefits are available to career government employees:

1. Liberal vacation with pay
2. Generous sick-leave allowances
3. Low-cost life insurance plans wherein cost of premiums is partially paid by the United States government
4. Voluntary health plans
5. Modern retirement system
6. At least eight recognized and observed holidays
7. Training and education programs
8. Credit unions
9. Insulation from politics
10. Professional status
11. Civil service and security

Promotions. As do private employers, Uncle Sam recognizes that government employees desire to advance, succeed, and improve their positions in life. Opportunities for promotion, therefore, are handled on much the same basis as original appointments—by competitive examination. Again, advancement depends on merit and ability. No consideration is given to employees' political affiliation, race, color, or religion. If a government employee has initiative, incentive, and ability, he can forge ahead as quickly and as advantageously as he can in private employment.

Due to the great extent and scope of criminal violations of the laws of the United States, there are plenty of career opportunities in the field of criminal investigator in the Federal service. In fact, there are almost 10,000 positions of investigator in the United States government. These positions are mostly in the Treasury and Justice Departments.

Specific Federal jobs

The following specific Federal law enforcement positions and those in related fields are described and explained in some detail so that the police science student can intelligently weigh employment opportunities and job demands in these fields and compare his own personal qualifications with the requirements.

The U.S. Department of Justice offers numerous law enforcement job opportunities. Positions in the Department's Federal Bureau of Investigation, United States Immigration and Naturalization Service, and Office of United States Marshal are discussed below.

Federal Bureau of Investigation. The Federal Bureau of Investigation has an impressive set of initials which also stands for "fidelity," "bravery," and "integrity." There is still another word, "loyalty," which might be used to describe the unswerving devotion of the FBI to duty, the law enforcement profession, and our nation. It would be very difficult to mention a single important case in which the FBI has not cooperated or contributed at least in a small way to its solution. The FBI laboratory, Identification Division, which houses the vast number of fingerprints, the FBI bulletin, uniform crime reports, law enforcement conferences, police training programs, and the FBI National Academy all are avenues through which the FBI cooperates with and assists local law enforcement at all levels.

JOB REQUIREMENTS. To those police science students who aspire eventually to become FBI agents, the following eligibility factors should be understood and appreciated before making application:

1. Must have absolutely no criminal record whatsoever.
2. Must have absolutely no adverse, reckless traffic record.
3. Credit record must be good.
4. Previous employment record must be good.
5. Reputation and character must be above reproach.
6. Loyalty and patriotism must be unquestionable.
7. Must have ability to get along with people such as neighbors, coworkers, and the public.
8. Scholastic record must be above average.

9. Law or accounting degree is preferred; however, on a probationary basis, a B.S. or B.A. college degree plus five years experience as a police officer is acceptable.
10. Must be from 23 to 41 years old. Minimum height is 5 ft 7 in., with no maximum limitation. Most applicants qualify between the ages of 25 and 30.
11. Must be in good physical health and able to perform arduous work. Overweight applicants should reduce their weights to meet life insurance height and weight standards.

PAY. Special agents enter on duty in grade GS-10 at $7,690 per year. After performing duties in this grade for at least two years, they become eligible for consideration for promotion to grade GS-11 at $8,410 per year. After about three years, they would usually be eligible for promotion to GS-12 at $9,980 per year. Finally, when they have rendered at least four years of satisfactory service, special agents may be promoted to GS-13 at a salary of $11,725 per year. It should be noted that at present there is a flat overtime pay of $1,081 per year for each agent in addition to his regular pay.

TRAINING. Training of employees in the FBI is a continuing program. From the initial 14-week academy-type training which the new special agents receive to the brief indoctrination classes or meetings for noninvestigative personnel, training is a never-ending part of their job. Advancement in the FBI is contingent upon knowledge, ability, and effective effort. J. Edgar Hoover and his associates do everything possible to encourage and assist every employee to learn, to improve, and to advance in the organization.

HOW THE FBI WORKS. One of the most exhaustive investigations ever conducted by the FBI was the Weinberger baby-kidnapping case. This investigation began on July 4, 1956 at 3:30 P.M. when Mrs. Weinberger discovered her baby had been taken from the carriage located on the porch of her home in Westbury, Long Island, New York. A ransom note was left behind.

After the routine investigation failed to develop either a witness to the kidnapping or any logical suspects, attention focused upon the handwriting on the note. Immediately, specially trained agents from the FBI began the difficult task of examining the voluminous handwriting specimens which were maintained by the New York State Motor Vehicle Bureau, Federal and state probation offices, schools, aircraft plants, and municipalities. Two million handwriting samples were examined. Then agents located a handwriting sample at the U.S. Probation Office, Brooklyn, New York, that bore a marked similarity to the note left at the scene of the crime. The sample was in the probation file of Angelo La Marca. Handwriting experts of the FBI compared the ransom note with that of La Marca's handwriting sample. They established that La Marca had prepared the ransom note. When confronted with the evidence, La Marca confessed to the kidnapping. His information led the FBI to the recovery of the remains of the abandoned baby. La Marca was found guilty and electrocuted.

The United States Immigration and Naturalization Service (Border Patrol) THEIR WORK. The Immigration and Naturalization Service is the agency of the U.S. Department of Justice that is responsible for administering the immigration and naturalization laws of the United States. Its officers, members of the Border Patrol, are on duty throughout the United States and at stations in Europe, Bermuda, Nassau, Puerto Rico, Canada, Mexico, and the Philippines. These officers perform a variety of assignments. In the performance of these responsibilities, officers are required to conduct investigations, detect violations of the law, and determine whether aliens may enter the United States. They collect and evaluate evidence, adjudicate applications for benefits, and preside over and present the government's cases at hearings. Also they prevent illegal entrance of aliens into the United States and make recommendations to the courts in such matters as petitions for citizenship.

These duties present new challenges to be met and many different problems to be solved. To cope with these challenges and problems it is necessary to obtain dedicated and hardworking men who are able to adapt themselves to new situations and different environments.

The Service maintains an employee-development program. This program, through organized training, furnishes the employee with the "know-how" to enable him to prepare for advancement.

The Immigration and Naturalization Service is a career service in which advancement is based upon merit. Vacancies from the basic level up to executive levels are filled by the promotion of officers who have demonstrated their capacity for advancement.

JOB REQUIREMENTS. No experience is necessary to become a member of the Border Patrol. Any qualified applicant will be considered for employment without regard to race, creed, color, or national origin. Every applicant for patrol inspector is required to take a written examination. This test measures verbal abilities, judgment, and aptitude for learning a foreign language. Future officers, too, are rated on the basis of the written examination. Upon completion of the written test with at least a grade of 70, applicants are required to appear for an oral interview in the order of their standing in class averages and only in such numbers as the Service may require at a given time.

Applicants must possess a valid driver's license and at least one year of driving experience. After entry to duty, appointees will be required to pass a road test before they can be issued a United States government motor vehicle operator's identification card. Applicants must be citizens of or owe permanent allegiance to the United States and have reached or passed their twenty-first birthday on the date of appointment. There is no maximum age limit.

PHYSICAL DEMANDS. Because of the rigorous conditions as well as the long hours of hard work, applicants must be in sound physical condition and of good muscular development. Applicants must be at least 68 inches in height and of proportional weight, at least 140 pounds.

Physical requirements are very important to a future patrol officer. Eyes, without glasses, must test at least 20/40 Snellen. Ability to distinguish colors is also important. Applicants must also be able to hear the whispered voice at 15 feet with each ear. Any type of tooth disease or decay will disqualify applicants. All other parts of the body such as lungs, heart, nervous system, nose, mouth, and throat must be free from conditions that would in any way endanger the life of the patrol officer. The dangers involved in this job necessitate sound physical and mental health.

SALARY AND BENEFITS. Salaries are based on the standard Federal workweek of 40 hours. Salary for overtime is provided for any time over the 40-hour week. The GS-7 entrance salary amounts to $5,795 per year. Any salary is subject to a deduction of 6½ percent for retirement benefits. Upon completion of the probation period, trainees are promoted to the position of patrol inspector, for which the basic salary is $6,390 a year. For employees in special prescribed fields, the basic salary is increased until the maximum rate for that particular grade is reached. Besides the basic salary, employees receive other benefits such as vacation leave each year, sick leave with pay, low-cost group life insurance, health insurance, and a retirement plan.

Travel expenses of trainee for transportation to the written tests, oral interviews, and physical examinations are at the expense of the applicant. Also, if appointed, transportation to the first duty station will be applicant's responsibility.

New appointees are required to buy a rough-duty and an official uniform. These must be purchased immediately. The cost is about $90. Later, within three months on duty, an official uniform costing $100 must be purchased. Other uniforms costing $150 must be purchased before the end of the probation year. Shortly after appointment, an allowance of $100 is provided by law for those officers of the Service who are required to wear uniforms in the line of their official duty.

TRAINING AND ADVANCEMENT. While attending the Boarder Patrol Academy at El Paso, Texas, new appointees are required to live in dormitories provided by the government. Three meals a day are served at a slight cost. Application forms are available at the United States Civil Service Commission, Washington, D.C.

A new officer in the Border Patrol has many important duties. His principal responsibilities are to prevent the smuggling and illegal entry of aliens into the United States, and to detect, apprehend, and initiate departure of aliens illegally in this country. Patrol inspectors guard areas along international boundaries and their vicinities. Areas may be patrolled by car, on foot, by boat, or by aircraft. Many times it is necessary to halt cars passing over the boundary lines of our country in order to search the car. This means that the officers are involved in numerous arrests including those of dangerous criminals.

After a man has been selected for the Patrol, he is assigned to duty stations on the Mexican border. For the next three months he attends the Border Patrol Academy to learn the history and responsibilities of the Service. Courses in Spanish, marksmanship, and physical training are emphasized. After the training period, the men return to duty posts on the Mexican border, where they continue to receive training for the next 10 months. At the end of the 5½ and 10-month periods, the men also receive written and oral examinations. After their first successful year, officers become qualified for future advancement as investigators, immigrant inspectors, and (for officers who have graduated from recognized law schools) for the position of general attorney.

Office of United States Marshal

DUTIES. The Office of United States Marshal was created by an act of Congress on September 24, 1789. This was five months after the inauguration of President George Washington, who appointed 13 marshals whose districts conformed to the Federal judicial districts. Thus, the Office of United States marshal is the oldest Federal law enforcement agency in the United States.

There are now 91 marshals, including those in Alaska, Hawaii, Guam, the Canal Zone, Puerto Rico, and the Virgin Islands. The marshal's appointment is made by the President of the United States and approved by the Senate. His term lasts four years. Upon expiration of his term, a marshal continues to perform the duties of his office until his successor is appointed and qualifies, or until he is removed by the President. The jurisdiction of the marshal still conforms to the Federal court district, which in the case of southern California extends from the northern border of Merced County to the Mexican border.

Where Federal law is involved, the marshal and his deputies have the same power as a sheriff, although their power is not limited to county or state lines. However, at present, the marshal does not operate as an investigator. Under normal circumstances, the marshal makes arrests only when warrants are issued, upon indictments by the Federal grand jury, by United States commissioners, by the parole board in the case of a parole violator, and in a riot against the Federal government. The marshal and his deputies have the power to make arrests without warrants for any offense against the United States committed in their presence or for any felony under the laws of the United States if they have reasonable grounds to believe that the person to be arrested has committed or is committing such felony.

All Federal prisoners, even though they may be arrested by

other agencies, are placed in the custody of the marshal after arraignment. Unless they furnish bail, they remain in his custody until tried. If convicted and sentenced, the marshal transports the prisoners to the institution to which they are assigned.

In addition to the handling of criminal matters, the marshal has a great many other duties involving civil actions. He seizes and auctions property to satisfy a judgment in Federal court. Since the marshal also has the responsibility of enforcing all admiralty laws, he seizes and auctions ships and all types of vessels. In some cases, the marshal is even required to supervise the operation of a business to get income for satisfying a judgment; and, if the income is not enough to satisfy the judgment, the marshal is required to auction the business.

Another function of the marshal is that of paymaster for Federal officials and their staffs. He is the paymaster for the judges, referees in bankruptcy, court clerks, probation officers, United States attorneys, and all juries and witnesses. He may even be required to protect government witnesses, judges, and congressional committees whenever that need arises. The numerous duties and responsibilities of the United States marshal require that he obtain men of high integrity and sound health. To accomplish this objective, the marshals have been authorized by the Attorney General to appoint deputies. The marshal also has the authority to remove a deputy from employment within the scope of civil service regulations.

As a subordinate officer, the work of the deputy marshal consists of:

1. Serving civil and criminal processes
2. Making arrests
3. Transporting prisoners
4. Maintaining order in Federal courtrooms
5. Conducting sales
6. Preparing official reports and correspondence
7. Operating motor vehicles
8. Carrying firearms and being proficient in their use

SALARY. Recruiting of deputy United States marshals is conducted by filling trainee positions at the grade of GS-6 level. The salary of trainee ranges from $5,505 to $7,170 per year. After a one-year trial period, the salary schedule increases and the deputy marshal grade GS-7 is received. This raises the salary to the $6,050 to $7,850 per year level.

TRAINING. Persons appointed as trainees receive indoctrination and training during a one-year trial period. The areas emphasized are the duties and responsibilities of the deputy marshals. This training is accomplished during the first three months under the direct supervision of experienced personnel. For the balance of the first year, trainees are given minor assignments which they are able to handle. Usually, trainees are promoted to GS-7 positions when they have satisfactorily completed the first year of training. Those trainees who do not progress satisfactorily during the course of their trial period are separated from the service.

EXPERIENCE. The position of deputy United States marshal has certain experience requirements that must be met. Applicants must have had 1½ years of general experience and 2 years of specialized experience. Substitution of specialized experience may be made for general experience. General experience is defined by the marshal as employment in which the applicant has had the opportunity to meet and deal effectively with the public. Experience in working with people involving the protection of property or custody of prisoners is preferable. Service in the Armed Forces of the United States and occupations such as salesman, manager, counselor, and instructor usually provide the experience necessary to qualify.

Those applicants who have had experience as a police officer, deputy sheriff, highway patrolman, or Federal officer, including military police, usually qualify as having had specialized experience. The United States marshal recognizes the experience of peace officers because they have already had specialized experience in making arrests and in use of firearms, exhibiting tact and courtesy, and practicing good public relations. Experience obtained as building guard, jail guard, night watchman, or work with similar duties, however, does not fulfill the specialized-experience requirement.

Substitution for general and specialized experience may be granted for college study. Up to a maximum of three years, one year of academic college study may be substituted for nine months of general or specialized experience. Also, one year of successful study in an accredited law school may be substituted for one year of general or specialized experience. One who is a member of the bar qualifies for three years substitution, and a six-year law graduate with a law degree receives the maximum of four years for substitution in both the general and specialized experience requirement.

SCREENING OF APPLICANTS. Before appointment, all applicants are processed by the FBI. An applicant's qualifications pertaining to loyalty to the United States government, honesty, integrity, and general character are completely and thoroughly investigated. Evidence of disloyalty, perjury, moral turpitude, disrespect for law, unethical dealings, habitual drunkenness, or other adverse conduct is sufficient basis for rejection.

PHYSICAL REQUIREMENTS. The physical condition of each applicant is carefully evaluated. A physical examination is required before appointment by a Federal medical officer. Any physical deformity or disability which may prevent the applicant from performing the duties of his position efficiently disqualifies him for employment. All deputies are required to have an annual physical examination after employment in order to ascertain their current physical condition to perform the arduous work of the service. Normal vision and hearing are required. The use of a hearing aid is not permitted. The minimum height is 5 ft 7 in., and the minimum weight is 126 pounds. Weight must be proportional to height. Applicants must possess emotional and mental stability.

AGE AND RESIDENCE REQUIREMENTS. The maximum age is 40 and cannot be waived. The minimum age is 21 and may be waived for veterans. Veterans may submit application for consideration, but they will not be employed until they reach the age of 21. All applications must be filed with the United States marshal for the Federal judicial district in which the applicant resides or desires employment. The final determination of qualifications of applicants and selections for appointment is made by the United States marshal, subject to approval by the Department of Justice, Washington, D.C.

U.S. TREASURY DEPARTMENT JOBS

There are five distinct bureaus, or divisions as they are often called, in the U.S. Treasury Department. They are:

1. Bureau of Customs
2. United States Coast Guard
3. Federal Bureau of Narcotics
4. United States Secret Service
5. Internal Revenue Service
   a. Intelligence
   b. Alcohol and Tobacco Tax Division
   c. Inspection Service

The organization chart in Figure 7 shows the relationship of these five divisions. The law enforcement responsibilities of each are briefly described in the sections which follow.

Bureau of Customs. The Bureau of Customs' Investigations and Enforcement Division has charge of the suppression of the smuggling of all types of articles into and out of the United States. This includes diamonds, gold, narcotic drugs, implements of war, and other merchandise in violation of the Tariff Act, Export Control Act, Mutual Security Act, Gold Reserve Act, and the Narcotic Drug Import and Export Act. Their investigations also involve the importation or the attempted importation of merchandise by means of false invoices for the purpose of evading payment of duties and taxes. Finally, investigations covering the ownership, documentation, and trade of vessels registered under the laws of the United States come under their jurisdiction.

All of these investigations play an important role in the health, welfare, safety, and economy of our country. Since our government has frozen the price of gold in the United States at $35 an ounce, criminals endeavor to smuggle the gold out of the United States to some foreign country where the gold may be sold for twice and maybe three times the price set in the United States. The mission of the Bureau of Customs is to prevent these illegal dealings.

United States Coast Guard. The Intelligence Division of the United States Coast Guard assists in carrying out the maritime safety program under which the Coast Guard inspects merchant vessels, reviews shipbuilding plans, licenses and certifies merchant marine officers and men, investigates marine casualties, and takes remedial action concerning violations and regulates the handling of dangerous cargoes.

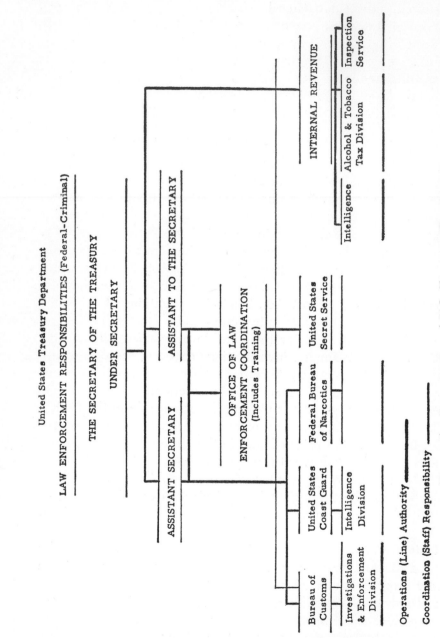

Figure 7. *Organization of U.S. Treasury Department.*

United States Treasury Department

LAW ENFORCEMENT RESPONSIBILITIES (Federal-Criminal)

THE SECRETARY OF THE TREASURY

UNDER SECRETARY

ASSISTANT TO THE SECRETARY

ASSISTANT SECRETARY

OFFICE OF LAW
ENFORCEMENT COORDINATION
(Includes Training)

United States
Secret Service

Federal Bureau
of Narcotics

United States
Coast Guard

Intelligence
Division

Bureau of
Customs

Investigations
& Enforcement
Division

INTERNAL REVENUE

Intelligence

Alcohol & Tobacco
Tax Division

Inspection
Service

Operations (Line) Authority

Coordination (Staff) Responsibility

The Coast Guard's jurisdiction also extends to the maritime police measures which cover enforcement of Federal laws on boating, oil pollution laws, and international treaties relating to the use of the high seas. Another important Coast Guard function is the port security program which deals with the protection of port and waterfront facilities against subversive action.

Figure 8.   Marijuana plant.

Federal Bureau of Narcotics. This bureau endeavors to control the legitimate narcotics trade in order to ensure that an adequate supply is available for medical purposes. It also has charge of the suppression of illicit narcotics traffic by eliminating illegal sources of supply in the United States and abroad. A large part of the Bureau's time must be spent suppressing traffic in marijuana and heroin.

Marijuana (see Figure 8) is a plant that grows like a weed in temperate climates in the United States, Mexico, and many other countries. When the leaves, stems, and flowers are dried like tobacco, the marijuana may be rolled into brown paper cigarettes, folded at both ends, and smoked as a cigarette. The results are unpredictable. The marijuana drug acts as an intoxicant and generally distorts the user's sense of time, space, sound, and balance. It is possible for the user to graduate from marijuana to heroin addiction.

Heroin is a derivative of opium and is obtained by a process of synthesis from morphine. It is very similar to morphine but is even more potent. This drug may be taken orally, sniffed, or even rubbed into the gums. The most common method of use is by hypodermic injection into a vein. Tolerance builds up very rapidly and chances of becoming addicted are very pronounced. The United States government has prohibited the manufacture of heroin and has declared heroin 100 percent outlawed.

Secret Service

DUTIES. Special agents of the Secret Service are generally appointed from a Federal registry list of men who have successfully passed a United States civil service examination for the position of treasury enforcement agent. Agents must be able to recognize and develop evidence to present in court and to write clear, intelligent reports. They must participate in raids, keep suspects and buildings under observation, make arrests, and do other hazardous work. If assigned to protect the President of the United States, they must be prepared to sacrifice their own lives, if necessary, to save the life of the President.

Although the Secret Service has other important duties, the one that carries the greatest responsibility is that of the protection of the President, his family, the Vice-President and his family, the President-elect and Vice-President-elect. This was not originally a function of the Secret Service. Unfortunately, the President who authorized the creation of the Secret Service, Abraham Lincoln, did not profit by its existence, for it was not until after President McKinley was assassinated in 1901 that Congress delegated the Secret Service to protect the President. Even then, it was not until 1903 that extra funds were appropriated by Congress for the protection of the Chief Executive. In the meantime, the responsibility of protecting the President of the United States was handled on an informal basis.

In June, 1913, Congress authorized the Secret Service to protect the President-elect. This protection was extended to the members of his immediate family on June 12, 1917. Operating under the United States Treasury's Secret Service, the White House detail is charged with the security of the White House and its premises. Personnel assigned to the White House detail are trained in the techniques of warfare, in detection of the mentally ill, and even in the mechanics of flying a helicopter.

Federal authorities report that the outlook and opportunities in the Secret Service are better and improving. With the increasing and pressing responsibilities, the Secret Service is especially interested in recruiting promising young people. The additional personnel is needed to continue their great services and to fill the progressively responsible positions that are available for qualified candidates.

Secret Service men work at regular hours in all kinds of weather and may have to do considerable traveling. They may be stationed anywhere in the United States.

JOB QUALIFICATIONS. Applicants without investigative experience must be college graduates. Special consideration is given to college graduates who have successfully completed an accredited college course in police science, police administration, criminology, or in other law enforcement subjects.

All competitors must take a written examination to test observation and memory, arithmetical reasoning, matching parts and figures, vocabulary, and ability to interpret statements. The applicant must score 70 or better to be eligible for further testing. Those who qualify in the written test and meet the experience and training requirements are interviewed. During the interview, they are rated on such factors as personal appearance, bearing, and manners. Ability to speak logically and effectively, to adapt easily to groups, and to evaluate situations is also considered.

Every applicant must be at least 21 years old. He must also be able to pass a thorough physical examination. All appointments are subject to an intensive investigation designed to obtain evidence of an applicant's loyalty to the United States government, his honesty, integrity, and general character.

TRAINING. The Secret Service has organized its own training academy in order to provide its personnel with intensive and specialized training in their various duties and responsibilities, such as protection of the President, suppression of counterfeiting and forgery, enforcement of the laws relating to gold, and investigations of certain offenses involving the Federal Deposit Insurance Corporation, the Federal land banks, and other finance institutions of the United States. In addition to academy training, the agents are frequently schooled in advanced and refresher courses to bring them abreast of the latest developments in scientific law enforcement.

SALARIES. The average four-year college graduate has the opportunity to enter the Secret Service as a trainee at a salary of $5,000 per year. He begins at the GS-5 level. If he maintained a B average or was in the upper 25 percent of his class, he may enter the Secret Service at the GS-7 level at a salary of $6,050 per year. The trainee remains at the GS-5 salary level for only six months and then is eligible for promotion to the next level. After one year probation, the agent is promoted to grade GS-9 at $7,220 per year, and in two years to grade GS-11 at $8,650 per year. The trainee may also receive an additional $500 to $1,000 for necessary overtime and hazardous occupation in Federal employment.

Internal Revenue Service

IRS INTELLIGENCE DIVISION. The Treasury Department maintains several outstanding investigative agencies. One that would appeal to police science students for the dedicated work of its special agents is the Internal Revenue Service. IRS agents make exhaustive investigations of income tax frauds, and they develop comprehensive reports based largely on documentary evidence. Through their diligent, relentless, often unheralded efforts, national crime kings like Al Capone of Chicago and Mickey Cohen of Los Angeles were imprisoned. These arrests and imprisonments struck damaging blows to organized and syndicated crime.

Since the early 1950s, the IRS has had jurisdiction over organized gambling. The Federal government has a law requiring that anyone engaging in the business of bookmaking must purchase a "wagering stamp" from the Federal government for fifty dollars. Bookmakers are also required to pay a tax of 10 percent of their "handle" (gross wagers). The IRS has convicted some of the nation's top gamblers under this statute. In addition to the above work, this division enforces Federal laws and regulations regarding willful attempts by taxpayers to evade such Federal tax obligations as estate taxes, gift taxes, excise taxes, stamp taxes, and social security taxes.

Applicants with four years of college are eligible to apply. Recommended courses for study include: law, police science, police administration, criminology, accounting, economics, and finance. Written and oral examinations are used to test the aptitude of applicants for this kind of investigative work.

IRS ALCOHOL, TOBACCO, AND TAX UNIT. All the investigative divisions or bureaus of the U.S. Treasury Department (except the Secret Service) are involved primarily in Federal tax violations. The Alcohol, Tobacco, and Tax Unit is vitally interested in those who secretly manufacture alcohol and make cigarettes but try to avoid paying the Federal tax. The Alcohol, Tobacco, and Tax Unit investigates the following violations:

1. Manufacture and sale of bootleg (illegal) whiskey.
2. Manufacture and sale of bootleg (illegal) cigarettes.
3. Manufacture and possession of sawed-off shotguns (possession means a $200 tax). Acquiring machine guns and other gangster-type weapons.
4. Prohibition of transportation of certain weapons across state lines, primarily by ex-convicts.

IRS INSPECTION SERVICE. This division investigates alleged violations of laws and other improper conduct involving IRS employees, tax experts, and other nonservice persons when their actions may adversely affect the integrity and reputation of the revenue service.

Investigations of accidents involving IRS employees and property are also conducted by the Inspection Service, as are background investigations of employees, prospective employees, and applicants for enrollment to practice before the IRS. Special investigations, studies, and inquiries also are among the duties of the inspection service.

Positions as intelligence specialists are available mostly in the Department of State, Army, Air Force, and Navy. A four-year college education is required, and written examinations must be taken to qualify for these positions. Police science courses also would be advantageous.

As intelligence specialists, the employee collects, analyzes, evaluates, interprets, and disseminates political, economic, social, cultural, or military conditions in foreign and domestic areas concerning national security.

PRISON ADMINISTRATION WORK

Jobs in this area of Federal employment include positions as corrections officer, training officer, instructor, and parole and classification assistant. Since there are over 2,900 prison administration positions in the Federal government, there are many desirable career opportunities in this field.

A four-year college degree qualifies an applicant for the entrance examination. Courses in criminology, penology, correctional administration, and crime control are recommended. The responsibilities and duties of a prison administrator include training, supervision, correction, and rehabilitation of inmates.

Job opportunities for policewomen

WOMEN IN POLICE SERVICE

Gone are the days when police work was almost exclusively a man's job. There was a time when the only police job open to women was that of a matron, and this work was usually performed by a civilian employee who was responsible for the care and custody of children and women who became involved with the law. At first, policemen resisted the employment of women in this field. However, police executives inevitably came to recognize the need for matrons.

New York City has the distinction of employing, in 1845, the first police matron. Thereafter, primarily on a part-time basis, police matrons were appointed by most of the major cities. The matrons' duties consisted of searching female prisoners at the time of arrest and during the booking process. They supervised detention facilities and saw to the security, comfort, feeding, and clothing of arrested women and children; they witnessed confessions and guarded female prisoners to and from court or en route to other institutions.

In 1893, Chicago recognized that women could be an asset in investigations. A policewoman was hired to assist the detective bureau in problems involving children and women. By 1905, Los Angeles and Portland had also hired policewomen. Before the end of World War I, policewomen were accepted as essential in large cities.

DUTIES OF POLICEWOMEN

With the continuous increase in population and the growth in the number of cases of juvenile delinquency, neglect and dependency, domestic cases involving parents and children, sex crimes against women and children, and vice, law enforcement administrators are finding women increasingly valuable as police officers. Women are usually assigned to juvenile divisions, where their work includes crime prevention, juvenile control, and patrol of areas and establishments where youths congregate. In the jail division, they are concerned with rehabilitation of women prisoners as well as with custodial care. There are also a few special assignments in vice cases, laboratory work, fingerprint examination, and in the investigation of crimes committed by adult women.

Women are also in demand as speakers for groups who want to know what the community in general, and the police department in particular, are doing to meet the problems of women and children. Recognizing the need to meet these problems, Berkeley, California, in 1925, selected a woman as the first head of its newly created crime prevention division. The trend toward more widespread use of women in police work, while it has been gradual, has been accompanied by great success.

At the present time there are about 3,500 policewomen in the United States. Since 1915, policewomen have had a national organization known as the National Association of Policewomen.

Many states have policewomen's associations, officially called the Women Peace Officers' Association. There is also an active International Association of Women Police.

GENERAL JOB REQUIREMENTS

Due to the nature of their work, it is obvious that policewomen must have special aptitudes and training. Although the requirements for appointment as a policewoman differ considerably, there is a definite attempt by the various women's peace officers' associations to promote uniform entrance requirements and standards for policewomen. Since cities vary in size, population, types of crimes committed, and depth of juvenile problems, entrance requirements often are not consistent. Where diagnosis, referral, choice of treatment, and rehabilitation programs are relegated to the court and probation departments, specialized training is not required and qualifications for appointments are not so strict. However, the educational requirements range from high school diploma to college degree, with the trend toward a college degree. Although social case work, as such, is not considered a typical function of a policewoman, training and experience in this field are encouraged. Many police departments refer juvenile cases directly to various social agencies, depending on courts only where there is no other resource or when an authoritative approach is necessary. To select the appropriate referral agency and to participate in community development of needed resources require specialized training.

WORK OF POLICEWOMEN

Duties and responsibilities. A policewoman, in general, investigates criminal cases involving women and juveniles, performs crime prevention work, and performs related work as required. Specifically, the policewoman makes investigations and does crime prevention work among juveniles; inspects women's sections of jails and cares for women and juvenile prisoners; guards, searches, and transports female prisoners; receives and releases prisoners; makes arrests; enforces laws and ordinances; serves subpoenas and warrants; prepares findings for use as evidence and

64 Introduction to police science

presents evidence in court; works with civic groups, social agencies, and youth organizations to promote crime prevention; keeps records and prepares reports; and does miscellaneous typing and filing as required.

Minimum job requirements. Women applicants for law enforcement should meet the following minimum requirements:

1. Graduation from high school or possession of a high school equivalency certificate
2. Age 21 to 35, inclusive, as of date of application (some departments have a minimum age of 23)
3. Minimum height, 5 ft 3 in. (without shoes); minimum weight, 115 pounds (height and weight must be in proportion)
4. Possession of a valid driver's license
5. A record free from all arrests except those for which the applicant has been fully exonerated by the arresting authority or by a competent court of law

Applicants providing a transcript showing the completion of 60 semester units or 90 quarter units of college-level courses at a recognized junior college, college, or university, with a grade of C, its equivalent, or better, may be appointed at the second salary step. Thus, a candidate seeking the position of policewoman is encouraged to obtain as many college credits as possible.

Salary. The salary schedule for policewomen varies. As a rule, the salaries are excellent. Many large police departments and sheriffs' offices have the same wage scale for men and women peace officers. This means that in some instances an entrance salary for policewomen of over $7,000 per year plus favorable fringe benefits is possible.

Probation and parole jobs

OPPORTUNITIES FOR MEN

Probation officers as well as parole agents are society's rehabilitation workers. They endeavor to restore the violator to his community as a useful citizen. In addition, they protect the community from persons who will not obey its laws.

An offender may be placed either on probation or on parole, depending upon his legal status. A juvenile or an adult released by a court without sentence or imprisonment is invariably released on probation. But the violator who has served time in a Federal or state correctional institution, because of the nature of his crime or because he cannot qualify for probation, receives parole.

Most probation officers are employed by the county. Parole agents, however, are usually employed by the state because a release to parole status is a conditional release from a correctional or penal institution. The Federal government employs combination parole-probation officers who work with persons falling within the jurisdiction of the Federal district courts.

Nationally, there are more than five times as many probation officers as there are parole agents. In most parts of the United States the demand for qualified persons for probation and parole work far exceeds the present supply. States with dynamic population explosions have been having a difficult time expanding their correctional machinery fast enough to keep pace with the need for these services. State correctional institutions are full and court calendars are crowded.

As an example of the expanding need for probation and parole services, one probation department has requested new positions for the next three years totaling ten times the number added in the last three years. As the public increasingly recognizes the savings that a probation officer makes in institutional costs by keeping just a few offenders a year out of correctional institutions, it is expected that budgets will be expanded and demand for qualified probation officers will be increased.

OPPORTUNITIES FOR WOMEN

The ratio of women to men employed in probation and parole work has increased in recent years from about one in ten to about one in four. This is just about the ratio of women to men offenders. Women now work extensively with family and juvenile problems, especially those involving women offenders. The number of women employed in all probation departments will probably increase as both the case load and the scope of probation services increase.

Duties. The presentence investigations that probation officers make are perhaps their most important duty. Officers also counsel persons involved in unlawful acts. They investigate home conditions. It is the probation officer's job to refer offenders to specialists in the community for medical diagnosis, personality studies, and vocational guidance. If the officer is working with a juvenile, he tries to establish the facts and underlying causes of the juvenile's crime. Then, he summarizes this information and reports it to the proper court in writing and, if necessary, serves as a witness. Not only does he supervise the offender released on probation, but he may also bring him back into court for a review of his case if the person becomes involved in additional lawbreaking.

The parole officer, on the other hand, devotes much of his time to the supervision and counseling of the offender after his return to the community. Like the probation officer, he gathers social, economic, and psychological data about the parolee. One report is made for each offender at the time of his commitment. Another is a preparole report which is presented to the parole board prior to the parolee's release.

All work of both the probation officer and the parole agent has the same goal—to reduce the possibility of future criminal acts by each person under their supervision. Through acceptance of the offender as a worthy person, able to learn to live by the law if he desires to do so, the professional worker helps the offender to relate his outlook and habits to those of the worker and society. This positive identification with the parolee or probationer and the personal influence the worker exerts on him are believed to be the most important factors in the rehabilitation of an offender.

Salary. Salaries in county probation departments vary with the size of the county and with the amount of education and experience required. Some of the more densely populated counties with high entrance requirements start probation officers at salaries from $505 to $543 per month with annual raises within grade up to $616 to $660 per month. Smaller counties have salaries ranging from $436 to $491 per month.

The parole agent working for the state starts at $530 per month with in-grade raises up to $644 per month. Federal probation-parole positions begin at $6,434 per year. Most agencies have a trainee or student-intern classification that starts at from $350 to $450 per month.

Education and experience. Although related experience may occasionally be substituted for education requirements, a bachelor's degree is the rule rather than the exception in most probation and parole departments. At the graduate level, most authorities recommend either social work or criminology. At the undergraduate level, social work and criminology are again recommended; however, sociology, psychology, and anthropology are also favored. Leaders in probation and parole work agree that future workers will need more and more professional preparation. A master's degree, usually requiring two years of additional study past the Bachelor of Science, is highly desirable.

Candidates in the 22 to 40 age group will have the advantage. Also, good health, emotional stability, and a pleasing personality are assets for this type of work. The probation officer or parole agent must always have his own biases and prejudices under control. He must refrain from making moral judgments if he is to accept each probationer or parolee as a unique and worthy person. He must be able to communicate easily with all kinds of people in all walks of life. He must be able to obtain the cooperation and assistance of his coworkers as well as those in related agencies. Most of all, he should enjoy his work and accept the challenges that it brings. He cannot let failures interfere with his present and future successes.

Regardless of the major field of study or how much graduate work is done, local authorities recommend that the prospective probation officer or parole agent obtain a very broad education and also take special courses in as many related fields as possible. Some of these recommended related fields are: causation and prevention of crime, treatment and rehabilitation of adult and juvenile offenders, legal aspects of social welfare and criminology, criminal procedure and rules of evidence, principles and procedures in probation and parole, psychology as it relates to criminology, and family and domestic welfare.

High school students planning to enter this field should be sure that they are able to qualify for college.

Opportunities for advancement. Since this is a rapidly expanding field, promotional opportunities are good for those who are well qualified. Advancement to positions of greater stature in probation and parole is normally dependent upon passing promotional examinations after securing sufficient experience. Large departments have several levels of classification above the entrance level. In short, promotions are available, and those who have the initiative and application will receive them.

Job opportunities in private security forces

DEVELOPMENT OF PRIVATE POLICE

Early history. When the early colonists came to America, they brought with them not only the public police systems but also the concept of private police (for those who could afford the luxury of special protection). Hence, the private security organizations in existence in America today trace their origins to the private police of England's seventeenth century.

From 1600 to 1850, the government or public police organizations did not have the training, manpower, or equipment to cope with the fast-rising crime problems of an increasing population. Crimes against property were so acute in the larger cities that merchants and other business establishments employed commercial private police as watchmen and patrolmen to guard their properties. These private police were under the control and supervision of the owners of the business or industry, and the owners paid for the special service.

The Pinkerton Detective Agency, founded in 1850, is one of the oldest private detective agencies of its kind in the United States. The history of this private police organization covers some of the most exciting periods in the development of our country. As an example, on November 22, 1861, the Pinkerton Detective Agency uncovered valuable information that materially assisted in exposing and preventing the carrying out of a plot to assassinate President Abraham Lincoln while the President was in Philadelphia, en route to his inauguration in Washington, D.C.

Banks have used guards and companies have used private detectives for many years. Railroad concerns such as Wells Fargo,

Union Pacific, Southern Pacific, and Santa Fe hired special agents as private police to guard and protect their valuable equipment and property. The legendary exploits of these railroad special agents are written indelibly in the pages of American history in the winning of the West.

Recent history. During World War II, private security forces received their greatest impetus for growth. Defense contracts required that company management provide the necessary security to protect government property and military secrets. Management, of necessity, had to create special security divisions in their companies. To achieve this, management, realizing that security had become a specialized type of private police protection, had to make a rapid transition from simple plant protection to effective industrial security. Hence, qualified, competent leadership had to be secured.

In order to acquire the necessary high caliber of leadership needed to ensure an efficient security program, industrial management drafted experienced, reliable personnel from Federal, state, and local law enforcement agencies. These well-trained executives, having experience in law enforcement with the FBI and with various local law enforcement agencies, made great contributions through their organized and effectively administered security operations in the industrial plants of America. Large department stores, aircraft companies, and utilities took this path to modern security operations.

Once efficient security supervisors were employed, the next logical step was to improve the quality of all employees classified as security officers, guards, patrolmen, and investigators. This was not an easy task because, traditionally, private police were not recruited from the ranks of colleges, nor did they have the knowledge or background required. Substandard candidates were usually hired from the ranks of older men, retired pensioners, and those rejected by public police agencies. Since no special qualifications were required, it was inevitable that the reputation of private police suffered by the admission of poorly qualified men. Higher specifications and qualifications, therefore, had to be formulated to attract a "new breed" in order to meet the standards of modern security. This goal was accomplished by appropriate advertising, careful screening and hiring, and intensive training.

Obviously, there was no alternative if management expected to assume the responsibilities and duties of modern security.

Security duties included being "on guard," "on watch," and "on patrol" constantly during the entire tour of duty. Gone were the days when a watchman could punch a few time clocks and then sleep for the rest of his watch or patrol. The new requirements meant that he had to be ready to handle any emergency. Fires, floods, disasters, and disturbances had to be controlled calmly, promptly, and intelligently. Only security officers who possessed common sense, good judgment, and quick reflexes were wanted. Alertness and ability to react quickly became key qualities for this type of work as did good judgment and early recognition and prompt thwarting of any possible destruction of valuable property and loss of life.

With these criteria and objectives, management has improved the rank and file of retail and industrial security forces. Moreover, higher wages and better fringe benefits have helped to ensure this improvement. Security officers now attend colleges, and a general upgrading in all categories of modern security forces has been the trend.

DUTIES AND QUALIFICATIONS

The modern security department today has as its primary function the responsibility of providing an effective security program for its company. In order to accomplish this goal, the security department must be staffed with employees who are dedicated to this principle and have the ability and knowledge to develop, coordinate, and administer a protection system for its company's products, facilities, property, funds, employees, and customers.

Carrying out this function calls for individuals trained in security, who have both a good educational background and a detailed knowledge of the business of the company. Although the security department of a company has many investigative responsibilities, this is not its primary responsibility. Nor is police work. The primary responsibility of a security department is to prevent an occurrence rather than to investigate after the occurrence, and to encourage effective security procedures in all operations of the company.

To be of most benefit to the company, the security department must maintain a close liaison with law enforcement agencies at all levels of city, county, state, and Federal government. Such liaison ensures proper handling of the company's image in the community in all matters involving criminal proceedings. It likewise helps the law enforcement agencies to understand the problem of a corporation in combating external and internal criminal elements.

Many of our corporations today either are directly involved in government contracts or provide materials and services for companies which have prime contracts with the Department of Defense. Guarding the information and products involved in these contracts requires additional security measures to prevent the possibility of secret-information leaks which could affect our national defense effort. Therefore, it is necessary that specially trained individuals be employed to protect the country's secrets and coordinate the necessary security measures from a centralized security department within the corporation.

The old-fashioned private police no longer exists in modern industrial plants. A security department of a corporation today consists of educated individuals with considerable knowledge of their company's operations. These men are specially trained to coordinate and administer an effective security program for their company.

Practically every modern security organization has the following duties:

1. To screen applicants for employment
2. To determine corporate liability pertaining to accidents and all other matters involving possible litigation
3. To detect and prevent thefts against the company
4. To detect and prevent frauds against the company
5. To detect and prevent shoplifting
6. To detect and prevent vandalism
7. To maintain liaison with governmental agencies
8. To develop and maintain adequate physical security measures for protection of company property and materials

Special agents. In order to perform the above duties, an elite corps of investigators, known as special agents, has developed in major security divisions of business and industry. These investigators are usually college graduates who have intensive knowledge of their companies' operations. Some are recruited from investigative divisions of law enforcement agencies. They are capable, ethical operators commanding salaries comparable to public investigators. Delicate and difficult investigations are assigned to them, and their jobs often call for liaison and cooperation with governmental agencies. Future predictions are that this field of endeavor holds many career opportunities for police science students.

Watchmen, guards, and patrolmen. Depending upon the type of business or industry, security police responsibilities at the watchman, guard, and patrolman level include such protective services as:

1. Controlling entrances and exits to facilities
2. Preventing and controlling fires
3. Promoting safety
4. Safeguarding equipment, valuables, and confidential material
5. Patrolling restricted areas

Distinction between private patrolmen and private watchmen. To understand accurately the jurisdiction and function of private patrolmen, a distinction between private patrolmen and private watchmen must be made. Although both are usually classified as private police, it must be pointed out that private patrolmen or merchant police are used essentially for patrol. They may operate both on and off the premises of the owner and may have a list of customers, such as owners of stores and warehouses, to check periodically during a specified period of time. On the other hand, private watchmen are detailed to stay on the property to safeguard the premises from theft, sabotage, arson, and prowlers. For example, local store watchmen and plant guards are private watchmen.

Status of night watchman and merchant patrolman. It is also important that the police science student understand the distinction between the modern security officer employed by large industrial concerns and the night watchman or merchant patrolman employed by small local firms. The security officers employed at modern industrial plants are carefully screened, are well paid, and are trained and qualified to perform required duties. On the other hand, night watchmen and those employed on a uniformed merchant patrol assignment cannot be classified in the same category. This latter type of employment attracts employees who are retired, need only temporary work, or seek a second job to augment their regular income. As a consequence, the wages of the night watchman and the uniformed merchant patrolman range from only $1.25 to $1.75 per hour. This places employment of this kind on the bottom rung of the private-security ladder, economically, socially, and professionally.

COMPANIES EMPLOYING PRIVATE SECURITY FORCES

Industrial security organizations vary in size and operation. There are security organizations that are only one-man operations, and there are others that consist of several special agents or security officers. There are also large and growing numbers of security divisions using both uniformed and nonuniformed personnel, with several levels of command, and supervised by chief special agents, managers, and directors.

Research recently conducted by the Industrial Security Committee of the State of California Peace Officers' Association, Inc., showed that 50 large companies operating in California alone possessed a combined net worth of about 50 billion dollars. These companies had over 1,700,000 stockholders and more than 854,000 employees; and they paid annual taxes of over $1,887,000,000. These statistics clearly reflect the tremendous economic growth that is influencing the need for security operations and security personnel in the United States.

The following are types of business, education, industrial, and other organizations having plant protection, security, or other specialized units:

1. Aerospace industry
2. Armored-car service
3. Automobile industry
4. Banks
5. Car rental agencies
6. Chain stores
7. Chemical industry

8. Commercial airlines
9. Credit agencies
10. Department stores
11. Electric power companies
12. Express agencies
13. Finance companies
14. Food concerns
15. Freight lines
16. Gas companies
17. Graphic arts concerns
18. Hotels
19. Insurance companies
20. Loan agencies
21. Manufacturing plants
22. Motion-picture companies
23. National auto theft companies
24. Petroleum companies
25. Pharmaceutical firms
26. Professional ball clubs
27. Public transportation companies
28. Race tracks
29. Railroads
30. School districts
31. Steamship lines
32. Steel and aluminum companies
33. Taxicab companies
34. Telegraph companies
35. Telephone companies
36. Tire and rubber companies
37. Universities
38. Water companies
39. Television and radio companies

DIFFERENCES BETWEEN PUBLIC POLICE AND PRIVATE SECURITY FORCES

In order to explain the practical differences between public police and private security forces, the following observations are outlined:

1. Private security officers are paid with private funds by the owner of the store, company, or industry.
2. Public police receive salary from public funds obtained from taxes.
3. Security officers are responsible only to the employer, unless they also carry a commission in a public police agency.
4. The public police handle all public offenses and are responsible to the people in their area of jurisdiction.
5. Security officers are only on duty for a specified shift or period of time, such as an eight-hour shift.
6. The public officer is on duty 24 hours a day and is subject to call at all times.
7. Security officers have limited authority, and then only on the premises of the employer.
8. The public officer has full authority 24 hours a day.
9. Private detectives for hire are licensed by the state through a board of vocational standards.
10. Security officers are licensed by local authorities.
11. Public police are hired by the state, county, or city government but receive authority from the state Legislature as "peace officers."

RESTRICTIONS ON PRIVATE POLICE

In addition to the above differences, private security officers have the following restrictions that they must adhere to:

1. They have no more authority to make an arrest than does a private person, unless they are duly commissioned by the public police agency as reserve officers or deputies.
2. Security officers have no authority to carry a concealed weapon. Any weapon carried must be worn on the outside of the uniform, and then only when on duty. Wearing a weapon en route to and from work is permissible, provided the gun is worn on the outside of the uniform.
3. Uniformed patrols and guards may wear badges on uniforms. However, the uniforms and badges must not resemble regular police uniforms and equipment.
4. Private guards and watchmen in some states are not required

to be licensed if all their work for their one employer is only on the employer's property.

5. The trend is for the states to license and conscientiously supervise private police in order to elevate standards and guarantee qualified, capable, and ethical employees in the field of security.

Careers in related fields

Not all students interested in employment as public peace officers possess the desired interests and qualifications and are able to pass the rigid examinations—particularly the physical. Fortunately, there are now many other avenues of opportunity for desirable careers in fields closely related to law enforcement. Opportunities exist in the public services of probation, parole, and correction. Private employment offers careers in plant security, store security, and as private investigators, custodial officers, and insurance adjusters. In all of these positions, police science courses are considered essential and worthwhile. So, before overlooking the many advantages of police science courses, a review of the potentialities and opportunities in these allied fields should be arranged with a college counselor, in order that no possibilities may be overlooked.

QUESTIONS

POLICEWOMEN

1. What city in the United States employed the first police matron?
2. Were women police readily accepted by policemen in law enforcement work?
3. How did policewomen overcome the resistance to their employment in police work?
4. What are the duties of a policewoman?
5. What are the educational qualifications for a position as a policewoman?

6. What are the physical qualifications for a position as a police-woman?
7. About how many policewomen are there in the United States, and what is the future outlook for their employment in law enforcement?
8. Name the policewomen's organizations.

9. Relate the origin and development of private police.
10. Explain the difference between private watchmen and private patrolmen.
11. Relate the security responsibilities and duties of security watchmen and patrolmen.
12. Describe the duties, qualifications, and functions of the *special agents* employed by security divisions of business and industry.
13. Name the restrictions placed on private police.
14. Explain the differences between public police and private police in the following areas:

    a. Authority of arrest
    b. Use of uniforms and badges
    c. Authority to carry weapons
    d. To whom each are responsible
    e. Source of authority
    f. Hours of employment

15. Enumerate at least 10 types of industrial and business concerns that employ private police.
16. What is the value of police science courses in the field of private police?
17. What are the other types of careers related to public police work in which there are many opportunities?

'tis education forms
the common mind,
just as the twig is bent,
the tree's inclined.
ALEXANDER POPE
Moral Essays

4. Criminal behavior and crime reporting

Theories of criminal behavior

Criminal behavior is human behavior that is in violation of criminal law. Many basic factors cause criminal behavior, and psychiatrists spend lifetimes studying these factors. Some police departments even retain full-time psychiatrists and psychologists for advice and consultation on human behavior in crime problems This chapter offers a brief, understandable discussion of the various motivations and influences that actuate human conduct so that the student will learn to recognize and comprehend signs of criminal behavior. By studying and recognizing the patterns of criminal behavior, all law enforcement officers can become more efficient in the apprehension of criminals and in the solution of crimes.

EARLY THEORIES

The very earliest explanations of antisocial behavior were quite simple and widely accepted. Primitive and medieval societies believed that spirits and demons lived within persons who were unable to comply with the rules of the community. When a person could not adjust, his behavior was considered "queer" and "crazy," and the nonconformist was labeled as being "possessed by the devil." This meant, in the thinking of those times, that the violator had to be tortured, banished, or executed, depending upon the gravity of the case.

During the colonial period of our country, witchcraft, sorcery, and other antisocial types of behavior were not tolerated. The wrath of the community was vented on unwanted "witches" and culprits by horrible punishments and inhuman treatment of the kind reflected in Nathaniel Hawthorne's novel *The Scarlet Letter,* published in 1850.

FREE WILL

With the gradual departure of paganism and the growing influence of Christianity, the concept of *free will* was introduced. Man was a human being, created by a divine power, and he possessed a free will, according to certain clergymen and scholars. Having his own will and the ability to choose right from wrong, man must be held responsible for his criminal acts. As a result, punishment of the wrongdoer was often severe, cruel, and inhuman.

As far back in history as the time of the Code of Hammurabi (2000 B.C.), the principal of free will was invoked to demand revenge, retaliation, and punishment for the violator of the Code. This prosecution of the person who failed to comply with the regulations of society was reflected in the Biblical expression, "An eye for an eye and a tooth for a tooth." No sympathy was felt for the criminal since he had within his power the choice of obeying the laws. If he elected, by reason of his free will, to commit a voluntary criminal act, he alone was held responsible for the crime. Hence, punishment of the individual was in order. This concept, like a strong, coarse thread, was tightly woven into the attitude of society toward crime and the criminal. Violators of the law were considered social misfits who deliberately decided on a life of crime. Society responded by creating institutions of isolation and detention for criminals, just as it isolated persons with contagious diseases.

And so, down through the centuries, society has been ashamed of crime and the criminal. Like the lazy housekeeper who sweeps the offensive dirt under the carpet, society has tried by laws, courts, punishment, revenge, and retaliation to hide the human debris of crime and criminals behind high prison walls. This unpleasant, unsightly weakness in our social structure, society feels, must not be visible and, like vice and abnormal sex, must be obscured from view.

Such an attitude and sentiment toward criminals encouraged very little investigation into the realm of criminal behavior. In fact, prior to the publication of Lombroso's *The Criminal* in 1876, there was no serious scientific approach to the study of the criminal.

BORN CRIMINAL

Cesare Lombroso (1836–1909), a noted Italian physician and anthropologist, rejected the philosophy of free will. He emphasized and initiated a scientific trend that led the study of criminal behavior into new avenues. His interpretation of criminal behavior was principally biological, and he considered bad conduct a return to the primitive uncivilized behavior of early man.

To back up his theory, Lombroso conducted many scientific studies of the physical characteristics of criminals in prisons. His research led him to believe that criminals could be *classified* as to their physical characteristics. By measuring the skull, bones, and all parts of the anatomy of known violators, he concluded that criminals had specific physical characteristics which made them different from noncriminals. He believed that persons who were criminally inclined possessed primitive physical traits such as the large jaws and receding foreheads of prehistoric man during the early years of his evolution. Lombroso insisted that criminals could be identified by these primitive physical characteristics. In fact, he prided himself in being able to identify criminals by these physical traits. Thus, he said, criminals are born criminals.

Lombroso's contention that man's criminal acts were due to his primitive, inner nature and not to free will has been proved wrong by psychologists and sociologists. It was not difficult to disprove Lombroso's theories because he restricted his studies to criminals and did not include noncriminal groups in his research. As a result, Lombroso and his associates did not explore the fact that criminal behavior existed in people whose bodily characteristics were different from the so-called primitive physical traits of the typical criminal.

In opposition to Lombroso's theory of the "born criminal," Albert Morris, in his book entitled *Criminology*, published in 1934, writes, "Criminals are not born so, they are made. If he becomes one it should be possible to find the starting point. Every bit of evidence we have points to the need of doing preventive work when the first signs of antisocial behavior appear. If those who deal with children could have at their disposal a trustworthy technique for detecting at the point of divergency those types which are starting in the wrong direction, society would have an effective means of checking crime" (Morris).

A former pupil of Lombroso, Enrico Ferri, an Italian scholar, insisted that society should be held responsible for crime prevention. He emphasized prevention instead of punishment. He believed that current social problems arising from the economy, industry, politics, climate, religion, and education influenced people toward crime. Through his study, he placed criminal types into five classifications: those who are born criminals, the criminally insane people, the habitual criminals, the accidental, occasional criminals, and the spontaneous, emotionally charged types.

Gland theory. Closely akin to Lombroso and his school of thought are the scientific advocates of the role of the human glands as an influence in human conduct. There are those who believe that intensive research into the realm of endocrinology, the study of internal gland secretions, would be most revealing and helpful in the study of human behavior.

Endocrinologists believe that the person best qualified to diagnose abnormal or antisocial behavior is the practicing physician. During the course of his professional career, the doctor attains the skills of the psychologist, the sociologist, and the therapist. So it is the family doctor who knows how to examine the body and intelligently extract a case history of present and past physical ailments. If the examination reveals glandular disturbances, the doctor can identify these and recommend treatment. For instance, he could prescribe drugs to regulate glands for those emotional disturbances and medical problems caused by the thyroid, pituitary, gonads, pancreas, and the adrenals. Imbalances of the glandular system could be thus remedied, and the source of adverse behavior could be reached and rectified, thus helping to solve problems in behavior.

Twentieth-century criminologists agree that there is no one specific cause of crime. They hold that crime is due to multiple, interrelated causes. Hence, heredity, environment, mental illness, physical defects, temperament, poverty, and adverse living conditions at home, at work, and at play may all either directly or indirectly play an important role in man's antisocial behavior.

At this stage of research, it is suggested that the theory of hereditary tendencies alone may not be accepted as the sole cause of the majority of crimes. Environment, particularly the social environment, must also be understood as a vehicle by which inherited traits are carried into right or wrong avenues of expression.

In short, man is not born a criminal. He may inherit certain traits which make it possible for him to become antisocial. For example, physically and mentally handicapped persons may be unable to adjust to their environment because of their hereditary defects. Also criminal behavior may be due to the inability of a person to adapt himself to the community or the society in which he lives. Furthermore, the community or society sometimes fails to create the kind of environment in which people can adjust favorably to the laws of society.

HEREDITARY ASPECTS OF CRIMINAL BEHAVIOR

Heredity versus environment. Just like "Which comes first, the chicken or the egg?" is the question of what is more important, heredity or environment, in criminal behavior. Modern criminologists agree that both play an important role in the makeup of the total human being and must therefore be taken into consideration in the study of criminal behavior.

Heredity can be defined as the passing on of physical or mental traits and tendencies from a parent to an offspring. Among those who adhere to the theory that the individual is a creature of his heredity are biologists, anthropologists, psychologists, and endocrinologists. They believe that weakness or failures in the physical makeup of the body, glands, or brain (all inherited) cause criminal behavior.

Effects of heredity. Geneticists have discovered that genes are the basic units of heredity. The genes determine all the inherited characteristics that a human being receives from parents and distant ancestors. Although all people inherit thousands of genes, the possibility of inheriting "bad" genes is remote. Our population is too fluid and constantly mixing to permit bad genes to dominate. The possibility of a person's inheriting bad genes occurs generally when a group of related people are isolated for generations and inbreeding causes undesirable traits to become dominant in offspring.

The opportunity to research the passage of genes from generation to generation was made possible by the study of a religious sect known as the Amish. They emigrated from Switzerland and southern Germany in the early and middle 1700s and settled in Pennsylvania and Ohio. A little later, they banded together and increased in number from 200 to about 8,000. Relatively few outsiders have been admitted to the fold since prerevolutionary days. Recent studies of these Amish by Dr. Victor A. McKusick of Johns Hopkins University show that new, previously undescribed derangements of health among the Amish are hereditary in nature.

For instance, in 1742, a member of the Amish sect, Samuel King, left Europe and settled in Lancaster County, Pennsylvania. Either King or his wife carried a certain recessive gene that produces an effect of dwarfism only when inherited from both parents. The offspring is 40 to 60 inches tall, with an extra finger on each hand and possible heart malformation. Forty-nine such cases have appeared since the initial case existed around the time of the Civil War (Schmeck). This recent study has given scientists a chance to make a realistic evaluation of heredity as it applies to human beings and as it reveals possible clues to criminal behavior.

Psychological aspects of heredity. The physical characteristics which we inherit have a profound effect upon us psychologically. Our size, shape, or other physical characteristics often have a strong influence on the kinds of feelings we may have about ourselves. How we feel about ourselves goes a long way toward influencing the ways in which we behave toward other people we meet.

The feelings of a person whose physical appearance is unusual or different from that of others may cause behavior which is also different from the normal behavior expected in the social group. Yet these different behaviors are not necessarily bad when other factors are taken into consideration. The comedians Jimmy Durante and Bob Hope, with their famous noses, or the comedienne Martha Raye, with her oversized mouth, are examples where apparent physical liabilities have been capitalized upon with overwhelming success.

But the reactions of some individuals to unusual physical appearance may be quite different. The person who feels himself to be undersized or abnormally short in stature, for example, may react to this supposed deficiency by becoming overly aggressive in his behavior in order to compensate for his feelings of inadequacy. A member of a different race may find that the skin color he has inherited from his parents has a real effect upon his place in society or upon how he is accepted by his fellow workers on the job. His feelings about himself and the ways in which he sees himself treated by social groups can have a strong influence on his behavior toward others. Thus, the physical characteristics we inherit do have definite meanings for us and can cause us to have feelings about ourselves which can directly affect the way we behave.

In summary, it can be said that heredity plays an important role in determining behavior because of the ways in which each individual reacts to his perceptions of his physical self. Heredity is certainly not the only factor which influences behavior, but it does sometimes create boundaries and set limits within which the person may be forced to exist against his desires.

ENVIRONMENT AND BEHAVIOR

There is a strong school of thought that sees environment as the controlling factor in determining criminal behavior. Environment includes all physical, psychological, moral, spiritual, and social influences which exist around and within a person.

Influences for good or evil exist in all environments. The word environment comes from the French word for "to surround." In its broadest sense, environment includes not only the physical surroundings of man but also the social conditions in which he lives, works, and plays.

Criminal behavior cannot be predicted with any high degree of accuracy because there are too many obscure variables. Yet it is possible to recognize influences that create a setting in which criminal behavior seems to flourish. These forces which increase the chances of antisocial behavior can be identified even though our social sciences cannot yet predict with accuracy just how individuals may respond to these forces.

Social-distress signals. Modern sociologists and criminologists agree that there are certain storm signals that can warn of antisocial conduct ahead. Law enforcement officers, therefore, need to make a careful study of criminal behavior so that they will be able to recognize the warning symptoms and anticipate unfavorable behavior patterns as well as adverse attitudes toward police.

If law enforcement officers, social workers, criminologists, and penologists can learn to recognize these signals and take appropriate action with the assistance of community resources, considerable progress may be made toward the prevention of antisocial behavior.

The following are representative environmental factors that may divert human behavior into channels of crime.

Broken home. The very foundations of society are in the home. Anything that tears down that foundation is an evil influence. Divorce is the number one offender in cases of broken homes. In 1890, 1 out of 17 marriages ended in divorce. Recently, the Governor of California announced that 1 out of every 2 marriages terminates in divorce in California. He also claimed that 75 percent of the juvenile delinquency and 50 percent of the imprisonments are directly attributable to the high divorce rate resulting in broken homes. The significance of these figures is obvious to the student interested in studying the influence of broken homes on criminal behavior.

Absentee pappyism. A new phrase has been coined in our vocabulary, "absentee pappyism." According to the U.S. Children's Bureau in Washington, D.C., one million fathers have deserted their families. In addition, the Bureau reports that each year one hundred thousand more fathers join the one million who have abandoned their families. In California alone, it costs the taxpayers about 194 million dollars to support these deserted, dependent children. While no one can determine precisely the amount of criminal behavior resulting from absentee fathers, it is clear that absence of a father reduces family stability and can have a devastating influence on the young.

Neglectful parents. Some parents may abandon their offspring on the steps of a church or leave their children in cars to be rescued by police or cleverly "ditch" them in a department store. These are cases of outright abandonment.

But there are other kinds of parental neglect which may predispose the young to crime. Such is the neglect of parents who turn the home into a domestic shambles by constant quarreling and fighting which drives young adolescents into the streets in search of some relief. Such is the neglect of parents who have little or no time for their children, yet seem to find plenty of time for their own work and play. The family is supposed to be a bulwark against the adverse forces of a sometimes destructive environment. If the family is disorganized by negligent parents, it seem more likely than not that the products of such a family environment would be inclined to extend this disordered thinking to society at large. Parental neglect is apparent in the backgrounds of numerous criminals.

Lack of discipline. An editorial in the Inglewood, California, *Daily News* very neatly sums up the problem of discipline as an environmental factor affecting human behavior as follows: "Today there are too many homes which have lost all influence because they have become only places to sleep. There are also too many parents imbued with the idea that character development makes discipline impossible. Adults and children continuously test authority and will go as far as allowed in that testing. Children want to have rules to obey and will obey them if they are spelled out."

Some authorities believe that the pendulum of discipline in administering to the needs of the modern child has swung to the opposite side. This is illustrated by a parent who admitted she had lost parental control when she appeared before a local judge.

When asked to explain her son's delinquency, she complained, "I can't do anything with him, Judge." The wise old judge admonished, "Have you ever done anything for him, such as giving him constructive discipline?"

Socially acceptable behavior reflects positive, adequate training and education—and discipline. The word discipline itself means "learning." This learning, or discipline, needs to be part of the individual's experience from birth. Lack of early discipline is another predisposing force toward crime.

Poverty. In any description of the destructive influences that can lead an individual to crime, poverty must be included. Sociologists insist that poverty alone may not be a single specific cause of crime but that it does produce adverse conditions that can lead to crime. Police blotters are heavy with reports and accounts of burglaries, robberies, and petty thefts caused by the need for the necessities of life.

Human casualties and criminals seem to accumulate under conditions of poverty. For the poor there are few decent homes and many homes without a father. There is less family stability and much early delinquency. Children of the poor frequently know little normal affection. All of these are the environmental forces of poverty that can turn an individual from the paths of normal social behavior into antisocial acts.

Lack of religion. Even people who have no interest in religion will agree that religion is a strong, stabilizing, and favorable influence in a community. Many people have been rescued from a life of crime by religion, and many have avoided criminal behavior under the influence of religious training at home, at church, or in a parochial school. The value of religion is immeasurable as an environmental factor controlling human behavior.

Law enforcement officers invariably tell you that they would rather interrogate a criminal with a religious background than one without one. The person with a sincere religious belief is apt to have developed a conscience so that he can distinguish right from wrong. Moreover, he can be reached and helped. But often a person with no religion—an atheist or an agnostic—is difficult to treat because he seems to build an invisible wall between himself and the police or social worker. This prevents treatment and rehabilitation because often that wall is insurmountable.

Although the philosopher Colton once said, "Men will wrangle for religion, write for it, fight for it, die for it—anything but live it," his comment is not true to real life. There are many people who try to live a religious life, and who can be rehabilitated when they fall, as police records will verify.

Understanding problems of environment. The above social danger signals are only a few of the many environmental conditions that may adversely influence human behavior. Each police science student is urged to pursue additional research and continuously study current social problems for a realistic understanding and awareness of behavioral patterns in order to understand criminal behavior and appreciate crime trends.

Classification of criminal types

SOCIOPSYCHOLOGICAL APPROACH

Criminologists have investigated criminal behavior mainly through three approaches.

1. The *biological* approach, which is concerned chiefly with the effects of the functioning or malfunctioning of various bodily organs on criminal behavior
2. The *psychological* approach, which is concerned primarily with disorders of the human mind as the source of criminal behavior
3. The *sociological* approach, which emphasizes the effects of poor environment and social conditions on criminal behavior

No one of these approaches, criminologists now agree, is completely satisfactory. The search for a broader approach to criminal behavior has evolved into the sociopsychological approach. This is really a combination of all three earlier approaches.

The sociopsychological approach rejects the theory that criminal behavior is the result solely of either biological or psychological factors. Instead, the two sciences, biology and psychology, agree, with reservations, that criminal conduct develops from previous experiences. Sociologists usually accent the social causes in those experiences while the psychiatrists emphasize the mental factors. By combining the two approaches, however, patterns of criminal behavior can be discussed intelligently. But it must be kept foremost in mind that the word "criminal" embraces many kinds of persons whose antisocial conduct could have been developed in completely different ways. Reducing criminals to types is simply a convenient way of identifying certain outstanding characteristics of criminals. Few criminals are completely "pure" types.

AMATEUR CRIMINALS (NONPROFESSIONALS)

Petty violators. Petty violators commit minor infractions of the law. The petty violator breaks traffic laws by speeding, running through stop lights, overparking, drag racing, or disregarding regulations on required standard car equipment. A petty violator may become overexuberant during certain holidays and wind up in jail. He may be an enthusiastic sports fan and become involved in a fight at an athletic event. However, he usually obeys laws and rarely gets out of line.

Accidental or occasional criminal. Some of the biggest headaches for those who must enforce the law are the family fights between husbands and wives and relatives. While not hardened criminals, participants in these fights violate the law as disturbers of the public peace, frequently in circumstances beyond their own control. Alcohol, social drinking, infidelity, and economic pressures may trigger an argument resulting in assault, battery, mayhem, or even murder. Those involved in crimes of this sort are designated as "accidental" criminals.

Officers who respond to police calls for help between battling husbands and wives must remember that, although these violators are not professionals, they may be dangerous in explosive circumstances.

Passion criminals. Closely related to the accidental criminal is the person who is thin-skinned. He is easily irritated and has a low boiling point. He takes offense easily, is quick-tempered, and is provoked to anger at slight provocation. Because of these tendencies, he may get involved in fights which may result in criminal violations as serious as homicide. This type of a person is placed in the class of violent criminals and commits crimes of passion such as those induced by rage, anger, hate, and other violent emotions.

White-collar criminals. There are some upper- and middle-class legitimate businessmen and women who succumb to illegal activities, mostly those which are undercover and carefully disguised. The crimes of these men and women take such forms as giving short weights and measures, fee splitting, embezzlement, fraud, false advertisement, illegal sale of liquor, and payola. These white-collar violators live in respectable society. They uphold all other laws, but violate one or two to get extra benefits. They become reconciled to the belief that their wrongdoing is "all right" because, they rationalize, "everybody has a little larceny in his heart." They shrug off the possible stigma of crime with belief that, if caught, it is most likely that they will experience only a fine or, at most, probation.

PROFESSIONAL CRIMINALS

The next distinct behavioral pattern is characterized by the professional criminals. These are in a class by themselves, because they are individuals who are either accidently or purposefully drawn toward a life of crime. Since they believe that crime pays, these criminals work hard at making it pay. Occasionally, they are sent to prison, but they calculate the odds and believe that the criminal life is worth the risk. These criminals become expert in some field of criminal activity. They develop techniques and utilize every scientific means to perfect a criminal role as bank robber, burglar, forger, counterfeiter, or confidence man. Some of the real professionals are bunco artists who prey on rich widows and fleece them out of their fortunes by fraudulent schemes, promises of marriage, or any other tricks or devices to get their victims to part with money and valuables.

A professional criminal becomes hardened and immune to any attempts at rehabilitation. Efforts to reform the professional criminal are almost invariably fruitless, especially when he operates in a gang or syndicate like the Capone gang and the notorious underworld crime syndicate, the Mafia. The FBI's Ten Most Wanted Criminal List usually contains several professional criminals.

Professor Walter Reckless, noted criminologist, calls the professional criminal "the most highly processed offender, the one whose career has represented a thorough schooling in criminal techniques, arts, attitudes, and philosophy of life."

No one knows with certainty the number of transients or hoboes crisscrossing our country, using any convenient, available mode of transportation. We do know that their numbers are legion. These "Knights of the Road" prefer the boxcars of our railroads. Embracing amnesia victims, missing persons, minor fugitives, absentee fathers, vagrants, runaways, and winoes, they compose a class of persons who are unable to face reality and conform to the standards of behavior of a community. Because of their inability to adjust to accepted social patterns, they become outcasts and hermits—essentially harmless avenues of expression. But they may also resort to petty theft, larceny, and embezzlement in order to satisfy their physical needs. The skid-row areas of metropolitan cities are teeming with maladjusted criminals exhibiting antisocial behavior.

Habitual criminals. Certain types of persons are unable to abide by the rules laid down by the majority. No matter how many times they transgress and are caught, they either repeat the same offense or commit some other act frowned upon by society. These people are criminal repeaters or recidivists. They persist in their life of crime. Examples of this type are prostitutes, pimps, madams, narcotic addicts, and alcoholics prone to public drunkenness like winoes. They fall into a rut and are unable to conquer their antisocial habits, so they are classified as habitual criminals. The largest expense to police budgets in many metropolitan cities is the processing of habitual drunks into and out of jail and to and from work farms.

Psychoneurotic (neuropathic) offenders. As many as 10 out of 100 people suffer from deep anxieties called pathological anxieties. They often display an overreaction to authority, high tensions, and self-consciousness. One type of neurotic is the kind with obsessions. He has certain ideas that keep constantly returning. As an example, Mickey Cohen, notorious gambler and hoodlum, was reportedly obsessed with the idea of cleanliness. He washed his hands at every opportunity. In fact, his obsession once saved his life. According to the newspaper accounts, Mickey Cohen was washing his hands in the lavatory of his haberdashery shop in the Sunset Strip area in Hollywood when rival mobsters charged his shop to "eliminate" him. Members of his gang served as targets, but Mickey Cohen, due to his penchant for cleanliness, was unscathed.

Sexual offenders (*neurotic*). There are two distinct types of sexual offenders. One type of sexual offender is the person with a neurotic degree of maladjustment. Examples of this would be the *voyeurist*, known in the vernacular of the police jargon as "Peeping Tom," the *fetishist*, who is the clothesline thief of women's intimate undergarments, the *transvestite*, who dresses in the clothes of the opposite sex, the *exhibitionist*, who exposes his private parts in public, the *passive homosexual*, who may be the victim of blackmail, and others of that ilk.

Psychiatrists believe that neurotics of this type are usually susceptible to rehabilitation if referred for treatment as soon as possible. After successful psychiatric assistance, they may again take their place in society as productive citizens.

Psychopathic criminals. Plato, in his *Republic,* stated that if one's objective was to ruin a person, the best way to do it was to shower that person with every gift and pleasure possible. This action would produce a person of weak character—one spoiled beyond redemption. That is just what parents are producing in our affluent society when they rear children in the lap of luxury, giving them no work, responsibility, or discipline. When every whim and caprice of youth is catered to by overindulgent parents, a child may become emotionally immature, unable to make moral and social adjustments, and subject to personality disorders. Psychologists describe anyone catalogued in this category as possessing a psychopathic personality. This means that egocentric, self-centered, selfish persons typifying this breed are prime potentials for robbery, bunco, burglary, forgery, and a host of other similar crimes which may satisfy the vicarious appetites of a *psychopathic criminal.* Such criminals can use other people for their own personal gain without remorse or pangs of conscience. They are social rebels who vent their deep-rooted feelings against law and order and practically any person or group that tries to help them.

Sexual offenders (*psychopathic*). Sexual patterns are learned during the formative years of growth and maturation. The great majority of people develop sexual maturity compatible to prevailing culture and social demands. There are some who deviate from what society rules a normal outlet for sexual practice. Of these there are two types of social offenders. One type is aggressive, and the other is passive; hence, their behavior is not the same. Instead, the aggressive sexual offender perpetrates rapes, has sadistic tendencies, and may get involved in child-molesting cases. He lends credence to the opinion that there is a psychopathic quality in this disregard for the rights of others. The psychopathic sex criminal is an extremely serious threat to a community.

For example, all too often a community is shocked by the revelation that a beautiful woman was tortured, brutally beaten, and ravished before she was dismembered and thrown into an open field. What kind of a person would do such a reprehensible crime? The answer is a *sadist,* because the sadist is one who enjoys inflicting pain, torture, and mutilation on the body of another. The unsolved Black Dahlia murder in Los Angeles, California, in which the victim's body was cut in half, was described by psychiatrists as the work of a sadistic sex criminal.

The opposite of the sadist is the *masochist,* the passive social offender who receives pleasure from experiencing pain inflicted by another person. A comic once quipped that "the ideal marriage occurs when a sadistic man marries a masochistic woman. He can beat her frequently, and she will love him for it. Hence, they remain happily married." Of course, it must be emphasized that this observation was made only in jest and is not recommended practice in any shape or form.

Occasionally a pyromaniac known as a "firebug" goes on a rampage and starts a series of fires. When he is finally apprehended, a psychiatric examination may reveal that he is a frustrated person with repressed, unfulfilled sexual desires. Perhaps, way back in his life somewhere, he was fired from his job at a lumberyard. He hates the owner of a lumberyard, so he sets the lumberyard afire. This is substantially the description of a young man who, when caught in a southern city, begged the officers to send him to a psychiatrist. He knew there was something wrong with him. He explained that he could not resist the urge to set fire to lumberyards.

The periodic wave of vandalism in churches, schools, parks, and other public buildings from coast to coast may be attributed to persons who hate their surroundings and the power structure of the community.

When one residential city suddenly became the target of a firebug, it appeared as though the whole city would go up in smoke before the arsonist was apprehended. However, coordination and cooperation of the police and fire department investigators finally trapped the violator through a series of stakeouts. When interrogated, the young arsonist, age 14, revealed that all his life he had been rejected because of a huge, hairy, discolored birthmark that covered one side of his face. As an unwanted outcast, he resented being shunted into the background. He never received any attention, so he struck back at society in the best way he knew. And he accomplished his objective. He was now receiving all kinds of attention from doctors, psychologists, sociologists, police, and fire officials.

Psychotic persons. Persons who lose adequate contact with reality and must be institutionalized are psychotics. Psychosis is a medical term which is just about tantamount to legal insanity. Persons in this class are a risk to themselves and others. They are unable to cope with daily personal affairs. Some psychotics can put up a good front when being tested. Hence, the average citizen is not qualified to testify unequivocally to this mental condition. Although not all psychotics are dangerous, they should be handled with care and caution. The officer who is called to remove such a person must remember to use the right approach. A pleasant demeanor, kind expression, and firm but gentle voice will reassure the psychotic that he is not alone in a hostile world. When psychotics have delusions of persecution, grandeur, and unusual body function, they may become a police problem. Violence concluding in murder or shrewd connivance in criminal activity is not out of the realm of possibility for *insane criminals.*

In the event the new officer permits himself to be lulled into a false sense of security when transporting persons for commitment to a mental institution, the following is one of many similar true cases that should be remembered.

Three officers were sent to the home of an alleged psychotic to escort him to a state mental institution pursuant to judicial decree. While in his home preparing to leave, the psychotic was quiet, docile, and cooperative. However, just as the officers were opening the patrol car door for him, this mental subject suddenly became uncontrollable. He savagely fought the three officers with almost superhuman efforts. Fortunately, the three officers were finally able to subdue the mental subject but only after a titanic struggle, torn clothing, and many bruises. Besides, one of the officers overheard one of the women bystanders who gathered at the commotion say, "Just look at those three officers beating up that poor, helpless old man."

To go alone on this type of case is suicidal, as was proven in one county when a deputy sheriff endeavored to take into custody a mental patient. The officer was overpowered and thrown from his speeding patrol car to his death.

Restraining devices such as handcuffs and plenty of manpower will prevent such tragedies.

Uniform Crime Reports

HISTORY OF CRIME REPORTING

Crime statistics. Prior to 1930, there were no national crime statistics available in the United States. As early as 1870, Congress passed an act to provide a national system for the collection of crime statistics, with the Attorney General's Office as the collecting agency, but the attempt was unsuccessful. Thus, police executives possessed only the crime reports from their own local departments. As a result, law enforcement agencies did not know how well or how poorly their departments compared with similar departments in the United States. Moreover, significant trends in crime could not be detected and charted. And since the value of crime statistics was not appreciated, the cost of crime was also in the realm of guesswork. Some departments kept accurate crime tabulations; others were indifferent; and still others kept only sketchy records that were conveniently "harmless" to their departments.

During the late 1920s, leading police administrators came to believe that a national crime picture for comparison purposes (such as city with city, state with state, and region with region) was of paramount importance and would be of great value and significance to all law enforcement agencies. So, under the auspices of the International Association of Chiefs of Police, a committee was formed in 1927 to explore the possibility of developing a national crime reporting system.

National clearing house for statistics. In 1930 the International Association of Chiefs of Police recommended that the FBI be designated as the central repository for all crime statistics. Consequently, since September, 1930, by an act of Congress, the FBI has been serving as a national clearing house for crime statistics. Since that time, all law enforcement agencies have been requested to report their crime statistics to the FBI for accumulation and distribution. To facilitate this reporting, a system of monthly and annual crime reports was devised so that all police agencies could report as accurately as possible the true picture of crime in their communities. The immediate response by law enforcement was excellent, and the system of reporting has improved steadily over the years.

USES OF UNIFORM CRIME REPORTS

Local uses. Police administrators now use the FBI Uniform Crime Reports to justify and explain to the city council their need for manpower and equipment to fight crime. For instance, a city with a small police force and a high incidence of crime can show, by meaningful use of crime reports, that another city of the same size has more personnel and consequently has less crime. Also, if a department in one city is holding back the pressure of crime better than other cities of the same size, a police executive may logically contend that this achievement is due to the efficiency of his department. However, in all instances, crime statistics should be used legitimately and not for ulterior purposes.

Dedicated police officials have reasoned correctly that an honest presentation of the crime picture both to the city council and to the public is the best policy. When the public and the press know the facts about an urgent crime problem, they willingly support law enforcement by approving needed financial and other aid.

Periodic FBI Uniform Crime Reports. By special issue of the Uniform Crime Reports in November, 1958, J. Edgar Hoover, Director of the FBI, announced that Uniform Crime Reports, published semiannually since 1941, would be published only once each year beginning in the fall of 1959. This complete an-

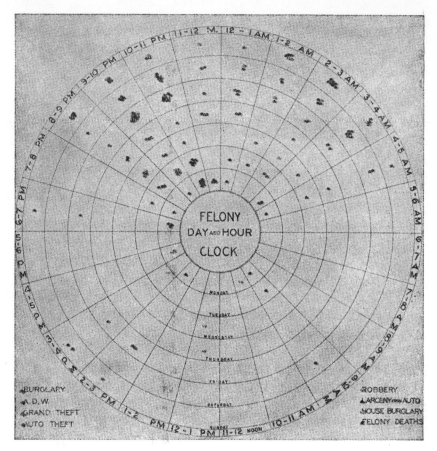

Figure 9. Felony day and hour clock.

nual FBI Uniform Crime Report covers all available statistics in considerable detail. It is now distributed in July of each year to all law enforcement agencies as one of the cooperating services of the FBI.

In this same special issue, Mr. Hoover explained that there would be an "issuance of intermediate publications of limited scope. . . ." As a result, since 1959 the FBI has released quarterly crime reports in the nature of preliminary data showing crime trends for the most recent available period for cities by population group. Also included is the number of offenses reported by individual cities with a population in excess of 100,000.

Public libraries and interested scholars, as well as newspapers, may receive copies of the FBI Uniform Crime Reports upon request.

Reports assist planning. More than 96 percent of the law enforcement agencies in the United States contribute crime statistics to the FBI. Free advice, counsel, and forms are furnished by the FBI to facilitate the preparation of the required reports.

Modern law enforcement administrators have learned that they are better able to administer to the basic needs to their departments when they have current crime facts which reflect the activities and requests received by the department for service rendered during each 24-hour period (see Figure 9, felony day and hour clock). With these facts they can make comparisons with conditions that occurred during the previous 24-hour periods. In this way, plans for future action can be formulated and crime traps avoided. By carefully analyzing crime trends as provided in the uniform crime reports, police executives may act swiftly to counteract criminal activities by deploying manpower strategically and opportunely.

HOW REPORT DATA ARE ORGANIZED AND CLASSIFIED

When the committee of the International Association of Chiefs of Police met to discuss the mechanics of organizing data on the national crime situation, there were many problems to solve. One of the most important problems was to group all criminal offenses known to the police into an index of the amount, extent, and trends of crime. The committee agreed on a practical classification of offenses, which has not changed substantially in the years since. By forming a strong partnership, the International Association of Chiefs of Police and the Federal Bureau of Investigation produced a reliable national view of crime in the United States. The participation of all police agencies is still voluntary, and each department is entirely responsible for compiling and submitting its own crime reports to the FBI.

The objectives of the FBI Uniform Crime Report are threefold: first, to present a crime index consisting of seven selected offenses in order to measure the extent, fluctuation, distribution, and trend of serious crime; second, to set forth a compilation of the total volume of all types of criminal offenses that are made known by police arrests; and third, to tabulate related police matters of significance, such as the number of police employees and the number of police killed and assaulted each year.

When the uniform crime reporting system was first instituted, 27 classifications of crimes were defined. At present there are 29 classifications, defined under Part I and Part II offenses.

1. Criminal homicide. Criminal homicide is classified as (a) murder and nonnegligent manslaughter and (b) manslaughter by negligence.

Murder and nonnegligent manslaughter include all willful felonious homicides, as distinguished from deaths caused by negligence. Excluded are attempts to kill, assaults to kill, suicides, accidental deaths, or justifiable homicides. Justifiable homicides are limited to: (a) the killing of a person by a peace officer in the line of duty and (b) the killing of a person in the act of committing a felony, by a private person.

Manslaughter by negligence includes any death which the police investigation establishes as having been caused by the gross negligence of some individual other than the victim.

2. Forcible rape. This is rape by force, assault to rape, and attempted rape. It excludes statutory offenses in which no force is used and the victim is under the age of consent.

3. Robbery. Robbery is stealing or taking anything of value from a person by armed force or violence, or by putting him in fear of violence. Strong-arm robberies, stickups, armed robberies, assaults to rob, and attempts to rob are examples.

4. Assault—aggravated assault. Includes assault with intent to kill or for the purpose of inflicting severe bodily injury by shooting, cutting, stabbing, maiming, poisoning, scalding, or by using acids, explosives, or other means. Excludes simple assault, assault and battery, fighting, and other assaults not aggravated.

5. *Burglary.* Forcible entry, housebreaking, safecracking, or any unlawful entry to commit a felony or a theft even though no force was used to gain entrance. Attempted forcible entry is also included.

6. *Larceny.* Includes thefts, except auto thefts. The Form A reports are used for (a) thefts of $50 and over in value and (b) thefts under $50 in value. A supplemental Form A has three categories: (a) thefts of $50 and over in value, (b) thefts of $5 to $50, and (c) thefts under $5. Larceny also includes thefts of bicycles and automobile accessories, shoplifting, pocket-picking, or any stealing of property or any article of value which is not taken by force and violence or by fraud. It excludes embezzlement, "con" games, forgery, passing worthless checks, etc.

7. *Auto theft.* Stealing or driving away and abandoning a motor vehicle is auto theft. Taking a car for temporary use and then returning it is not auto theft, nor is unauthorized use by those having lawful access to the vehicle. "Joyride" thefts, however, are counted as auto thefts.

PART II OFFENSES

8. *Other assaults.* Includes assaults and attempted assaults which are not of an aggravated nature, such as assault and battery, pointing a gun in jest, injury caused by culpable negligence, intimidation, coercion, resisting or obstructing an officer, hazing, and attempts to commit these acts.

9. *Arson.* Includes all violations of state laws and municipal ordinances related to arson and attempts at arson.

10. *Forgery and counterfeiting.* Includes making, altering, uttering, or possessing, with intent to defraud, anything false which is made to appear true. Attempts are also included.

11. *Fraud.* Fraudulent conversion, and obtaining money or property by false pretenses, such as bad checks or confidence games.

12. *Embezzlement.* Misappropriation or misapplication of money or property in one's care, custody, or control.

13. *Stolen property—buying, receiving, possessing.* Buying, receiving, and possessing stolen property; also attempts.

Criminal behavior and crime reporting 101

14. *Vandalism.* Willful or malicious destruction of public or private property without consent of owner or custodian.

15. *Weapons—carrying, possessing, etc.* All violations of regulations or statutes controlling the carrying, using, possessing, furnishing, and manufacturing of deadly weapons or silencers; also attempts.

16. *Prostitution and commercialized vice.* Sex offenses of a commercialized nature, such as prostitution, keeping a bawdy house, procuring, transporting, or detaining women for immoral purposes; also attempts.

17. *Sex offenses.* All sex offenses except forcible rape, prostitution, and commercialized vice. Statutory rape, offenses against chastity, common decency, morals, etc.; also attempts.

18. *Violation of narcotic drug laws.* All state and local offenses relating to narcotic drugs, such as unlawful possession, sale, use, growing, and manufacturing of narcotic drugs.

19. *Gambling.* Bookmaking (horse and sport book), numbers, lottery, etc.

20. *Offenses against the family and children.* Nonsupport, neglect, desertion, or abuse of family and children.

21. *Driving while under the influence of alcohol.* Operating vehicles (including train or boat) while intoxicated.

22. *Violation of liquor laws.* Includes violations of state and local laws but not of Federal laws.

23. *Drunkenness—drunk and disorderly.* Common or habitual drunkenness, intoxication.

24. *Disorderly conduct.* Breach of the peace, disturbing the peace.

25. *Vagrancy.* Vagabondage, begging, loitering (persons 18 or over).

26. *All other offenses.* All violations of state or local laws not included in classes 1 to 25.

27. *Suspicion.* Arrest made for no specific offense, followed by release without formal charges being placed. (Such arrests are made for investigative purposes in relation to an actual or suspected offense.)

28. *Violation of curfew and loitering laws (juveniles).* All arrests made for violation of local curfew or loitering ordinance, where such laws exist.

29. *Runaway (juveniles)*. All apprehensions for protective custody as defined by local statute. Runaways from reporting jurisdiction apprehended are reported by home department.

Part I and Part II offenses explained. While these 29 different crimes have been divided into Part I and Part II offenses, the distinction between Part I and Part II classes is not as marked as it originally was. The first seven relatively serious crimes were selected as Part I crimes because they were initially, and still are, the most frequently reported crimes; and they were more consistently described and defined in all parts of the United States. It should be noted here that there are some crimes that do not come readily to the attention of the police, mostly crimes of vice and sex.

Report forms used. The seven selected crimes, known as Part I crimes, are reported by a monthly report form entitled Return A —Monthly Return of Offenses Known to the Police. It does not matter how these offenses were made known to the police just so long as the police obtain the information. Later, if the report proves groundless or false, adjustments may be made on the subsequent monthly report.

Accompanying this monthly Return A report are two additional monthly reports. One is named Supplement to Return A, and the other Supplementary Homicide Report, which includes traffic collisions with fatalities. The supplement to the monthly Return A report involves values of property stolen and classifies recoveries by type of property and by the crime.

Annual Report B is the annual summary of the monthly Return A Report of Offenses Known to Police. Return C is also an annual report and only records persons charged with a crime. This report also reflects the disposition of the charges, and is designed to include all 29 classifications of crimes. Persons arrested, including those who have been released without having been formally charged, are categorized according to age, sex, and race in a separate report submitted on an annual basis.

A Police Employee Data Form is also submitted annually. This report states the numbers of full-time police employees, both officers and civilians, who are paid from police funds. The number of police officers killed or assaulted in line of duty, whether accidentally or otherwise, are also included. Assaults against officers are differentiated as to whether or not an injury was sustained.

Valuation of stolen property. To ascertain the value of stolen property for purposes of reporting is not an easy task. The following guidelines have been established in the uniform crime reporting system to ensure national uniformity in reporting the value of stolen property.

1. The fair market value is used for articles which are subject to depreciation because of wear, age, or other reasons which cause the value to be reduced with use.
2. The cost to the merchant (wholesale) applies to goods stolen from retail stores and warehouses.
3. The victim's cash estimate is accepted for the value of jewelry, watches, and similar items which do not decrease in price materially because of age or use.
4. The replacement cost or actual cost (cash) to victim applies for new or almost new clothes, auto accessories, and bicycles.

Necessity for accurate reporting. In discussing police reports of this nature, too much emphasis cannot be placed on the important role that each officer plays in the final compilation of the FBI Uniform Crime Reports. Since the entire reporting system is collectively based on the individual reports of each officer, it behooves each officer to submit each report as conscientiously, clearly, accurately, and factually as possible. Otherwise, inaccuracies will appear. Misdemeanors will be reported as felonies and vice versa. Lost property will be reported as stolen. If that happens, then the entire reporting system becomes valueless. However, law enforcement personnel are fully aware of the value and importance of and great need for a true crime reporting system in the United States.

QUESTIONS

CRIMINAL BEHAVIOR

1. Discuss historically the problem of criminal behavior.
2. What is meant by *free will* as it pertains to criminal behavior?

3. Discuss the Lombrosian theory of the "born criminal" for criminal behavior.
4. Explain how heredity may influence criminal behavior.
5. Explain how environment affects criminal behavior.
6. Why should peace officers study criminal behavior?
7. Explain what is meant by the term "social-distress signals" as it refers to criminal behavior.
8. What part does religion play in the problem of criminal behavior?
9. Why is the home so important in the foundation of our American way of life?
10. Discuss such environmental factors as poverty, discipline, and neglectful parents, and the effect of these factors on criminal behavior.
11. Name and describe 10 sociopsychological types of criminals.
12. Describe the difference between the amateur and the professional criminal.

GENERAL

13. How did the FBI Uniform Crime Reports originate?
14. Name the reasons that a national crime reporting system is valuable to law enforcement as a tool of administration.
15. When and how are crime reports sent to the FBI by police agencies?
16. When and how does the FBI distribute the FBI Uniform Crime Reports?
17. Name and define the crimes included in Part I offenses in FBI Uniform Crime Reports.
18. Name and define the crimes included in the Part II offenses in the FBI Uniform Crime Reports.
19. Explain the purpose and use of Return A—Monthly Return of Offenses Known to the Police.
20. Relate the use and purpose of Annual Return B.
21. Describe the function of Annual Return C.
22. How is the value of stolen property determined?

5. The purposes of criminal law

Maintaining law and order

Have you ever attended a night athletic event at any of our great outdoor amphitheaters and heard the master of ceremonies say, "When the lights are extinguished in the stadium, will each of you light a match?" The lights go down, and you obligingly strike a match, as does everyone else. Suddenly the amphitheater is bathed in the glow from thousands of tiny match lights. Awed by this spectacular demonstration of mass cooperation, you join in the chorus of appreciative exclamations.

Yet each night a somewhat similar spectacle occurs in every city and town across the nation. As the house lights in each community are switched off and citizens retire for the night, thousands of foot patrolmen's flashlights and squad car headlights are flashing on to protect the lives and property of sleeping families. How impressed people would be if they could fully realize the scope of this nightly spectacle which is too often taken for granted. Without the thin line of blue which the police form between the criminals and the rest of society, our present way of life could not last.

If the police were removed from their job of patrolling the

highways and streets of America, anarchy would soon take over. Consider what happens when a disaster or a riot paralyzes a community. Looting, vandalism, arson, and other criminal acts result. In moments of stress and crisis, men have been known to go berserk. Then, more than ever, the police, as the disciplinary arm of government, are needed to maintain law and order. They do it faithfully night and day—often unspectacularly.

To understand the role of the police in modern law enforcement, it is necessary to arrive at a working understanding of the law itself. What is the law which the police are charged with upholding and enforcing?

Laws in general

WHAT IS LAW

Law consists of rules by which the game of life is played. These rules, born of experience and necessity, prescribe and govern the conduct of men with each other, with the state, and with the nation. Society needs rules or laws to protect the rights of people and to fix boundary lines beyond which men must not go without injury to themselves and to their neighbors. The Bible tells us that there was a law in the Garden of Eden. Moses was instructed by God to write down certain rules or laws, the Ten Commandments. Every home, social group, and fraternity has rules and regulations. Transgressors are punished by fines, loss of privileges, or banishment from society.

In a great society such as ours, all people cannot always agree on what the rules of that society ought to be. Bootleggers are opposed to liquor laws. Thieves and robbers would oppose the enactment and the enforcement of laws against larceny and robbery. Even honest and intelligent men cannot agree, always and consistently, on what laws or rules are necessary and proper. So, we have developed a constitutional form of government made up of three departments: legislative, judicial, and executive. We elect representatives to our government and they, guided by their experience and such wisdom as they may possess, make rules or laws designed to promote the general welfare of all citizens. From past experience, it must be admitted that the rules and laws enacted by our representatives do not always suit all of the people. But they are fixed, established, constitutional rules or laws that govern all of the people in the United States.

A frequent complaint of the average citizen is that there are too many laws. "Obsolete," "arbitrary," "unnecessary," devious," "too easy to circumvent" are terms people sometimes use to describe some laws. After listening to the numerous denunciations of our complex web of local, state, and Federal laws, one cannot help but speculate and wonder how all these laws originated.

During the formative years of our civilization, those charged with the responsibility of protecting life and property and keeping the peace had to rely largely upon common sense and good judgment because there were few laws. But soon accepted human behavior developed into customs that served as guides for people. When early tribal custom evolved methods of handling important matters such as marriages, stealing, or murder, patterns were set to guide the handling of similar matters in the future. These gradually developed customs were not the same for all peoples, since custom differed from tribe to tribe and from time to time. But, once these methods of handling tribal problems were accepted and usage proved them practical, they became rules, then regulations, and eventually, the unwritten laws of the tribe. It was from this pattern of long usage and general acceptance that our system of unwritten common law received its binding force.

Criminal laws. As the student of police science will soon find out, there are many different kinds of laws and there are laws to meet almost every situation and occasion. But the laws every officer must know, understand, follow, and appreciate are the criminal laws. Such laws are punitive; that is, they provide for punishing the violators. They regulate conduct regarding the health, welfare, safety, morals, and protection of the members of society. Frequently, criminal laws are legislated into a penal code, such as the laws of a state. When such laws are enacted by the Legislature of the state, they become statutory laws. The alert officer keeps abreast of all new laws being enacted and any changes or modifications in the existing laws.

For example, here is a statutory law that was passed by the California Legislature and is contained in the state Penal Code:

Section 148.5 *False Reporting of a Criminal Offense*
Every person who reports to any police officer, sheriff, district attorney, deputy sheriff, deputy district attorney or a member of the California Highway Patrol that a felony or misdemeanor has been committed, knowing such report to be false is guilty of a misdemeanor. (Stat. 1957—Chap. 813)

Civil law. Another vast body of law is civil law. Civil laws are noncriminal. They pertain to transactions between private individuals such as contracts and property law. Also included in the civil law are the laws involving grievances of a personal nature such as torts, which are civil wrongs (not involving a breach of contract) against the person or property of another. It is important for the student of police science to understand that the peace officer is traditionally not a civil officer and is not usually authorized to become involved in or be a party to civil matters. Where civil disputes and suits exist, such as personal grievances or family feuds, the peace officer merely keeps the peace. He does not interfere until a violation of a criminal law has been committed. By prudently keeping the peace, he may avoid and prevent a criminal violation. Many sheriffs' offices have a civil division which is separate and distinct from the criminal division.

Duties and responsibilities. The International City Managers' Association has written that "the entire governmental structure is built upon the foundation of law and order, which in turn is entirely dependent upon efficient and honest police administration." Obviously, this places a tremendous responsibility directly upon the shoulders of the peace officer. Hence, it is absolutely necessary that a peace officer know what his primary duties and responsibilities are as well as what duties are intimately related. All his duties are important and have a definite purpose. Police executives agree that the primary duties and responsibilities of the peace officer are classified into five categories, as follows:

1. Protection of life and property
2. Preservation of the public peace
3. Prevention of crime
4. Enforcement of the law
5. Apprehension of violators and recovery of lost and stolen property

The above enumerated five duties and responsibilities of police are fundamental. They represent the basic purposes of law enforcement and have been an integral part of law enforcement for many years. A sixth responsibility of the police originated with the advent of the automobile and has grown in importance with our population explosion and related problems. The sixth responsibility is defined as *traffic control and regulation of noncriminal conduct*. The following sections discuss these six principal duties.

PROTECTION OF LIFE AND PROPERTY

If the many duties of the peace officer could be boiled down to one responsibility that would cover almost every aspect of his job, that one would be the *protection of life and property*. The police officer has no greater responsibility. In fact no greater responsibility can be given to any person than the obligation of protecting the life and property of his fellowman. To carry out his first and broadest of his responsibilities, an officer must of course know the law. But he must also know and be capable of rendering first aid, in order to handle the many emergencies that arise from accidents in the home, school, church, street, park, playgrounds, freeways, lakes, and industrial areas.

PRESERVATION OF THE PUBLIC PEACE

One of the mistaken ideas that a student of police science may have is that the average officer is always busy during an eight-hour watch making arrests, stopping fights, shooting it out with robbers, and rescuing maidens in distress. True, during his career an officer may have to handle and solve many such difficult assignments. But more often his tour of duty will be a tedious routine which leaves him chafing at the lack of continuous, exciting activity. Therefore, the mature student of law enforcement needs to prepare himself for long periods of routine operations with infrequent exciting moments. Patrol duty requires an even temperament, generously sprinkled with tolerance and understanding. By merely walking his beat in uniform or patrolling the streets in a squad car, the police officer is actually keeping the peace and protecting life and property.

It is common knowledge that criminals will "case" a city to ascertain whether the city is policed efficiently. If the criminal observes a lack of police activity, he is encouraged to go ahead with his lawbreaking plans. However, if he notes that crime-prone areas are under the constant watch of the police, the criminal very likely moves elsewhere, to look for soft spots in the armor of the law. So, keeping the peace means many things: being seen conspicuously on duty; being at the right place at the right time to handle neighborhood feuds, complaints of noise, and family fights; and being on the scene to control unruly crowds that could develop into mobs and thus precipitate riots and disaster.

In preserving the public peace, an officer must be careful to conduct his inquiries or investigations so as not to provoke additional breaches of the peace. Many times an officer is dispatched to handle very sensitive situations. These situations, from start to finish, must be approached with tolerance and understanding. An officer must not take sides or become personally involved in any way. Tact is one of his greatest assets in handling delicate situations.

PREVENTION OF CRIME

In recent years, greater emphasis has been placed on crime prevention as one of the primary functions of police. This is a healthy trend. By developing programs to prevent crime, law enforcement agencies, supported by the necessary public cooperation, see ways of reducing our unbelievably staggering national crime bill. Crime prevention activity on the part of the police is an encouraging development. Although the brunt of crime prevention work is carried on by the juvenile bureaus, every police officer must be trained, educated, and motivated in the field of juvenile control and crime prevention. Teamwork by all officers provides much of the answer to the problem of crime prevention.

Each year a million and a half youngsters get into trouble with the law. Every teenager saved from a life of crime means another good citizen to reinforce the foundations of our society. It also means the saving of life, property, and tax dollars.

In addition to employing its youth programs and cooperating with youth-serving organizations, the police frequently use other excellent methods to stop crime before it happens. One of these methods is to inform and educate the public in crime prevention. For example, police now issue publications advising the public how to protect their property and valuables when on vacation or away from home. These police pamphlets are mailed to the public and they explain:

1. How to reach the police in an emergency
2. What to do when victimized
3. How to prepare a home before leaving on vacation
4. How to keep serial numbers on personal property in order to identify it when recovered
5. How the public can help the police

Suffice it to say that the police are alert to ways in which the public can assist in curbing crime and take adequate steps to convey this information to the public in order to obtain the needed cooperation. For example, one dedicated county sheriff recently started an effective well-publicized crime prevention program against burglars and other night prowlers in which he recommended that everyone keep lights in their homes at night during a certain one-month period. A follow-up survey showed that crime in this county decreased in the proportion to which houses were illuminated.

ENFORCEMENT OF THE LAW (CRIME REPRESSION)

Enforcing the law is not an easy task. There are some officers who can make an arrest without any difficulty whatsoever and, like the Pied Piper of Hamlin, lead the criminals to jail without incident. Then there are others who look as if the whole Russian army had walked over them each time they enforce the law. Tact, understanding, adequate training, and proper indoctrination are the ingredients that make for successful enforcement of the law.

There are a few basic principles which the student of law enforcement might do well to bear in mind as key factors in effective law enforcement. These principles can be summed up in these ideas: proper timing, good example, and impartial judgment.

Proper timing in law enforcement means not jumping to conclusions but rather taking action only when the pertinent facts have been weighed. Such timing prevents mistaken arrests that may produce needless hardships.

Good example reflects an officer's own firm belief in the law. His adherence to the law encourages others to follow his example. His own exemplary conduct makes it easier for him to enforce the law.

Impartial judgment suggests that police act legally and justly in apprehending felons so that needless sacrifice of life may be prevented and stolen property may be returned rightfully to owners. Impartial judgment depends principally on facts revealed by intensive investigation, not on guesswork. Lastly, decisions of the courts must be followed so that physical evidence will be obtained legally, thereby assuring successful prosecution and conviction of violators.

Even after the last word has been written about law enforcement, it is clear that before an officer can enforce the law equitably and intelligently he must know the law. Hence, every officer has to keep informed of new laws and legal changes. Studying and keeping a personal copy of the current penal code for ready reference will help. Attending meetings called by the district attorney or other experts to discuss the law is a prime source of information. College courses in criminal law likewise have greatly added to the policeman's knowledge of the law. Personal development is undoubtedly the key to keeping informed and up-to-date on the law and its enforcement.

APPREHENSION OF VIOLATORS AND RECOVERY OF LOST AND STOLEN PROPERTY

No arrest is routine. Arrest is one of the most important and dangerous functions of a law enforcement officer. Hence, an officer must exercise good judgment and common sense in all apprehensions. An alert officer will remain a live officer.

In order to reduce the hazards of an arrest to a minimum, the following seven basic principles of arrest are recommended:

1. *Superiority of manpower.* If an officer needs help, he should arrange to have assistance *before* the arrest—after may be too late.
2. *Superiority of firearms.* The advantage of the use and availability of greater firepower cannot be overemphasized.
3. *Surprise.* Whenever possible, an arrest should be made when the suspect least expects an arrest, when all the advantages are in favor of the officer.
4. *Speed.* No time should be lost. All action must be swift and sure.
5. *Movement.* All officers involved must function as a well-informed team.
6. *Concealment.* No officer should be exposed. He must be protected at all times.
7. *Simplicity.* A simple plan of arrest that is understood by all officers will invariably accomplish the desired results.

Coupled with arrest is the problem of the recovery of stolen property. This is especially important to the victim of a robbery or burglary. The victim often judges the effectiveness of police by the amount of property recovered. The average citizen is not aware of the tremendous amount of cars, bicycles, jewelry, appliances, money, and other valuables recovered annually by law enforcement agents. Fortunately, abandoned, lost, and unidentifiable property recovered by police may be sold at public auction, after a legal lapse of time. The money obtained from such sales is added revenue to the city and county involved. When property is recovered by law enforcement, it helps to prove that crime does not pay.

TRAFFIC CONTROL AND REGULATION OF NONCRIMINAL CONDUCT

Protection of life and property, preservation of the public peace, crime prevention, enforcement of the law, and apprehension of criminals and recovery of lost and stolen property, all revolve about the matters pertaining to criminal control. Besides these crime control responsibilities, the police provide many noncriminal services to the public and other subdivisions of government.

Foremost among these noncriminal services is traffic control. The student of police science will spend many hours of concentration in this subject. Traffic control is such a pressing police responsibility that it often taxes the ingenuity of local police. Take the case of the local chief whose community was plagued by transcontinental motorists illegally speeding through the community in utter disregard for the lives and safety of its citizens. Lack of manpower and equipment left the chief practically helpless to cope with the problem. Finally, he hit upon the idea of strategically placing an abandoned car, painted to resemble a black and white police squad car, at the city limits. Speeding motorists, seeing this apparently vigilant police car, burned rubber for at least a block in their hasty, reflex action to comply with the law.

In addition to traffic control there are many other miscellaneous noncriminal services rendered by police. In fact, some police executives fear that law enforcement is accepting too many such responsibilities by providing services that are not part of the primary responsibility of the police. For instance, it is now common for officers to be detailed to rescue cats and dogs, open locked doors for people, deliver babies in emergencies, act as escorts for visiting foreign dignitaries, serve as guards in large deliveries of money to banks, and participate in many other similar public assistance services. Despite the fear of concerned police administrators over the direction police work is taking toward public-assistance activities, this trend is not likely to be reversed. And so the police student should recognize that the public now looks to police for all kinds of additional services—not only those that protect people from criminals, but also those that make the community a healthier, happier, and more convenient place in which to live. It appears, therefore, that as long as the people are paying the bill, the police will provide new public-assistance services along with traditional police services. It must be noted that many of the duties or services discussed under traffic control and regulation of noncriminal conduct fall under the category of protection of life and property.

The purposes of criminal law   115

Our constitutional form of government provides for checks and balances among its three branches—the legislative, the executive, and the judicial. The legislative branch makes the laws. The executive branch enforces these laws. And the judicial branch interprets them.

The policeman's primary job. It is the job of the police to enforce the law. Thus, police officers must remember that they are primarily fact finders for their department and have no authority or control over the judicial or legislative branches of our government. If the police effectively enforce the law, that is all that is expected of them. No officer attempts to tell the judiciary how to interpret the law. Yet some officers never get over the feeling that they have to follow a case to its bitter end and, if the defendant is not sentenced to life, or at least ten years, in prison, then the courts are all wrong. As a result, police may criticize prosecutors and the courts while the courts and prosecutors may criticize law enforcement. The result is animosity, and this causes lack of cooperation which ultimately helps only the lawbreakers.

Hence, students need to realize that a peace officer need not lose heart when his case is lost or even mishandled. His main job is to exercise good judgment at the time of an arrest. The police officer who makes a legal arrest, gets the necessary evidence, identifies witnesses, writes a good report, and acts as a truthful, effective witness has done his work completely. The rest is up to the prosecutor, judge, and jury.

Getting the facts. Policemen who concentrate on doing a better job every day direct their energies and time to getting the facts in a case. Officers who do this make fewer mistakes and obtain better results. Law enforcement, therefore, must know its limitations. What is legal and within the jurisdiction of police officers? They cannot prosecute and judge a case. They have only the authority to investigate. The single example in early Greek history in which a single group was vested with the authority to investigate, prosecute, and judge failed. The Ephors, as this group was called, were unpopular, and their authority was soon divided into three branches, much like those we have in the United States now.

116 Introduction to police science

It is usually the new and inexperienced police officer who is upset when he loses a case or when his case is reduced or when it does not proceed as he expected. After a number of years in the profession, an officer becomes philosophical about the outcome of cases. The sooner he learns to do his own job well and lets the others do their jobs, the sooner his work of investigation will bring him pleasure and enjoyment. Police records show that the officer whose cases most often result in conviction is the one who concentrates on making an efficient investigation, who pays attention to detail, and who gathers all the pertinent facts. The officer who is griping constantly and finding fault continuously with the prosecutors and the courts is the one who does a sloppy job of investigation. Attempting to place blame on someone else for his ineptitude and inefficiency, he uses the old method of fault-finding to cover up his own deficiencies.

Probation and parole

During the student's introduction to police science, questions concerning probation, parole, pardon, commutation of sentence, and reprieve often arise. This is evident especially during discussions of the purposes of criminal law. In the study of the fundamental duties of a law enforcement officer, the police science student is curious about what happens to the persons who are brought to the bar of justice as a result of a police officer's enforcement of the law. These questions are answered on the following pages.

DEFINITION OF PROBATION

Probation is a legal arrangement which allows a person convicted of a criminal offense to be released, under certain conditions prescribed by the court, from serving sentence. However, the violator is placed under the supervision and guidance of a probation officer. Adults as well as juveniles may be placed on probation.

PRESENTENCE INVESTIGATION

One of the most important aspects of probation is the gathering of pertinent information concerning the offender so that the judge may equitably and justly determine if probation is warranted, feasible, and practical. This background inquiry is conducted and completed before sentence and does not include data revolving about the guilt or innocence of the violator. Rather, a personality and social background investigation is instituted by the probation officer covering the following items:

1. *History of offender* including the date and place of his birth
2. *Family background* plus data about his immediate relatives
3. *Physical condition* with description of all physical deficiencies, if any, that are the proximate cause of instant difficulty
4. *Results of psychiatric examinations* reflecting mental capacity, emotional stability, and disturbances, if any
5. *Educational background* reviewed for scholastic achievements or deficiencies (needed to report any handicaps or failings that could throw light on the problem)
6. *Employment record* revealing work history so that evidence of earning ability, capability, and reliability may be ascertained
7. *Recreational hobbies,* habits, and sports (also may be revealing)
8. *Religious affiliation,* if any, and degree of participation
9. *Personality evaluation* explaining faults, strengths, and other illuminating characteristics
10. *Reports from other welfare and social agencies* having contact with offender and family
11. *An objective summary* of the pros and cons concerning the offender
12. *Recommendations* for the best disposition of the individual

CONDITIONS OF PROBATION

The judge does not casually release a violator. Instead, there are necessary judicial strings attached. Compelling conditions are included in the terms of the probation in order to control the behavior and activities of the probationer, to protect both him and the public.

When juveniles are involved, the following general terms of the probation may be imposed:

1. No truancy
2. Obedience to all lawful authority including parents, teachers, and police
3. Regular hours
4. Refrainment from fraternizing with bad companions
5. Refrainment from frequenting places of ill repute
6. Any change of address reported to court and probation officer
7. Cooperation with probation officer

Special significant conditions may also be added, such as:

1. Damages assessed and paid
2. Enrollment in a special institution such as a school
3. Membership in a local recreational association
4. Medical treatment, if needed

Adult conditions may be more stringent. For instance, the terms may insist that the adult violator abstain from alcohol, drugs, association with convicted criminals; live in a certain area; have steady, desirable employment; support his family; pay a fine or make restitution; and obtain the permission of the probation officer if he moves, changes employment, or performs any act that might interfere with the terms of the probation.

DEFINITION OF PAROLE

Parole is a method whereby a convicted criminal is released from a correctional institution prior to the completion of his minimum sentence. It may be described as a type of conditional release which means that the offender has to conform to specific rules and regulations under the supervision of a parole agent. If the offender violates the restrictions imposed, he forfeits the conditions of the parole and he is returned to the correctional or penal institution from which he was released.

Parole must not be confused with probation, pardon, or clemency. To reiterate, *probation* is granted by the judge instead of commitment to a correctional institution. On the other hand, *parole* occurs after the offender has been placed in a correctional institution. Both probation and parole require supervision and guidance of the offender in order to rehabilitate him, if possible.

Pardon is the official release from legal penalties of an offense and is under the complete control of the governor of the state. The full pardon rectifies legal wrongs that are recognized by the governor, and the recipient of the pardon is restored to full citizenship.

COMMUTATION OF SENTENCE

This is a method of substitution of a lesser sentence for a greater punishment. However, it is not like full pardon in that it does not forgive, nor does it restore civil rights. Usually, it is invoked to commute a death sentence to life imprisonment or to a reduced number of years in prison.

REPRIEVE

Reprieve is the act of postponing the execution of one who is sentenced to death. It merely gives the condemned convict an extension of time but makes no other concessions.

PURPOSE OF PAROLE

Parole is an integral part of our entire correctional system which includes law enforcement, the judiciary, probation, reception, and diagnostic centers, penal and correctional institutions, and finally parole itself. Each has its own influence and impact upon the offender, and each follows a logical sequence. Under the correctional system, society is protected, and the offender has an opportunity for rehabilitation. When this is the case, the safety of the community is improved and the adjustment of the offender is more likely.

PAROLE BOARD

The parole board is also known as the "adult authority" and "youth authority." In California, these are part of the Department of Corrections. The authority governing parole is relegated to a centralized board, and its six members are appointed by the governor. Their appointment is confirmed by the state Senate, and they usually serve for four staggered terms of office. The offenders committed to the youth authority by the criminal courts are those who are under the age of 21 and have not been sentenced to death or life imprisonment.

PAROLE HEARING

In order to ascertain whether an offender is eligible for parole, a hearing is held to evaluate the offender's ability and willingness to cooperate. It must be determined that the offender is able to fulfill the conditions for living in society on a conditional release.

The hearings are scheduled only when the applicant is legally eligible for release. Such hearings should be made a part of the entire process of treatment for rehabilitation. Sufficient time should be allowed to permit a just hearing. Consequently, all avenues and sources of information should be explored so that an equitable decision may be made by the paroling authority.

QUESTIONS

GENERAL

1. Describe the need for police and what would happen if there were no police.
2. Trace the genesis of police authority.
3. What is the law? Describe its derivation and purpose.
4. Differentiate between criminal and civil law.
5. Enumerate the five primary duties of the police.
6. Explain and give an example of the duty of police to protect life and property.
7. How do the police preserve the public peace?
8. Describe the crime prevention activities of police.
9. What is meant by crime repression, and how is it related to law enforcement?
10. Explain the limitations of police jurisdiction.

The purposes of criminal law 121

11. What is the purpose of probation?
12. What is the purpose of parole?
13. What is meant by the statement that "an offender may be placed either on probation or parole depending upon his legal status"?
14. What important factor may influence the increase in personnel for probation and parole departments?
15. Define probation and give an example.
16. Define parole and give an example.
17. Define pardon and give an example.
18. Define commutation of sentence and give an example.
19. Define reprieve and give an example.
20. Why is a presentence investigation conducted? Describe the procedure.

*History in illuminating the past,
illuminates the present and
in illuminating the present
illuminates the future.*
BENJAMIN N. CARDOZO
Nature of the Judicial Processes
53 (1921)

6. Historical background of English police

Development of English police

EARLIEST BEGINNINGS OF POLICE

The development of law enforcement is a fascinating story of slow but continual progress. It begins at the time in early human history when small, roving family groups banded together for mutual protection against marauding animals and people. It was quite natural for these early communities to select the strongest and most dependable men to stand guard while the other members of the tribe slept.

As these early roving bands organized themselves into tribes and settled down in small communities, they began to evolve rules and regulations governing personal and property rights. Along with the development of these rules and regulations went the problem of upholding and enforcing these personal and property rights. It is quite probable that the earliest law enforcement groups were a kind of military police, detailed, during peacetime, from the ranks of the warriors to uphold the early tribal laws.

Even in Biblical times, there were patrols of watchmen which went about the cities. More precisely, the military origin of police systems can be traced to the Romans. Caesar Augustus, who was the Roman Emperor when Christ was born, used his soldiers to police Rome. Other nations copied the Roman military police system.

Origin of word "police." Authorities differ as to the origin of the word "police," but the the origin most widely accepted is the Greek word *polis*. This word means "city," and is defined as a judicial and executive system such as an organized civil force in a town or city for the preservation of the life, property, and health of the community, and for the enforcement of laws.

The French word for police is *policer*, meaning the power of the people. Historically, the title of "police" was officially designated in the famous Act of Parliament in England in 1829 under the leadership of Sir Robert Peel. This act has been a milestone in the progress of law enforcement throughout the world and particularly in the United States.

Origin of Penal Code. In the United States, the Penal Code clearly defines the function of the peace officer and designates the law enforcement agencies qualified to have peace officers. Our courts have ruled time and again that the police of today are members of an organization empowered with the authority vested in them by the people to enforce the laws of the city, county, and state. The development of the Penal Code, like that of the police system, was a long, gradual process which takes its roots far back in man's history.

As our civilization progressed, the laws of the people in different countries were reduced to writing, formalized, and codified. One of the earliest codes of written law was that known as the Code of Hammurabi in ancient Babylonia about 2000 B.C. This code was a body of accepted customs dealing with the responsibilities of the people individually and collectively.

In the same vein, the Jews in the Near East had the first five books of the Old Testament, the Pentateuch, to obey and follow. Other civilizations were also governed by codes. The Assyrians had a code of law. The Chinese had a penal code. The rulers of India used the Code of Manu, and the Romans established a digest of Roman law first in A.D. 450 and again in A.D. 550, at the time of Justinian. But not until A.D. 1215 were the English able to wring from King John the celebrated Magna Carta, "The Great Charter." The Magna Carta is also the foundation of the Constitution of the United States. No greater legal documents than these two were ever written, for together the Magna Carta and the Constitution guarantee to the people of England and the United States the fundamental rights and liberties of a free people. As long as they exist, these documents preserve our most precious heritages and ensure that no man will be deprived of life, liberty, and the pursuit of happiness without the due process of the law.

The American police system is patterned after the English police system. The beginnings of these systems date back to the Anglo-Saxon period.

Town system. Prior to A.D. 700 the people in old England lived in small rural *tuns,* or towns. These early Anglo-Saxons loved home rule and local control. When at war—and that was frequently—they fought in squads of tens and hundreds. So this arrangement became practical for living purposes when peace prevailed. Hence, ten families in a tun equaled a *tithing.* Each tithing elected a leader who was known as the *tithingman.* Since 10 tithings amounted to 100, the leader of the 100 families was named the *reeve.* Both tithingman and reeve were elected officials, and they possessed judicial power as well as police authority.

County system. With the inevitable growth in population, the size of the tithings expanded until this urban type of community developed into a *shire,* which is the equivalent of our American county. The leader of the shire became the *shire-reeve,* subsequently abbreviated to sheriff, and the tithingman eventually became the undersheriff.

During the period A.D. 700 to 800, the Kings of England rewarded loyal subjects with titles, such as "nobleman," and granted them large estates. These noblemen in turn appointed sheriffs to rule the people residing in their county (shire). In areas still belonging to the Crown, the King appointed his own sheriff, and in time these small towns also developed into counties (shires).

Since the King in early England assumed the responsibility of keeping the peace, it was natural for him to delegate that authority. The logical person to execute and enforce the law of the land was the sheriff. So the primary duties of the sheriff in old England were to maintain law and order and to preserve the public peace, just as is the case today in the United States. Thus, our modern police systems, in many respects, are a direct, gradual development from the old English methods of law enforcement. Hence, it is important that the police science student understand and appreciate the period from the eighth to the nineteenth century in English police history. It is during that eleven-century period that the system of police service and our system of criminal law evolved.

Actually our codes of criminal law are based not only on the Magna Carta but also on the old unwritten and traditional common law of England. Just as many of the English customs and procedures were brought to America by the colonial settlers, so too was the common law of England transported to our shores.

Hue and cry. The Anglo-Saxon tithingman was delegated the authority to see that members of the tithing obeyed the laws. This was not a difficult job because there were only two major laws to observe: killing of human beings and stealing. If a member of the tithing was guilty of either, all members had the solemn duty to bring the guilty person to the shire-reeve for justice. This procedure was known as the "hue and cry," the forerunner of our citizen's arrest procedure in the United States. Hence, it was as elementary in England at the time of the Anglo-Saxons as it is today for every Englishman to keep the law himself and to see that the law was not violated by others. Perhaps this ingrained principle in every Englishman is the leading reason why crime is at a minimum in England.

Trial by ordeal. Although the Anglo-Saxons did not believe in capital punishment, they practiced a most cruel form of judicial punishment known as *trial by ordeal.* In this primitive method of ascertaining innocence or guilt, a suspect might have to walk over hot coals of fire, or immerse his hands in boiling water, or be bound, weighted, and thrown into a river. If the suspect's feet were burned by the coals, if his hands were boiled by the hot water, or if he was drowned, he was considered guilty. If not, he was innocent. As you may readily see by this procedure, the court calendar was never cluttered, and justice was dispatched speedily, if not humanely. This period is also most significant because all crimes were adjudicated on the basis of civic restitution, i.e., money damages for the injured person. This procedure is woven into the procedure of American courts today.

Watch and ward. When observing the transitions in law enforcement, it is important to note the influence that these changes have had on our modern concepts of law enforcement. For instance, the *watch and ward* system was the brainchild of the Anglo-Saxons and the germ of our modern American police system. Initially, the tithingmen were responsible for maintaining the watch and ward. The watch was the night guard, and the ward was the day guard. Anyone 16 or over was subject to call by the tithingmen to serve on the watch or ward duty.

With the increase in population, sheriffs were permitted to assign four to six men in each town for night watch. Those detailed to do so served without pay. They carried a lantern and a staff, forerunners of the flashlight and nightstick of today's patrol officer. When the early colonists came to America, they brought with them the English watch and ward system. This system prevailed in the United States until the middle of the last century.

NORMAN PERIOD

In A.D. 1066 William the Conqueror invaded England and established a national government which was almost the direct opposite of the Anglo-Saxon form of government. While the Saxons placed emphasis on local home rule, the Normans stressed national government and increased taxes and expenditures. The sheriff became the tax collector. In order to systematically collect the taxes, a list of all taxable property owned by each person was recorded. This record was named the *Domesday Book.*

While William the Conqueror reigned, the Normans and the Anglo-Saxons were two opposing forces he had to contend with. In order to ensure harmony, he required all loyal subjects to take the pledge of allegiance to the King. Since this oath was administered on the plains of Salisbury, it has been called the *Salisbury Oath.* Historians conclude that our familiar pledge of allegiance to the American flag has its origin in William the Conqueror's Salisbury Oath.

In 1116 the Laws of Henry classified arson, murder, false coinage, and robbery as felonies. These crimes were punishable by the King, and, since the Normans had established a national government, the King had the first right of civil suit and damages. This was a radical change from the Anglo-Saxon period during which the criminal was punished by his fellowmen. Now the authority to punish came into the hands of the King, and outmoded procedures such as the trial by ordeal were abolished. This development called for a more rational investigative procedure. To assist the Crown in finding the facts and the truth in a criminal case, selectmen were chosen to investigate crimes. From this beginning our modern grand jury system developed.

In 1215, when our country was an unmapped wilderness, a shaft of light broke through the gloom of despotism that ruled most men's lives. In that year, rebellious barons forced England's King John to relinquish much of his absolute rule. The episode took place on a meadow not far from London at a Thames-side site called Runnymede. There the historic document called the Magna Carta was signed, and British democracy was born.

The meadow is sacred soil to Britain. In 1965 one acre of this unique tract became United States territory forever—Runnymede, U.S.A. The British government made this unparalleled gesture in honor of the late President John F. Kennedy. Its decision to do this was taken, in democratic tradition, on the recommendations of Britain's three main political parties. A stone pedestal was built at Runnymede as a memorial to the memory of John F. Kennedy and as a symbol of freedom.

Bailiff. The Westminster Period derives its name from the Statute of Westminster, which was in effect from 1285 to 1500.

By the provisions of the Westminster statute, reforms were introduced for the benefit of freeholders who were permitted to invoke the assistance and protection of the royal courts and royal officers to stop great lords from abusing their tenants. In general, the aim of the provisions of Westminster was "to make everyday life easier for all kinds of freemen by protecting them in their free tenements and defining the limits of interference with their freedom." In this period the offices of bailiff and justice of the peace and the rank of sergeant developed. The bailiff was the chief law enforcement officer. His job was to periodically scan all new people in the community. As the cities grew in size, this became a difficult task. At curfew time, crowds would crash the town gates in order to spend the night in the protected area inside the walled towns. Hence, the bailiff appointed assistants named *sergeants* to help scrutinize incoming people for aliens and undesirables. Those who could not be trusted had to sleep outside the walls of the city and were called "outsiders."

In order to combat the prevalence and tolerance of prostitution flourishing during this period, a method of segregation was instituted. This attempt at control required that the prostitutes reside in specified sections of the city. In order to make identification possible, each house catering to this type of questionable business was compelled to use red lanterns, red lights, or other red insignia to reflect the nature of the district.

Justice of the peace. The justice of the peace also had its origin in this period, one was appointed for each county (shire). The justice of the peace had the power to free the accused on bail. Today the bail system is assailed by some legal authorities as one of the most corrupt and inequitable processes in our legal machinery of justice. Arrested persons who do not have money or friends to post bail often have to languish in jail for weeks and even months until their case comes to trial; whereas wealthy people, crooks with legal connections, and syndicated criminals have the opportunity and funds to take advantage of bail for immediate release.

To correct the inequities and abuses of the bail system, some judges are releasing suspects from jail on their own recognizance (OR). In order that the judge may release only persons held for trial who are deserving of this procedure and are good risks to appear for their trial, he usually bases his "OR" release on the recommendations of the probation officer. Judges have found that suspects who are employed, permanent residents are good risks. They have a higher "not guilty" record than persons admitted to bail.

Star Chamber. As with every period in the growth of police systems, in early England there were favorable advances as well as setbacks. One English development in law enforcement which received considerable notoriety was the courts of the Star Chamber. These courts of the King were tolerated, for it was thought that "the King could do no wrong." Some of the brutalities that resulted from this philosophy were the third degree, flogging for confessions, and multimethods of torture. Such flagrant miscarriages of justice eventually became so revolting that they were formally abolished in 1641 by Charles I. With the disappearance of the Star Chamber, two important legal guarantees came into being—freedom of speech and freedom from self-incrimination.

Severity in English and American courts. Excessively severe court punishment was, until recently, quite common in both England and the United States. Two examples will show how similar court severity was in both countries. The following is an excerpt from a punishment handed down by an English judge in 1660. The sentence of death was pronounced upon Thomas Harrison, found guilty of participating in the killing of Charles I.

The judgment of the court is and the court doth award, that you be led back to the place from whence you came, and from thence to be drawn upon an hurdle to the place of execution; and there you shall be hanged by the neck; and being alive shall be cut down and your privy members to be cut off, your entrails to be taken out of your body, and you, living, the same to be burnt before your eyes, and your head to be cut off, your body to be divided into four quarters, and head and quarters to be disposed of at the pleasure of the King's majesty, and the Lord have mercy upon your soul.

The following is a verbatim transcript of a sentence imposed upon a defendant convicted of murder in the Federal District Court of the Territory of New Mexico, many years ago, by a

United States judge, sitting at Taos in an adobe stable used as a temporary courtroom.

Jose Manuel Miguel Xavier Gonzales, in a few short weeks it will be spring. The snows of winter will flee away, the ice will vanish and the air will become soft and balmy. In short, Jose Manuel Miguel Xavier Gonzales, the annual miracle of the year's awakening will come to pass—but you won't be here.

The rivulet will run its purring course to the sea, the timid desert flowers will put forth their tender shoots, the glorious valleys of the imperial domain will blossom as the rose; still you won't be here to see.

From every treetop some wild woods songster will carol his mating song, butterflies will sport in the sunshine, the busy bee will hum happily as it pursues its accustomed vocation, the gentle breeze will tease the tassels of the wild grasses, and all nature, Jose Manuel Miguel Xavier Gonzales, will be glad but you. You won't be here to enjoy it because I command the sheriff or some other officer or officers of this county to lead you out to some remote spot, swing you by the neck from a nodding bough of some sturdy oak and let you hang until you are dead.

And then, Jose Manuel Miguel Xavier Gonzales, I further command that such officer or officers retire quickly from your dangling corpse, that the vultures may descend from the heavens upon your filthy body, until nothing shall remain but the bare, bleached bones of a cold-blooded, copper-colored, blood-thirsty, throat-cutting, chile-eating, sheepherding, murdering. . . .

ENGLISH COMMERCIAL POLICE

During the 1500s, wars and colonization, as well as empire building and the demand for wool and other English products abroad, brought about many changes in England over the next three centuries. Tenants were uprooted by feudal lords from their small farms, causing mass movements from the country to the city. The social unrest, unemployment, poverty, health reverses, and welfare needs multiplied police problems. As a consequence, the bailiffs, the reeves, and the simple watch and ward methods of protection were not sufficient to cope with the avalanche of crime. Hence, business people hired private commercial police to guard their shops and property.

Oliver Cromwell, Lord Protector of the Commonwealth and strong man of England in the first half of the 1600s, also acted to meet the challenge of the steady increase in crime that accompanied the transition from rural to urban ways of life in England. Since England was deep in civil strife, Cromwell placed the country under military police. In order to handle the policing problems effectively, he divided England into 12 districts. He also created the provost marshal to be in charge of each district and to serve as mediator and judge. Under the provost's command there were about 6,000 troops, all but 200 mounted. With this force, the provost was able to keep both civil and military peace. Probably, this was the origin of mounted English police.

BEGINNINGS OF MODERN ENGLISH
POLICE SYSTEM

Special municipal police. As England struggled along with hit-or-miss methods of law enforcement, a number of police systems were tried. Eventually, a diversified law enforcement program was evolved through the use of merchant police, dock police, river police, market police, and the night watch. These specialized police forces, however, operated under different authorities, without coordination or cooperation. Naturally, this uncoordinated type of law enforcement was hardly adequate to combat the steady increase in crime. Realizing the situation, Parliament appointed a committee to investigate existing police systems—the first such survey of its kind.

Henry Fielding. No real progress in police English organization was made, however, until Henry Fielding, better known as the author of *Tom Jones,* was appointed magistrate for the Middlesex and Westminster areas. He made the first real police survey and promoted the idea that police should be paid and trained, and permanent police forces should replace voluntary ones. He also advocated special detectives to investigate and police courts to adjudicate crime. Putting his ideas into effect, he organized a foot patrol for the streets, a mounted patrol for the highways, and, in 1749, he established the Bow Street Runners as special investigators. They were specially trained detectives who sped to the scene to investigate crimes. Along with the police courts that he also established, Fielding goes down in history as having made outstanding contributions to the development of police systems.

Anthony Cooper. The inequities and unethical activities of police in the arrest and detention of prisoners resulted in the passage of the Habeas Corpus Act sponsored by Anthony Cooper. As a result of this act, a prisoner thereafter had the right to be advised as to why he was being held, and he could be held only within his own county. Again, English pioneering in the realm of human rights produced a favorable model for our American writ of habeas corpus.

Industrial revolution. The impact of science and inventions on the social and economic welfare of England, is most important in the history and development of law enforcement. Mechanized factories brought unemployment, depression, hunger, and inevitably an even greater upward surge of crime. Unfortunately, there were no social or governmental organizations in the cities to cope with the prevalent problems of poverty, disease, juvenile gangs, and adult gangs of thieves and robbers. Crime ran rampant. Moreover, in the attempt to check crime, laws were strictly and cruelly enforced. Offenders were deported to Australia and America. Public executions, while common, were ineffective in preventing crime. But once again, England was fortunate in producing a man who was equal to the giant task of solving the crime problem, Sir Robert Peel.

Sir Robert Peel. The name of Robert Peel shines as a beacon in the annals of modern police progress. In fact, the present English "bobbies" derive their name from this enterprising leader. Although the development of England's law enforcement progressed slowly toward an efficient police system, the most lasting and effective advances were made possible by the reforms of Sir Robert Peel.

In 1829, as Home Secretary, Peel introduced into Parliament the Metropolitan Police Act. This move consolidated and reorganized the numerous forces existing in London into one efficient, paid body of officers. Like Fielding, Peel was convinced that police must be dedicated, trained, ethical, paid personnel of local government. Peel's enthusiasm and logical police platform of suggestions were recognized by Parliament. Hence, in 1829, with official blessing, he compressed his ideas into Peel's Principles, the basis for an efficient, reliable law enforcement agency. These principles have weathered time and are followed by police management today throughout the free world. In fact, New York City adopted Peel's Principles as a foundation for organizing the New York Police Department in 1833. These are Peel's Principles:

1. The police must be stable, efficient, and organized along military lines.
2. The police must be under government control.
3. The absence of crime will best prove the efficiency of police.
4. The distribution of crime news is essential.
5. The deployment of police strength, both by time and area, is essential.
6. No quality is more indispensable to a policeman than a perfect command of temper. A quiet, determined manner has more effect than violent action.
7. Good appearance commands respect.
8. The selection and training of proper persons are at the root of efficient law enforcement.
9. Public security demands that every police officer be given an identifying number.
10. Police headquarters should be centrally located and easily accessible to the people.
11. Policemen should be hired on a probationary basis before permanent assignment.
12. Police crime records are necessary to the best distribution of police strength.

Putting Peel's Principles to work. In order to apply Peel's Principles, two qualified and worthy men were appointed as police commissioners with headquarters at the home office in London. They were Colonel Charles Rowan and Richard Mayne. Their job was not an easy one. The people of London were reluctant to accept the Metropolitan Police and showed their resentment of the "new breed" by mobbing the first police contingent to patrol the streets. In fact, one sergeant was killed and two constables were injured critically on the first patrol. It should be remembered that at this time the bobbies were not in uniform and were armed only with a truncheon (nightstick). Nevertheless, through courteous but firm enforcement of the law, the Metropolitan Police gradually won the respect of the people. This is the grand tradition that the present bobbies have inherited.

Permissive legislation. The success of the London police was contagious. Other cities in England desired similar effective and honest police protection. So, in 1835, Parliament passed legislation permitting a city of over 20,000 population to establish its own law enforcement agency. The city council was authorized to appoint a committee to establish a police force comparable to the London police. This permissive legislation was also granted to counties. However, the response in the counties was meager because vested interests, anxious to maintain low taxes, were reluctant to adopt an efficient system of paid police based upon taxation.

Obligatory Act of 1856. Since permissive legislation was not as successful as expected in creating effective, tax-supported law enforcement agencies in England, Parliament passed the Obligatory Act of 1856. This act made it mandatory for each county to create its own law enforcement body and to finance its operation.

Local Government Act of 1888. In 1888, the Local Government Act created county councils to supervise county government. These councils organized standing joint committees to act as a police authority. Today there are 125 police forces in England. These include 51 county constabularies, 72 county-borough and city departments, the Metropolitan Police of Greater London, and the police of Old London Town.

ENGLISH POLICE SYSTEM TODAY

Ratio of police to population. The ratio of police to population in England varies but is much higher than the 1.9 police officers per 1,000 population in the United States. At present, in rural England there is 1 officer per 730 people, while in urban England, the ratio is even higher, namely, 1 officer to 375 persons.

Scotland Yard. Each of the 125 police forces in England is a separate entity, responsible for matters within its boundaries. There is no national police or superimposed body either to assist or to harass the local police. Contrary to public opinion abroad, Scotland Yard is not a national police, nor is it exactly like the FBI. The FBI is a great coordinating and cooperating Federal police agency in the United States; it is without local jurisdiction and with Federal limitations. Scotland Yard, however, is like the FBI in one respect, in that it is the repository for the national collection of fingerprints in Great Britain and thereby serves as a national clearance agency for fingerprint matters. It also bears a resemblance to the Secret Service of our U.S. Treasury Department because Scotland Yard has the great responsibility of protecting the royal family of England, wherever they may be. Lastly, Scotland Yard comes to the aid of the small police departments in England, if requested to do so, especially if the crime requires resources beyond that of the small departments.

It should be noted that Scotland Yard is the headquarters of the London Metropolitan Police. The City of London has its own police force to protect the one square mile in which its inhabitants live.

Police organization. England is divided into eight different districts to administer the following three vital services provided by the 125 police forces: training of recruits, laboratory examination of evidence, and the national police radio. In order to ensure efficiency and uniformity in the police service, all citizens of England share in the expenses of the national police radio network, of police recruit training, and of the police laboratories. The Home Office is responsible for the National Police College at Bramshill in Hampshire.

New horizons. Queen Elizabeth II, on January 25, 1960, created a 15-man Royal Commission to study the entire British police system for improvements. Two years later, this commission returned a 200-page report that recommended:

1. Continuance of the separate local police agencies and rejection of a national police system, although it was conceded that a national system has many desirable features

2. Establishment of the optimum strength of a police force at 500. Smaller departments should consolidate for efficiency
3. Creation of a central planning and research unit
4. Elimination of nonpolice duties so that police are not burdened with such activities and are better able to cope with actual crime problems
5. Increase of the number of inspectors of the constabulary from five to eight, to correspond with the eight police districts
6. Creation of the position of Chief Inspector of the Constabulary for Great Britain to bring about better control, cooperation, and coordination among police agencies

QUESTIONS

1. Why is the period from the eighth to the nineteenth century in English police history important to the police science student of today?
2. Relate what is meant by the words "hue and cry." How is the "hue and cry" system related to present-day law enforcement?
3. Describe the early English procedure known as *trial by ordeal*.
4. What was the important difference between the Anglo-Saxon and the Norman forms of government?
5. Explain the significance of the *Domesday Book*.
6. How did the Magna Carta come into existence, and what impact did it have in England and America?
7. Describe the developments pertaining to law enforcement in the Westminster Period (1285 to 1500).
8. Explain fully the *watch and ward* system of policing.
9. Relate the reasons that commercial police were needed in England.
10. Who organized the military police in England? How and where did military police function?
11. Who was Henry Fielding, and what was he noted for?
12. Who was Sir Robert Peel, and what influence did he have on modern law enforcement?

13. Describe the jurisdiction and functions of Scotland Yard.
14. Does England have a national police force?
15. How does Scotland Yard resemble the Federal Bureau of Investigation?

7. Historical background of United States police

Development of United States police

EARLY DEVELOPMENT

East coast origins. When England, France, and Spain established colonies on the eastern coast of America during the fifteenth and sixteenth centuries, each brought its own police system. Each of these nations, therefore, has left its imprint upon the American police system. England, with its tithing, night watch, constable, and sheriff method of organization, had the greatest influence in shaping our law enforcement system.

Night watch. The English settlers lived in small settlements along the east coast of early America. Mutual needs banded them together. Quite naturally, they borrowed the night watch system and the military guard of their homeland. In most colonial towns, all able-bodied males over the age of 16 were detailed to the night watch without pay. The night watch system prevailed in the majority of American towns until about 1800. In the more rural agricultural districts of the South, as the farms flourished and areas grew into counties, it became natural to use the sheriff method of law enforcement.

Where the night watch system was in effect, citizens who became sick or suffered physical or mental impairment that would excuse them from duty were permitted to pay qualified persons to take their places on the watch. Such a system brought on inefficiency and encouraged many abuses, such as absence without leave and personal vendettas.

Boston's day watch. In the early 1800s, as towns grew into cities and crime became a day problem as well as a night problem, cities were forced to provide a day watch. Boston was one of the first cities to recognize this need, and in 1838 the city established the first day watch. Within eight years, the Boston police force increased to 30 men, but, unfortunately, the day watch had no coordination or liaison with the night watch.

New York's unified watch. Not to be outdone by Boston, the New York Legislature, in 1844, created for New York City a united day and night force of 800 men with a Chief of Police. This organization followed the London plan and served as a model for urban police organizations throughout the United States. In 1851, Chicago adopted New York's pattern, and in 1850, Boston consolidated its day and night watch because it found that the separation of the two units was not feasible.

Stephen Girard. When Stephen Girard died in Philadelphia in 1831 he stipulated in his last will and testament that a large sum of money be bequeathed to the city of Philadelphia to create a "competent police." So, by an 1833 city ordinance, Philadelphia came under the protection of a unit of 24 police by day and 120 by night. A captain appointed by the mayor was responsible for both units. Moreover, advancement was entirely on merit. This merit system is perhaps the first evidence of police promotion incentive based on ability rather than political favor.

Police uniforms. It was inevitable that police uniforms would be introduced as police became more highly organized. Police executives in 1855, however, were not prepared for the resistance which arose to police uniforms from both the police and the public. The complaints were that uniforms were undemocratic and un-American. Many of our forefathers had come to this country from foreign lands where the mere mention of a uniform brought visions of the mailed fist, extortion, torture, and horrors too revolting to mention. Hence, Americans shied away from putting their police in uniforms. Persistence, however, paid off, and, beginning with regulation hats, then badges, New York City police in 1856 adopted the full police uniform. In 1860, the same transition took place in Philadelphia.

Police boards. Because of corruption and local political interference, police boards or police commissions were adopted in many cities in order to take the control and direction of police operations out of the hands of local politicians. It was believed at first that state control would be an improvement over local control of police. Consequently, New York State took the lead, and the governor appointed the members of the New York City Police Board. In fact, as early as 1857, the state of New York experimented with state boards for local police. But it was soon found that this apparent solution was not successful because the administrative control was too remote from the local police problems and activities. Police cannot be supervised *in absentia*, it was concluded as a result of this experiment.

Municipal police. Many factors contributed to the development of the present American police systems prevailing in our cities today. Among the most prominent were the various political wars and corruption which stemmed from the philosophy that "to the victors belong the spoils." During the late 1800s, there were forces for reform in almost every city in the United States. But only when people became aroused from their usual apathy because of shocking crime waves did reform movements appear. Then, new procedures, such as the free election of police chiefs, were suggested and tried. However, the election of the chief of police to office usually involved the whole department too deeply in politics, and today this practice of electing the chief of police is almost extinct in our country. Whereas, in the past, the most common method of selecting a chief of police was through appointment by the city council, the modern trend is toward selection by open, competitive written and oral examinations. Usually, under this system, the members of the city council select a police chief from one of the top three successful candidates in the competitive examinations. If the municipality has a city manager or administrator, the city council usually acts on the recommendation of the city manager or administrator.

Pendleton Act of 1883. When Congress passed the Pendleton

Act in 1883, a real breakthrough to the establishment of civil service was accomplished for law enforcement. This act marked the end of the previous 75 years of "to the winner goes the graft and political plums." Then at last, a tool was forged that would take police appointments out of the reach of sordid politics. The example of the Federal government's success with civil service served to set up a model for state, county, and municipal police departments to follow. Now, police promotions at state, county, and city levels, based on a civil service system of merit via open examinations, have brought about noticeable improvement in municipal police service in the United States.

THE CALIFORNIA POLICE SYSTEM

Growth of San Francisco police. While police progress was being made through trial and error in the East, the western part of the United States was also going through the throes of developing a modern police system. By 1850, San Francisco, with the help of a city charter, had a chief of police and a police force of 7 to 12 men. With the Gold Rush and the spirit of "Go west, young man, go west" inspiring migration to California in great numbers, many problems appeared involving vigilantes, bounty hunters, gunslingers, and the vice of the Barbary Coast. To preserve law and order effectively, San Francisco's police force was boosted to 400 members in 1878.

DEVELOPMENTS IN LOS ANGELES

Early police. On September 4, 1781, almost 500 miles south of San Francisco, the city of Los Angeles came into existence by proclamation. But the nucleus of its present-day modern, highly trained, and efficient police department did not emerge until nearly 69 years later. Only when California was admitted into the Union in 1850 did Los Angeles legally incorporate as a city. It is at this point in time that the history of the Los Angeles Police Department rightly commences.

Initially, the city marshal was permitted by law to deputize citizens whenever it became necessary to maintain law and order. Those who violated the law were allowed to work out their fines on chain gangs at $1 per day.

In 1851 a voluntary police force of 100 members acting under the authority of the Common Council (city council) was formed in Los Angeles. White ribbon badges bearing the words "City Police" in both English and Spanish were issued to the volunteers as a badge of their police authority.

Vigilantes. To combat the organized bands of bandits, several volunteer organizations described as vigilantes were formed. One of the most famous volunteer groups to organize was the Los Angeles Rangers. In order to supply needed equipment, the California state legislature, in 1854, granted the sum of $4,000 to the Los Angeles Rangers. By 1869 this voluntary force was changed to a paid police department with an appointed city marshal. The new department consisted of two 6-man squads, each under the direction of a captain. Each squad worked a 12-hour shift under a two-platoon system. Compensation was based on fees rather than on a regular salary.

Board of police commissioners. The first board of police commissioners was appointed by the mayor in 1870, with the approval of the Common Council. Seven years later, the office of city marshal was abolished and the Common Council elected the city's first chief of police. Almost at once, the city police began to wear regular uniforms, and in 1885 the first telephone was installed in the chief's office.

By 1889, Los Angeles was divided into four policing districts, each under the supervision of a sergeant. In order to keep the officers in close contact with headquarters, an alarm system was installed in 1897. About this time, also, the Bertillon system of identification was adopted. Civil service, however, did not come into effect until 1903. By 1911, the modern concept of fingerprint classification superseded the Bertillon system of identification.

August Vollmer. August Vollmer, the patriarch of California law enforcement, was induced to come to Los Angeles in 1923 to assist in the reorganization of the city police department. Under his direction, the department was consolidated under a chief of police who, for the first time, was placed under the civil service. The administrative supervision of the department was delegated to the police commission appointed by the mayor, with the consent of the city council.

Today's Los Angeles Police Department. From a small adobe village, Los Angeles has grown rapidly to become the third largest city in the United States. From all reports, the police department cannot recruit new officers fast enough to keep pace with the great influx of newcomers. Aggravating this serious lack of manpower is the loss of personnel through retirement and to industrial jobs which offer lucrative pay and attractive administrative positions. As a result, the Los Angeles Police Department is accelerating its recruiting program and urges young American citizens between 21 and 31 to apply. As an inducement, application may be made at age 20, and, if the applicant is successful, he becomes eligible for regular police officer employment at the age of 21.

THE SHERIFF'S ROLE

His qualifications. With roots stemming primarily from Great Britain, the sheriff of today in the United States has become an integral part of American law enforcement. The past has proven that the American people like to elect the top law enforcement officers in their counties. Since the formative years of our country, this office of sheriff has been coveted. Even persons outside law enforcement often campaign for the office of sheriff. In the past, unqualified and questionable political hacks sometimes were elected to office; however, with the great professional advancement of law enforcement, many high-caliber men now seek the sheriff's office. Previously, political connections, popularity, and an easy conscience were the strongest factors in a successful election to the office of sheriff. Today, however, college graduates, ex-FBI agents, and dedicated law enforcement veterans who have worked their way up the ladder of success in police administration are seeking and winning the office of sheriff.

State laws affecting sheriffs. Each state has laws governing the qualifications, jurisdiction, duties, and limitations of the sheriff. Section 24000 of the Government Code of California stipulates that the sheriff is an officer of the county. Moreover, the Appellate Court of California has ruled several times that the sheriff is a public officer, as distinguished from a mere employee. The powers and duties of the sheriff are administrative in nature, and he is an officer of the court. Section 817 of the California Penal Code makes the sheriff a peace officer. Section 24001 of the Government Code of California requires that the candidate for sheriff, to be eligible for county office, must be 21 years of age or older, a citizen of the state, and an elector of the county.

While the office and powers of the sheriff cannot be changed by the voters of the county, certain indirect methods of control do exist, namely:

1. The office of sheriff is an elective one which is filled by the choice of the electors of the county.
2. The organization of the sheriff's department is subject to the control of the county board of supervisors.
3. The county board of supervisors also determines the department's appropriations.
4. Finally, the county grand jury reviews the sheriff's record each year, and its findings are contained in an annual public report, which receives considerable public scrutiny.

Sheriff's legal authority. The Government Code of California vests the sheriff with broad policing authority. In order to preserve the peace effectively, the sheriff may sponsor, supervise, or participate in any project or crime prevention program. The rehabilitation of persons previously convicted of a crime or the suppression of delinquency also comes within his jurisdiction. He must arrest and take before the nearest magistrate, for examination, all persons who attempt to commit or have committed a public offense. He is charged with the responsibility of preventing and suppressing any public brawls, breaches of the peace, riots, and insurrections which come to his attention. Perhaps his most widely known duty is to investigate public offenses which have been committed. The sheriff is authorized to summon and to command a posse. He is also the custodian of the county jail and the prisoners confined there.

Sheriff's jurisdiction. By law, the sheriff is required to serve all residents of the county. However, in practice, he actually provides police service primarily to the unincorporated areas and cities that contract for the police services of the sheriff.

Normally, law enforcement within the confines of each municipality is left to the police department in each city government.
However, if the city police department is unable or unwilling to
cope with such problems as vice or other similar police problems,
the sheriff may assume law enforcement responsibilities within
the city, especially if requested to do so by the duly elected city
officials, or when directed to do so by the attorney general of the
state.

County contract law enforcement. In 1954, contract law enforcement was initiated in Los Angeles County. Since then, Los
Angeles County has made over 1,000 city-county contracts that
cover services ranging from street lighting and fire service to law
enforcement. Almost every new city which receives a charter contracts with the county for police services. This trend is being followed by other counties throughout the state of California, particularly in the metropolitan areas.

How city-county police contracts work. The Los Angeles
County Sheriff's Department represents the most widespread application of city-county police cooperation in the United States.
At least 29 cities have now contracted for law enforcement services with the sheriff.

In order to handle this large volume of police service, the
sheriff's department is decentralized. There are 14 sheriffs' stations located throughout Los Angeles county to serve the unincorporated communities and contract cities. Each station operates its
own 24-hour radio car patrol service, and maintains detective and
juvenile units. The department is divided into seven major divisions, each headed by a chief who is responsible to the sheriff for
the division's activities. These divisions are: administrative, patrol, detective, technical services, jail, corrections, and civil.

Advantages of contract services. According to the sheriff's publications, the advantages of contracting for county police services
are many. In the first place, no initial cost outlay for law enforcement is necessary when the community incorporates because all
police buildings, jail facilities, police cars, and other equipment
are provided by the sheriff. Besides, there are no continuing maintenance or replacement costs. Instead, for an annual operating
cost of $101,937, the sheriff provides a patrol unit around the
clock, including one deputy during the day and two deputies at

night. The price quoted also covers a share of the costs of other departmental services, such as investigation, crime prevention, vice law enforcement, police records, prisoner custody, and crime laboratory. These additional services are available and rendered as needed.

Sheriffs' surveys show that the average contract city's policing budget is about half that of a city that maintains its own police department. The newly incorporated city of Pico Rivera is convinced of this economy, so the city contracts for police services from the sheriff and appropriates an annual law enforcement budget of $403,000. For this sum, the city receives the services of 31 deputies. These deputies work out of the nearby Norwalk Station of the sheriff's department 7 days a week, 24 hours a day. This contract provides for 2 general law enforcement cars around the clock, plus 8 traffic units 7 days per week and evenings.

Apparently, other city managers are convinced of this economy because practically all newly incorporated cities, such as Pico Rivera, enter into contractual agreements with the sheriff for police services in Los Angeles County.

Disadvantages of contract services. Taking the opposite position, police executives of established police departments insist that the savings through contract services, if any, are not worth giving up the "home rule" that every independent city exercises. By contracting with the county sheriff, they say, the city loses its law enforcement autonomy and has no control over police services because the needed control passes by contract to the sheriff so that he can adequately enforce the law.

Established chiefs of police also insist that the sheriff's deputies are not locally oriented or community-minded and are therefore not personally interested in the contract city. Usually the deputy lives in some other city, and so his interests and roots are centered in his home area. Thus, the contract deputy may not have the personal interest or consideration which the local police officer brings to his community. In addition, chiefs emphasize that contract cities are paying for services that they have already paid for through regular county taxes and assessments. So, it is felt that local communities which contract with the sheriff are paying twice for some police services which are available to them anyway as cities located in the county.

Signal Hill, California, is an example of a city that first had an established police department, then discontinued its regular police force and contracted with the sheriff for police services. However, after a relatively short time, Signal Hill officials did not renew the city's contract with the sheriff but, instead, reestablished their own police force. Another city that returned to the city police system after sampling the sheriff's contract services is Irwindale, California.

City or county police services? Obviously, each police system has merits. One system may be ideal for one city and not for another. All pertinent factors must be considered when a community decides which service to utilize. Moreover, it is the responsibility of each city to conduct surveys and to evaluate its own peculiar needs for police services. When these needs are clear, then the police system that provides the most efficient and economical services should be instituted.

STATE POLICE

Authority. Unlike the municipal or local police, the state police system does not trace its origin back to Biblical times, to medieval days, or to the English police. Rather, the state police is a creation of the state Legislature because police power is the reserved or inherent power of the states to legislate for the health, welfare, safety, and morals of the people.

Some states maintain a state police force endowed with general police power throughout the state. Still others have established a statewide force primarily to patrol highways and to enforce traffic laws. A number of states have developed state bureaus of identification and investigation which serve as a general clearing house for criminal matters pertaining to fingerprints, records, and laboratory examinations. Also, a state militia may be held in readiness for emergencies such as those which occurred during the civil rights demonstrations in Mississippi, Alabama, Georgia, and other states.

It should be remembered that not all state police organizations are granted general police power. Instead, some are permitted only limited, regulatory power. The states that have highway patrols usually limit police jurisdiction to traffic control and enforcement. Although the highway patrol officers have complete authority as peace officers, their assignment is exercised almost exclusively on the state highways and roads. They usually handle crime problems originating on the highway. Normally, the officers are not detailed as a general police force and so do not involve themselves in purely local matters. In most instances, the highway patrol does not function in cities except upon the request of the city. Some freeways passing through municipalities in California are policed by the California Highway Patrol under contracts between the cities and the state, but this is the exception rather than the rule.

Very close liaison is maintained between the state highway patrol and the city police and county sheriff's office. Consequently, there exists splendid cooperation between local and state law enforcement agencies. The key to this excellent relationship is accomplished by highway patrol membership in local law enforcement organizations and by attendance at official police zone meetings. Because of this participation at the local level, mutual crime problems are solved, criminals are apprehended, ideas are exchanged, training is accelerated, and the administration of justice is enhanced for the welfare of society as a whole.

State highway patrols. In 1749, the main purpose of the mounted patrol in England was to watch for criminals and thieves. Today, modern state highway patrols have the important responsibility of traffic control. This implies responsibility not only for enforcement of traffic laws but also for assistance to motorists in distress. Because of the nature of his work, the highway patrol officer must be versatile, for he may have to capture a fleeing criminal, assist local police and deputy sheriffs in the arrest and apprehension of known criminals, or set up roadblocks with checkpoints in order to bring to justice violators of the law.

The progress of the state highway patrols in finding new ways to make the job safer for the patrolman and the highways less hazardous for the public has been remarkable. In past years, there have been many scientific improvements in patrol cars. Helicopters and airplanes have been tested for practical use, not only in rescuing and helping traffic-accident victims, but also in enforcing the law. In California, for instance, two fixed-wing planes were recently used to patrol U.S. Highway 99 between

Sacramento and the Kern County line to determine whether the use of aircraft was practical in spotting and aiding motorists in need of help. This test proved so effective that thereafter helicopters were used to patrol remote areas of the San Bernardino freeway. In the constant search for improvement, another test revealed that installing push bumpers on patrol cars could help keep freeways clear of stalled cars.

Tests of many other devices and techniques for traffic control, such as use of bucket seats for squad cars, wearing of harnesses and helmets for drivers, conduction of psychological interviews with motorists involved in accidents, post-mortem examination of fatality victims to determine the role that carbon monoxide may have played in certain accidents, and study of noise to establish acceptable noise limits for vehicles, have been made and are continuing.

FEDERAL LAW ENFORCEMENT

Origins. Federal law enforcement is a product of our United States Congress. The first Federal law enforcement office created by Congress was that of United States marshal in the year 1789. Forty years later, in 1829, Congress passed the Postal Act, which conferred police powers on a Federal agency. This act required the services of inspectors to enforce the postal laws.

Secret Service. Subsequently, when counterfeiting became prevalent, Congress passed the counterfeiting law of 1842. However, the Secret Service was not organized to investigate and control the Federal violations established by this act until July 5, 1865. When it finally did assume jurisdiction in 1865, it became one of the first general investigative agencies of the Federal government. In the years since 1865, its agents have established a record that ranks with that of the world's finest investigators. In numbers, Secret Service agents do not compare with such enforcement bodies as the FBI or Scotland Yard, but in skill, courage, and effective accomplishments, they have proved to be equally respected, loyal, and dedicated public servants.

With the establishment of national headquarters of the Secret Service in Washington, D.C., 11 cities were selected for field-operations sites. The Secret Service went into action then and has been busy ever since. At first, agents' credentials were handwritten letters of appointment. Badges were not provided. Instead, when the Secret Service was established, the Treasury Department simply sent out a formal circular letter to the United States marshals and other peace officers announcing the formation of the Secret Service and describing its functions.

Early problems of the Secret Service. Because handwritten credentials were not acceptable and did not prove satisfactory, the work of the Secret Service was often made difficult. Bankers and other law-abiding people were suspicious and reluctant to cooperate with "strangers" about clues and suspects in criminal cases. Furthermore, during the formative days of the Secret Service, the agents carried handcuffs but not guns.

The following case clearly illustrates what could happen in those days through lack of positive and adequate identification of Secret Service agents. In June of 1871, a very presentable but clever impersonator by the name of Ira W. Raymond came to the San Francisco office and introduced himself as a Secret Service agent to the agent in charge, explaining that he had been appointed to handle the affairs of the Secret Service in the California area. To prove his authority, he presented official-appearing documents from the State and Treasury departments. When he had apparently convinced the agent in charge, he demanded the keys to the office vault and a complete report of the property, including any contraband held as evidence. Naturally, the agent in charge was amazed and at a loss to understand why he had not been informed of the new man's appointment. So he sent a telegram to his chief in Washington, D.C. An immediate reply advised the agent that Raymond was an impostor and unknown to either the State or Treasury Department officials. Arrested, Raymond pleaded guilty and was sentenced to the state prison.

In order to counteract other similar schemes, distinctive badges and printed credentials were issued to all members of the Secret Service in 1873. The shape of the new badge was a five-pointed silver star with a lacework design similar to the pattern appearing on the borders of our paper money. It carried the engraved inscription, "U.S. Secret Service." Even today the badges are the same. Each agent now carries a replica of the original badge and a commission card which bears his photograph and signature.

Justice Department investigators. The next indication of any police action by our Federal government was taken on June 22, 1870. Then, several investigators were hired by the United States Attorney General to investigate allegations concerning the transportation of European women to the United States for immoral purposes. This investigation was the forerunner of the problems involving the White Slave Traffic Act, which was introduced in Congress by Representative Mann and is frequently called the Mann Act by police and vice lords alike.

Beginning of the FBI. In 1908 President Theodore Roosevelt recognized that the Department of Justice needed investigators. On July 26, 1908, his Attorney General, Charles J. Bonaparte, organized the Bureau of Investigation, as it was known at that time, and this small group of investigators became the investigative arm of the Department of Justice. This organization has grown as new violations have been added to its jurisdiction by Congress, until now it is one of the largest and most respected law enforcement agencies in the world.

During the reorganization of the Bureau by Harlan Fiske Stone, United States Attorney General, in 1924, John Edgar Hoover was appointed Director at the age of 29. On July 1, 1935, the present official name of Federal Bureau of Investigation came into being. Under the leadership of Mr. Hoover, the FBI has created a favorable public image. As a result, the FBI has successfully withstood Congressional and political scrutiny since 1924.

FEDERAL INVESTIGATIVE AGENCIES

Although the FBI has investigative jurisdiction in more than 160 Federal matters, there are also other important investigative agencies of the United States government. The most prominent of these, and the ones that the police science student should be familiar with, are:

Executive branch
  1. *U.S. Department of Justice*
     Attorney General-chief legal officer of the government. The Federal Bureau of Investigation is the primary investiga-

tive agency of the government and investigates both criminal and security violations under its jurisdiction, such as espionage, counterespionage, sabotage, subversive activities, and all violations of Federal laws not specifically assigned to other agencies. The Immigration and Naturalization Service enforces immigration and naturalization laws and patrols the border.

2. *Executive Office of the President*
Central Intelligence Agency—foreign intelligence.

3. *Department of State*
Office of Security—passport and visa applications, munitions control; personnel.

4. *Department of the Treasury*
   a. Coast Guard—maritime law enforcement, safety, and port security.
   b. Bureau of Customs—smuggling activities, customs, and navigation laws.
   c. Internal Revenue Service, Intelligence Division—enforcement of internal revenue tax laws, national and Federal firearms acts, and alcohol tax laws (Alcohol and Tobacco Tax Division, Inspection Service).
   d. Bureau of Narcotics—Federal narcotic and marijuana laws.
   e. Secret Service—protection of President; offenses relating to coins, obligations, and securities of government; other laws under direct control of Treasury Department.

5. *Department of Defense*
Assistant Chief of Staff, Intelligence (Army).
Office of Naval Intelligence (Navy).
Office of Special Investigations (Air Force).
Army, Navy, and Air Force matters and espionage, counterespionage, subversion, and sabotage, in accordance with Delimitations Agreement.

6. *Post Office Department—Bureau of the Chief Postal Inspector*
Postal laws and regulations, including schemes to defraud; lotteries, obscene matter, and certain extortions (threats against character and reputation).

7. *Department of the Interior*
   a. Fish and Wildlife Service—Migratory Bird Act; Fish and Wildlife Restoration Acts; international agreements and restraints upon interstate transportation.
   b. Bureau of Indian Affairs—maintaining order and suppressing liquor and drug traffic on Indian reservations.
   c. Bureau of Mines—mine accidents, explosions, and fires.
   d. National Park Service—laws and regulations relating to national parks.
8. *Department of Agriculture*
   More than 50 regulatory laws protecting farmer and consumer public; enforcement of Sugar Act of 1948 and Commodity Exchange Act of 1936.
9. *Department of Labor*
   Wage and Hour Division—Fair Labor Standards Act.
10. *Independent Agencies*
   a. Civil Aeronautics Board—Federal Aviation Agency—civil aircraft accidents.
   b. Civil Service Commission—applicant and employee investigations and administration of civil service laws and rules.
   c. Federal Power Commission—Federal Power Act and licenses, rules, regulations, and orders thereunder.
   d. Federal Communications Commission—regulation of interstate and foreign commerce in communication by wire and radio.
   e. Federal Trade Commission—unfair competition and deceptive practices in interstate commerce.
   f. Interstate Commerce Commission—regulation of common carriers in interstate commerce; investigations of railroad accidents.
   g. Securities and Exchange Commission—malpractices in the securities and financial markets.

Legislative branch
1. General Accounting Office—matters relating to receipt, disbursement, and application of public funds.
2. House and Senate Investigating Committees—investigate national problems pertaining to crime, juvenile delinquency, un-American activities, and similar vital matters.

American opposition to strong national police. The basic functions of police have been conducted on a local level in the United States since the arrival of the earliest colonists. Thus, the concept of a national police force has never really taken root in the United States. Always there has been the fear of a strong national police organization or a mighty military force that could subtly or openly take over our government. The frequent revolutions in some of the Central and South American countries on this continent are constant reminders of what a national police force can mean.

This philosophy, favoring local police over national police, has been upheld consistently by J. Edgar Hoover, who has directed the destinies and the many successes of the FBI since 1924. Time and again Mr. Hoover has advocated strong, well-trained and well-paid local law enforcement agencies to fight crime. Often he has been the strongest voice supporting local law enforcement. His universal popularity and influence on the American public has held in check those elements of our society who recommend a semimilitary national police organization such as those which prevail in some European countries.

For these reasons, and unlike many other countries, the United States does not have a national police force as the sole law enforcement body. Moreover, the consensus in our country is that we neither need nor want a national police force. This opinion stems from our founding fathers and our revolutionary forebears, whose aim was to avoid the tyranny of centralized power. Throughout our system of government, the separation and diffusion of powers is constantly enunciated and practiced so as to carry out the aims of those who designed our system. The Tenth Amendment of the United States Constitution makes explicit this diffusion of power. It delegates specific powers to the national government but "reserves" to the states and the people all other powers not prohibited to them. The power of the police is one of the great powers of government.

If this power is centralized in the hands of a single agency and is then used in a political and abusive fashion, the damage to democracy can be irreparable. We of the twentieth century need

Historical background of United States police   155

hardly be reminded of this fact when the mind conjures up the dark and sinister images of Hitler's Gestapo or the Russian OGPU (secret police).

Moreover, a nation the size of America, with her diverse population and pluralistic society, could not conform harmoniously to a single national police force with a uniform system of operation. Local conditions vary greatly in America, and local people feel they know how to handle their own citizens best. The only condition which needs to be imposed on all the separate law enforcement agencies is that every citizen is entitled to his full constitutional rights, without exception.

Federal jurisdiction explained. Investigative jurisdiction is spelled out by our United States Constitution, by Federal law, and by state constitutions and state laws. Usually, a police science student can determine whether a crime is under Federal or state (local) jurisdiction by applying this test: if the criminal act occurred entirely within the state, it is usually a matter for investigation by the interested law enforcement agency *within* that state. For instance, if a motor vehicle was stolen in New York and driven entirely within the state from New York City to Albany, it would be a case for the police or sheriff from the city or county where it was stolen. If the violation proves to be (inter) between states or involves a foreign country, then the Federal law enforcement agency has jurisdiction. As an example, if a motor vehicle, stolen in Chicago, Illinois, is recovered in New Orleans, Louisiana, it would be a Federal violation over which the Federal Bureau of Investigation has jurisdiction. Of course, there are exceptions to this rule. One exception is the FBI's jurisdiction over crimes which occur on Indian and United States government reservations and over thefts of government property, even though these crimes occur solely within a certain state. This applies only when the Federal government has exclusive jurisdiction in such areas. Also, the FBI has concurrent jurisdiction with local police and sheriffs in robberies of Federal banks, such as those insured by the Federal Deposit Insurance Corporation, those organized and operated under laws of the United States, and those that are members of the Federal Reserve System. This FBI jurisdiction applies when Federal savings and loan associations and Federal credit unions as well as banks are involved.

Federal and local cooperation. In past years, a feeling of animosity, jealousy, and ill will often existed between local and Federal law enforcement agencies. This situation has been remedied successfully in recent years. By mutual participation in training, conferences, seminars, institutes, and official cooperation at all levels, the old suspicions and competition arising from concurrent jurisdiction have been reconciled in most instances.

With higher local police standards, pay increases, and retirement and fringe benefits closely equaling and resembling Federal civil service, the entire police profession has achieved a relatively favorable outlook and a comparatively secure future. As a result much of the conflict between local and Federal law enforcement agencies has been swallowed up in an era of cooperative police effort.

HISTORY OF METHODS OF IDENTIFICATION

Bertillon system. Criminal identification has progressed from the branding and maiming of early history, through the "photographic memory" of law enforcement officers, through the Bertillon measurements introduced in 1870, to the present infallible system of positive identification through fingerprinting. The Bertillon system was utilized for over 30 years but lost its reputation for reliability when, in 1903, a man by the name of Will West was convicted and sentenced to the United States Penitentiary in Leavenworth, Kansas. Upon arrival at Leavenworth, Will West was subjected to the customary Bertillon measurements. While referring to the Bertillon measurement file, the clerk learned that one William West had been entered previously in the files, and even the photographs of the two men appeared to be identical. When the Leavenworth clerk reversed William West's card, he learned that this man was then in detention in Leavenworth, serving a life sentence. Upon fingerprinting the two prisoners, it was learned there was no resemblance between the two pairs of fingerprint cards. The unreliability of three means of criminal identification—Bertillon measurements, facial similarity, and names—was thus proved, and the value of fingerprinting was established.

Portrait parle. The science of fingerprints has been accepted universally by law enforcement officials as the best method of identification known. However, a holdover from the Bertillon method of criminal identification by measurements of the human body is still used to great advantage. This method of identification is known as portrait parle. These two French words mean "speak-

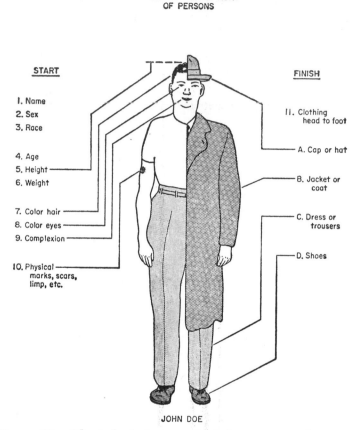

STANDARD DESCRIPTIONS
OF PERSONS

START

1. Name
2. Sex
3. Race

4. Age
5. Height
6. Weight

7. Color hair
8. Color eyes
9. Complexion

10. Physical
marks, scars,
limp, etc.

FINISH

11. Clothing
head to foot

A. Cap or hat

B. Jacket or
coat

C. Dress or
trousers

D. Shoes

JOHN DOE

Figure 10.   Chart depicting standard descriptions of persons.

ing likeness." Law enforcement officers are taught to be able to understand and appreciate the value of the head and facial differences in human beings. Every investigative file should contain a complete description of the suspect.

Figure 10, entitled "Standard Descriptions of Persons," is only a very minimum description, but coupled with a distinctive description of every feature of the face and head, it may be a valuable investigative technique, especially when a set of the suspect's fingerprints is not available from his file.

Identi-Kit. In June, 1959, the most constructive extension and application of descriptions to criminal investigation was made by Hugh C. McDonald, Chief, Technical Services Division, Los Angeles Sheriff's Department. He invented the Identi-Kit. This valuable investigative aid, which is now used extensively by law enforcement in the United States and in many foreign countries, is a scientific method whereby an officer or witness is able to "build a face" of a suspect from transparencies. Considerable success in the apprehension of fugitives and suspects has been realized by those law enforcement agencies that possess or have access to the Identi-Kit.

Fingerprint identification. Many centuries before the Christian era, man was conscious of fingerprint ridges. In ancient Babylon, fingerprints were impressed in clay tablets to record business transactions. The Chinese used fingerprints on legal documents in the eighth century A.D., although it is doubtful that the fingerprints did any more than add solemnity to the business transaction. The fact that fingerprints are individual has been considered repeatedly through the ages, however, and, in the fourteenth century a Persian governmental official observed that the fingerprints of no two people were identical.

Dr. Nehemian Grew of the Royal College of Physicians stated in 1684 that fingers possessed ridge patterns, but it remained for Marcello Malpighi, Professor of Anatomy at the University of Bologna, in 1686, using a new instrument called a microscope, to comment upon "diverse figures on palmar surfaces, and loops and spirals." In 1823, John Evangelist Purkinje, Professor of Anatomy at the University of Breslau, wrote a thesis on the diversity of ridge patterns and identified nine variations in pattern.

Thirty-five years after Purkinje's scholarly treatise, Sir William James Herschel, British chief administrative officer for the Hooghly district, Bengal, India, began to use fingerprints officially. He required natives to affix their fingerprints as well as their signatures to legal documents, perhaps primarily to impress the native imagination and to prevent dishonesty. He seems to have become aware of the individuality of these ridges, however, for in 1877

Herschel requested official permission to extend the use of finger-printing as a means of identification for prisoners. Permission was withheld, but Herschel extended his system within his own province, although he did not produce a method of fingerprint classification.

At about the same time Dr. Henry Faulds, of Taukiji Hospital in Tokyo, began parallel observations. In 1880, a scientific journal titled *Nature* carried an article by Dr. Faulds in which he discussed criminal identification by means of fingerprints left at crime scenes, recommended use of a thin film of printer's ink as a medium for transfer, and detailed future possibilities of the science of fingerprinting. Faulds demonstrated a practical application of his theories by identifying the person responsible for drinking some "spirits" taken from the official supplies, probably one of the earliest latent fingerprint identifications.

The first authentic record of official fingerprint use in the United States was in 1882, when Mr. Gilbert Thompson of the United States Geological Survey placed his own fingerprint on official orders as a means of preventing their forgery. In 1883, Mark Twain published his book *Life on the Mississippi* in which he relates the identification of a murderer by his thumbprint; and in 1893, Twain's "Pudd'n-head Wilson" told the story of a court trial in which fingerprint identification proved its infallibility.

In 1880, Sir Francis Galton, renowned British anthropologist and a cousin of scientist Charles Darwin, commenced studies which produced, in 1892, his book *Fingerprints*. This was the first time anyone had established both the individuality and the permanence of fingerprints. Galton also devised the first scientific classification of fingerprint patterns.

Juan Vucetich, a noted criminologist as well as an Argentinian police official, using the patterns typed by Galton, first installed fingerprint files to provide official criminal identification. Fingerprinting was first used in conjunction with the Bertillon bodily measurement system but gradually replaced this. At present, the Vucetich system forms the basis of the systems used in many countries. In solving the Rojas murder case in 1892 at La Plata, Argentina, Vucetich holds the record for the first official criminal identification by the fingerprint method at the crime scene.

In 1901, fingerprinting was introduced officially for purposes of criminal identification in England and Wales. It was based upon Galton's observations and devised by Mr. Edward Richard Henry, later to become Sir Henry, Commissioner of the London Metropolitan Police. Henry produced a simplified fingerprint classification system, adapted to police needs. His system and that of Vucetich are the foundation of all present-day, 10-finger systems of fingerprint identification.

In 1902, Dr. Henry P. DeForest, the American pioneer in the science of fingerprinting, introduced the practice of fingerprinting to the New York Civil Service Commission as a means of ensuring applicants for civil service testing. This was the first systematic use of fingerprinting in the United States and was followed, in 1903, by the first systematic use of fingerprints in criminal identification. In March, 1903, the New York state prison took fingerprints for classification, and on June 5, 1903, it officially adopted the fingerprint system.

In 1904, the United States Penitentiary at Leavenworth, Kansas, organized a fingerprint bureau. In the same year the St. Louis Police Department organized its fingerprint bureau, with the assistance of a sergeant of Scotland Yard then on duty guarding a British exhibit at the St. Louis Exposition. The Leavenworth bureau was the first to offer a fingerprint service on an exchange basis, without cost, to nationwide police agencies.

The first official military use of fingerprinting was introduced in 1905 by the United States Army, followed in 1907 by the Navy, and in 1908 by the Marine Corps.

As more fingerprint bureaus were established by local police agencies, the International Association of Chiefs of Police organized the National Bureau of Criminal Identification to which many local departments forwarded copies of their criminal fingerprints. The obvious need for Federal handling of these prints, however, resulted in an Act of Congress which established, on July 1, 1924, the Identification Division of the Federal Bureau of Investigation. A nucleus of 810,188 fingerprint records was transferred to the Identification Division from the National Bureau of Criminal Identification files and from Leavenworth Penitentiary.

In 1932, an international exchange of fingerprint information between nations was organized; in 1933, the single fingerprint section (for technical examination of latent prints) was initiated. Also, in this year the FBI civil identification section was established. It is estimated that in 1966 the total number of fingerprints on file in the FBI Identification Division will be more than 178 million.

Interesting facts about fingerprinting. Fingerprint experts estimate that there is only one chance in 64 billion that a fingerprint of one person may be the same as that of another person. Since there are less that 4 billion people in the world, the odds are tremendously in favor of no duplication.

Fingerprints form in a child during the fourth month of the mother's pregnancy, and there is no change in the prints during life. Only after death, when the skin actually becomes extinct, do the fingerprints disappear. The only positive method of removing or changing fingerprints is to burn the fingers to ashes. Ordinary plastic surgery cannot permanently change fingerprints satisfactorily. It is a criminal violation for a doctor even to attempt to change anyone's fingerprints. The notorious fugitive, John Dillinger, bank robber and escape artist of the early 1930s, had his face lifted, and a doctor endeavored to mutilate Dillinger's fingerprints. However, after Dillinger was killed in a gun battle with FBI agents, his body was positively identified by his fingerprints.

QUESTIONS

1. Describe the police system that the early colonists brought to the United States and the manner in which their police were actually utilized.
2. Who was Stephen Girard, and what did he contribute to law enforcement?
3. Why were state police boards first adopted, and why were they abandoned?
4. Explain the significance of the Pendleton Act of 1883.
5. What are the qualifications, jurisdiction, duties, and limitations of the sheriff?

6. Explain county contract enforcement and its effect on local law enforcement.
7. What are the duties, authority, and limitations of the state highway patrol?
8. Describe the history and development of the FBI under J. Edgar Hoover.
9. Explain the duties and functions of the Secret Service.
10. What Federal department has jurisdiction over passport and visa applications?
11. What department has jurisdiction over extortions involving threats against character and reputation?
12. What are the advantages of local law enforcement over a national police force, if any?

*Before you organize you ought
to analyze and see what
the elements of the business are.*
GERARD SWOPE

8. Orientation to police administration

How police organize

ORGANIZATION AND PERFORMANCE

Chapter 5, The Purposes of Criminal Law, discussed the primary duties and responsibilities of police. There, perhaps for the first time, the student of police science was able to develop a broad overall view of what the job of law enforcement is and what the police officer is expected to do. What was not emphasized in Chapter 5, however, was the way police agencies have organized themselves in order to carry out their duties and responsibilities. Performance of police duties depends upon proper organization. It is true that any group of people who band together to achieve common goals must organize or fail. But good organization is especially crucial to law enforcement work because of the split-second timing, the accuracy, the care, and the speed with which much police work must be accomplished. Indeed, the police organization must be fully equal to its demanding, difficult, and often hazardous work.

Understanding police organization is important to the police student. Police are highly organized—almost as highly organized as the military. The police student, therefore, as a future officer, needs to understand the type of organization he will become a part of, and, through that understanding, to visualize his own future place within the law enforcement structure. Moreover, knowing the interacting elements within a police department will give the student a good idea of how the whole machinery of law enforcement works.

Nature of police organizations. Police organizations are both similar to and different from other organizations. Like any business organization, police agencies combine the necessary personnel, materials, equipment, and facilities to achieve their goals efficiently and harmoniously. There are command officers, supervisors, supporting staff, and line employees. The biggest difference between the typical business organization and police organization is that business organizes for profit, while the police organize for public service.

The police organization, perhaps, resembles the military more closely than it does the business organization. In fact, the police frequently have been described as a semimilitary organization. The symbols of the police—uniforms, insignia, arms, special vehicles, and equipment—are obviously military in aspect. But it is in a somewhat deeper sense that the police structure resembles the military more than it does business. Police work involves danger to life in a constant battle against a tough enemy—crime. The demands made on the police by the fight against crime call for a well-disciplined force, one high in morale and often subject, in crises, to an almost absolute control by superiors. Consequently, the police's tighter, military type of organization is completely consistent with the nature of their law enforcement duties and responsibilities. It is this kind of organization which the student of police science will one day enter.

It is clear, then, that police organization is not an end in itself, but simply a means to the end of law enforcement. Some features of this organizational structure came into being by chance, some developed out of a long tradition of experience, and some were the outcome of careful planning and design. No matter how the structure came into being, a study of police organization provides a necessary part of the student's background.

There are three ways in which the police organize men, materials, and equipment for law enforcement: (1) by line functions, (2) by staff functions, and (3) by both line and staff functions. These important types of organization are carefully blended in a well-organized department.

Line organization. A line officer is one who does his work in the field. He performs the basic police functions for which the police department was created. He protects life and property and preserves the public peace. The patrolman in uniform is a practical example of a line officer because, like the soldier, he is on the firing line.

Staff organization. Staff personnel render services to the line personnel. An officer performing a staff function is one who supports the line officer in his efforts to accomplish the objectives of law enforcement. The staff officer supervises or provides necessary services, such as planning, preparing, coordinating, and supplying the line officer with needed equipment, services, and information. A staff officer may be a supervisor, such as a sergeant, a lieutenant, a captain, or an inspector. He may also be a radio dispatcher, a police photographer, a records officer, a fingerprint expert, a laboratory technician, or a criminologist.

Line-staff organization. It should be noted that an employee of a police department may be functioning in a dual or line-staff capacity. When sergeants or lieutenants work in the field, they are line officers; and when supervising at headquarters, they are staff officers.

Rank. Since staff officers are supervisors, they are provided with rank and authority equal to their responsibility in the department. The patrolman is not a ranking officer. The chain of command, with the chief as highest ranking officer, is as follows:

Chief
    Assistant chief of police
      Inspector

Captain
Lieutenant
Sergeant
Patrolman

Organization charting. An organization chart does no more than show how line and staff police work is divided and arranged and how the authority within the police organization should flow. The organization chart is a convenient picture that tells how police activities are organized. It is a recommended procedure to provide all police personnel with a copy of the organization chart. It would be well to examine several types of organizations according to the way they have been charted.

Organization of small department. The duties of the small police department are divided, under a chief, into two channels, operations and service.

The secret of success in getting work done is to group together employees who are performing similar and related tasks. This simplifies their classification as well as their supervision. Following this principle of administration, all officers doing basic police work, such as line officers (patrolmen), are listed under operations. Where the size of the police department merits it, a ranking officer is placed in charge of operations.

Using the same principle, a ranking officer such as a sergeant, lieutenant, or captain, according to the size of the department, is placed in charge of the staff functions designated as services. Under this simple type of organization, the police activities could be organized along two *vertical* lines as follows:

CHIEF

Sergeant—Operations	*Sergeant—Services*
Patrol	Records
Detectives	Identification bureau
Traffic	Jail
Juvenile	Laboratory
Vice	Communications
	Maintenance
	Equipment and supplies
	Business office
	Property recovered

Organization of growing department. As the department grows, however, the various police functions that increase in importance and that require closer supervision may be moved out of the vertical chain of command and be recombined on a horizontal level as follows:

CHIEF

Captain—Operations		*Captain—Services*	
Sergeant	Sergeant	Sergeant	Sergeant
Detective division	Patrol Traffic	Records Identification	Jail facilities Recovered property
Juvenile bureau	Traffic education	Laboratory	Maintenance
Vice		Communications	Equipment
Policewomen	School patrol guards	Business office	Supplies Court procedures

Thus, it will be seen that this type of organization has spread horizontally and that there are now two sections under operations and two under services.

Organization of large department. As the department continues to grow in size, it will need to provide for additional services and coverage. Such an expanded organization is shown in the chart on page 169.

Relationships in police organization

Organizing, as we have seen from the previous discussions, divides the total job of law enforcement among the various units or work groups within the department. But good organizing goes a step further. It establishes the relationships of the various units to one another—spells out the authority and the responsibility of each unit and each individual. These organizational relationships are most important in police work, and the principles by which these relationships are worked out should be understood by the student of police science.

MODEL ORGANIZATION CHART
(To be anticipated for growing cities)

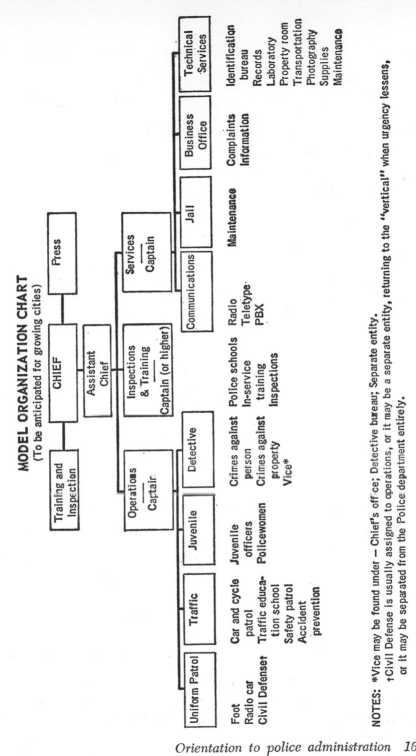

Training and Inspection — **CHIEF** — **Press**

Assistant Chief

Operations
Captain

Services
Captain

Inspections & Training
Captain (or higher)
- Police schools
- In-service training
- Inspections

Operations / Captain:

Uniform Patrol	Traffic	Juvenile	Detective
Foot	Car and cycle patrol	Juvenile officers	Crimes against person
Radio car	Traffic education school	Policewomen	Crimes against property
Civil Defense†	Safety patrol		Vice*
	Accident prevention		

Services / Captain:

Communications	Jail	Business Office	Technical Services
Radio	Maintenance	Complaints	Identification bureau
Teletype		Information	Records
PBX			Laboratory
			Property room
			Transportation
			Photography
			Supplies
			Maintenance

NOTES: *Vice may be found under — Chief's office; Detective bureau; Separate entity.
†Civil Defense is usually assigned to operations, or it may be a separate entity, returning to the "vertical" when urgency lessens, or it may be separated from the Police department entirely.

Orientation to police administration 169

There are four basic principles which police use to establish the working relationships within an organization. Understanding these principles provides an excellent insight to how the police organize men, materials, and equipment to get the job of law enforcement done. These principles are:

1. Chain of command
2. Unity of command
3. Span of control
4. Definition of authority

CHAIN OF COMMAND — AUTHORITY

Authority in any law enforcement organization works through its chain of command. Authority is the right to act or to get others to act within a certain well-defined area. The chain of command is simply the path along which this authority flows.

By checking an organization chart, one can readily trace the chain of command that relates each employer to his supervisor, subordinate, and fellow officer. The chain of command is simply explained as the number of superiors placed between the patrolman and the chief. As a rule, the patrolman proceeds officially up the chain of command through the sergeant, the lieutenant, the captain, and on up to the chief. The patrolman does not skip or deviate from this chain unless in a critical emergency. For a patrolman to skip, or bypass, the vertical upward flow of the chain of command is to commit the serious mistake and almost unforgivable sin of "short circuiting."

By the same token, in order to maintain order and avoid administrative tangles and confusion, the chief also proceeds down the chain of command to the patrolman. He also does not skip or bypass the chain of command unless for the most urgent reasons.

UNITY OF COMMAND

Another basic principle in organizational relationships comes from the Bible: "No man can serve two masters." In law enforcement, no officer should have more than one immediate superior.

When an employee has only one direct superior, he will be spared conflicting orders and directions. To fall under the direction of several commanders leads personnel into confusion and lack of coordination. Only in an emergency and for good reason does a ranking officer give orders and assignments to another's subordinates.

In considering the relationships that should exist among units of the police organization, the question often arises: how many persons can a police supervisor manage effectively? The answer depends on three elements: people, distance, and time.

Number of persons. The number of subordinates a supervisor can efficiently control depends on the duties and abilities of the subordinates. If the work is routine, one supervisor can control ten or twelve subordinates. But if the work is varied, technical, or complicated, one man may have difficulty in supervising even four or five subordinates. Theoretically, the limits have been set at not less than three nor more than eight subordinates for any one supervisor.

Distance. Distance also affects a supervisor's span of control. If his subordinates work within a short distance of him, his problem is simpler than it is if they are spread over a large area. Since the essence of good supervision is personal attention, a supervisor must be in close touch with his subordinates at all times. Absentee management works no better for the police than it does for any other type of organization.

Time. Time is the third aspect of the span of control. There are time limits for any kind of work. And time is especially crucial in the field of law enforcement which operates on a 24-hour basis each day, every day of the year.

Law enforcement personnel must be deployed to cover the equivalent of 1,095 working days each year. Employees in private industry or government civil service are engaged on an average basis of 232 eight-hour work days per year. But the police must man each station, not 8 but 24 hours a day. Hence, the ratio of 1,095 police work days as compared with 232 work days for employees outside of law enforcement is 4.72 to 1. This means that it requires the employment of 4.72 officers to maintain an around-the-clock watch for each station every day of the year. By the same analysis, equipment used in regular police work for a period of 5 years would actually sustain wear equivalent to more than 20 years of normal private service. This poses a budget and financial problem for the chief in regard to personnel and equipment.

To provide the services required of law enforcement, chiefs of police and heads of other similar types of investigative operations conduct 24 hours of police functions on three watches or work periods. Personnel should be assigned to the three watches according to need. The deciding factor is work peak load. For instance, the greatest activity for traffic and uniform patrol occurs during the hours that people are going to work in the morning and coming home late in the afternoon or early evening. On the other hand, the detective division is usually very busy in the early morning and the late evening. Each eight-hour watch needs a supervising officer or a watch commander. In larger departments each division, such as the detective division, patrol division, and traffic division, has a division commander for overall administration. Watch commanders act as division commander in the commander's absence.

In deploying personnel, many departments use a functional chart to show exactly how and where the officers are distributed. The functional chart is a continuation of the organization chart. With the help of the functional chart, police administrators can organize duties, authority, responsibility, and hours of employment for the department's entire personnel. Such a functional chart appears on page 173.

Such a functional chart appears on page 173.

DEFINITION OF AUTHORITY

When the organization and functional charts are completed, they resemble the foundation and framework of a building with vertical and horizontal lines for strength and control. Being also like a stepladder, they emphasize authority step by step from the patrolman on the lowest rung to the chief on the highest. Every employee knows his exact position in the structure and thereby reduces problems of administration to a minimum. Organization

FUNCTIONAL CHART

DISTRIBUTION OF PERSONNEL (25 including chief, captain, and secretary; city of 13,000 – 15,000 population)

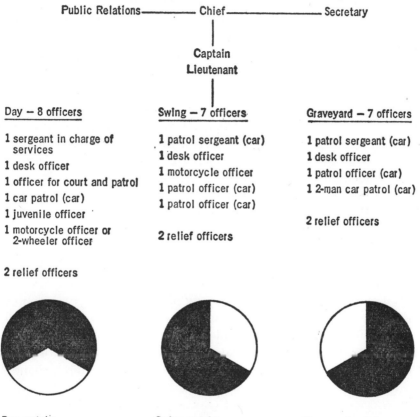

Public Relations———— Chief———————— Secretary

Captain
Lieutenant

Day – 8 officers

1 sergeant in charge of services
1 desk officer
1 officer for court and patrol
1 car patrol (car)
1 juvenile officer
1 motorcycle officer or 2-wheeler officer

2 relief officers

Swing – 7 officers

1 patrol sergeant (car)
1 desk officer
1 motorcycle officer
1 patrol officer (car)
1 patrol officer (car)

2 relief officers

Graveyard – 7 officers

1 patrol sergeant (car)
1 desk officer
1 patrol officer (car)
1 2-man car patrol (car)

2 relief officers

Day watch:
8 A.M. to 4 P.M.

Swing watch:
4 P.M. to 12 midnight

Graveyard watch:
12 midnight to 8 A.M.

charts, therefore, are an important technique for defining the authority of policemen.

Two other devices in addition to the charts are used by most police departments to clarify in greater detail the authority of various units within a police organization. One is the manual of instructions which sets forth the duties of all members of the organization. The other is the manual of rules and regulations

Orientation to police administration 173

which spells out procedures for guidance of personnel within the organization.

Manual of instructions. The manual of instructions is a duty manual. Each officer receives a copy of his duties with his responsibilities appropriately clarified. Through the manual, each officer learns his limitations and what is expected of him. Explanations of the manual of instructions are usually made to all personnel by a superior officer. Such a manual prevents duplication, overlapping, and confusion of function, and promotes an orderly distribution and administration of the work of the department. It also creates a sense of security and confidence and provides proper guidance for the new officer as well as the veteran.

Manual of rules and regulations. The manual of rules and regulations in police organizations is essentially a policy manual. The manual of rules and regulations specifically defines the desired code of conduct for personnel and the procedures for handling police misconduct. A copy of this manual is issued to all personnel so that all will be governed, equally and fairly, by the same rules. All rules and regulations are carefully explained either at special meetings or at roll calls prior to tours of duty. Thus, every person in the department is made aware of the high ethical standards expected in police service. Having and using a manual of rules and regulations prevents many of the disciplinary difficulties that occur in a police department where personnel operate only under custom, tradition, conjecture, rumor, or loose controls. Moreover, surveys reveal that police officers enjoy working in a department that has definite guidelines organized into a manual.

Police operations and service functions

As pointed out previously in this chapter, there are two major functions within a police department—operations and services. Operations are generally line functions, while services are staff functions which support the line operations. These two functions are explained in detail in the following sections.

POLICE OPERATIONS

Investigations. It is common knowledge that the detective division handles the bulk of investigations of crimes against the person and property of the people of the community. Needless to say, investigations must be handled intelligently, effectively, and ethically.

Police executives have found selective law enforcement an excellent procedure in such investigations. The first step in selective law enforcement is the determination of how much crime exists in the city. Next, when, where, and how specific crimes occur is ascertained. Finally, a practical plan of action is formulated to solve prevalent crime problems by strategic placement and deployment of personnel. The entire approach is greatly aided by the use of spot maps with colored pins to reflect the times, dates, and places of burglaries, robberies, sex crimes, traffic accidents, and other problems in the city. Stakeouts and raids are then planned according to all the facts obtained through selective law enforcement studies. This procedure eliminates guesswork and utilizes a scientific approach to the control of crime.

Traffic. Selective law enforcement studies must also be made of traffic problems. Spot maps and colored pins are used to show traffic accidents, hit and run areas, and other expanding traffic control problems. The three E's in traffic control, engineering, enforcement, and education, must be utilized in law enforcement. When all three are applied, safer highways and more sane drivers will help to reduce traffic accidents and fatalities. Assignment of manpower and equipment is made on the basis of actual rate obtained through surveys and studies. Traffic training for all officers is planned so that every member of the police department can handle, understand, and appreciate the problems of uniform enforcement. Good public relations through traffic education programs for both adults and juveniles is a desired objective in traffic. Defensive and conditioned driving should be stressed as recommended by the National Safety Council.

Parking control—both day and night—requires careful planning and execution. Otherwise parking will become a knotty problem during peak daytime shopping hours. Requiring all cars to park off public streets from midnight to 6:00 A.M. is an excellent technique to reduce burglaries by transients and to simplify patrol checks of suspicious cars during the morning watch. Moreover, street cleaning procedures are greatly facilitated and expedited when motor vehicles are in garages or driveways and the streets are empty. Similarly, thefts of cars and thefts of accessories and belongings from cars are reduced.

Juvenile. Frequently police science students are interested in becoming juvenile officers. There are many opportunities in this field. The FBI Uniform Crime Reports reflect that juvenile crime is increasing. Moreover, the types of crimes committed by youth are becoming increasingly more vicious. Special problems such as vandalism, narcotics, curfew, liquor, and gangs should be recognized. Squads with specialized training are organized to control and cover problem areas, giving special attention to juvenile crime and offenders.

Community approach to juvenile program. A program to coordinate all the community resources to combat juvenile problems is a practical approach to juvenile control. A coordinating council consisting of representatives from schools, churches, homeowners, PTA, civic groups, fraternal organizations, welfare agencies, and health and recreational facilities is organized. If every representative pledges the assistance of his organization to cooperate in a community program for all youths, an effective crime prevention program can be launched and a successful battle against juvenile crime may be waged.

A *trained juvenile officer* in the police department is most desirable. Juvenile officers are schooled in the problems of the young and are capable of coping with police situations involving youth.

A police department crime prevention program needs to be carefully planned. Police work with "hot rod" clubs, bicycle clubs, scouts, and similar youth groups brings gratifying results. In fact, police officers often develop into outstanding supervisors and leaders in youth character-building activities.

Patrol. The patrol division has been described correctly as the *backbone* of law enforcement. Each patrolman, whether he works day or night, is the visible symbol of his department. The attitude and methods he brings to the performance of his duties form the basis upon which the public judges the whole department. Obviously, therefore, this line officer must be adequately trained and furnished with modern police equipment in order to function efficiently.

Police equipment. The equipment needed for efficient patrol service will vary with the area under patrol. Special police equipment will be required for mountains, deserts, beaches, industrial areas, and residential districts. However, the following list of equipment is recommended for a patrol car no matter where the patrol service is located. At various times, the patrol car may become the officer's temporary office, his interview room, a roving crime laboratory, or a vehicle for errands of mercy.

1. Loose-leaf three-ring notebook from which pages can be removed and taken to court for reference, if necessary
2. Clipboard, two pens, two pencils, calendar card, and first aid pressure-point card
3. Police report forms in a portable file
4. Local city maps plus timetables of bus and train schedules
5. National Auto Theft Bureau booklet showing serial or motor numbers for most automobiles in the United States
6. Traffic report forms such as Vehicle Code Summary and Change of Address
7. Pocket directory which has emergency phone numbers of public buildings, industries, places of amusement, referral agencies, and other pertinent information
8. Sam Browne belt, key ring, revolver with ammunition (6 rounds in the revolver and 12 in carrier), handcuffs with key, whistle on chain, badge, and credentials
9. Pair of white gloves for night traffic enforcement and signals
10. Yellow-marking crayon to mark crime scenes
11. Pocket tape measure
12. 100-foot tape measure for large areas
13. Pocketknife to mark evidence and for miscellaneous use
14. Magnifying glass to locate small items at the crime scene
15. Citation traffic book with forms for traffic enforcement
16. Citation guide with reference numbers to most frequently used vehicle code sections
17. Nightstick (baton) for defensive or offensive action
18. Blackjack (sap) for defensive or offensive action
19. Three-cell flashlight to be carried day or night
20. All-weather gloves to protect hands from glass and other sharp objects
21. Copy of the Penal Code and Vehicle Code, indexed
22. Traffic-diagram tool with scale and uniform symbols

23. Cellophane envelopes for evidence
24. Portable spotlight for searching the crime scene
25. Highway flares (fusee) to warn and divert traffic (extreme caution must be exercised when using flares around gasoline)
26. Fire extinguisher (CO_2)
27. First aid kit
28. Sun glasses
29. Wool blanket to keep injured person warm
30. Venti-breather for resuscitation via mouth-to-mouth respiration
31. 100-foot nylon rope, yellow in color, with loop at one end for rescue and crowd control
32. Camera for photographing the crime scene and evidence (4 × 5 speed-graphic camera with accessories and film or Polaroid camera with accessories and film)
33. Fingerprint kit for developing and lifting latent fingerprints
34. Yellow rubberized raincoat
35. Rubber boots
36. Shotgun—12-gauge, Remington model, or Wingmaster 870, with 00 buckshot ammunition plus rifled slugs
37. 12-inch and 6-inch rulers
38. Pack of 3 by 5-inch cards
39. "Hot sheet" reflecting current stolen cars, supplemented by recoveries
40. Spanish pocket dictionary, in locality where needed

Many law enforcement agencies furnish the above equipment either totally or partially. Where this practical equipment is not supplied, some officers purchase their own at a financial sacrifice to themselves.

Vice problems. The majority of law enforcement officials agree that vice problems are the most trying and dangerous work in law enforcement. Traffic experts, however, insist that traffic problems are the most hazardous and difficult to handle. Doubtless, there are many difficult traffic problems. No one can dispute successfully the gravity of adverse traffic conditions on our freeways and in our metropolitan areas. Nevertheless, as experts explain, vice investigations involve habitual criminals and syndicated crime, such as the Mafia, while traffic enforcement involves the average, normally law-abiding citizen. Moreover, vice operators work undercover and are hard to detect, while traffic is open, visible, and therefore not difficult to observe and enforce. Also, many people who are intolerant of adverse traffic conditions are tolerant of vice operations such as gambling and prostitution.

Generally, vice conditions and vice investigations are ranked with espionage investigations as the most difficult. Both vice and espionage investigations require specially trained investigators. Both require patient, tireless, relentless investigation and the aid of paid confidential informants and modern scientific electronic equipment. Often, only by the use of paid informants, reliable sources of information, or the legal use of electronic recording equipment can gamblers, narcotic peddlers, and prostitution rings be located and successfully prosecuted.

The first logical step in vice law enforcement is to establish a basic policy on all phases of vice investigation, inform all personnel of this policy, and expect them to follow it. It has been found that a strict enforcement of vice laws is the best policy. Hence, officers must not conduct unsupervised, personal, secret, sporadic investigations but rather must investigate all vice cases under coordinated departmental control so that there are no legal entanglements. In this way, the department will be protected from false accusations and adverse publicity. Vice conditions may then be controlled if not completely eliminated.

Experienced vice law enforcement supervisors periodically rotate personnel assigned to the vice detail. This procedure keeps the officers from becoming involved personally in local conditions. It also prevents adverse criminal influence and associations that may hamper vice investigations from materializing.

POLICE SERVICES

The primary responsibility of police services is to provide staff support to the line police officers. These services take many forms, as will be seen in a study of the sections which now follow.

Personnel services. A police organization, to remain strong and efficient, must depend largely upon the caliber of new men appointed to serve. In small departments, the chief of police assumes the task of recruitment. He has complete control over assignments, promotions, and discipline.

As a city or county increases in size, a central personnel department such as a city or county civil service commission may handle the recruitment of personnel for law enforcement along with that of other employees of the city or county. If such centralized recruitment exists, the police department establishes a workable, cooperative relationship with the members of this recruiting agency so that well-qualified personnel who meet police standards may be available for appointment.

Frequently, the municipal personnel agency advertises and handles the preliminary examinations and tests for the law enforcement agency. Then, the chief of police, or his personnel officer, depending upon the size of the department, conducts all personnel investigations. The police department retains control over the screening and selection of all personnel.

When a new employee reports for duty, provisions are made for proper indoctrination. The first day at work is most important. The impressions, information, and understanding that the recruit receives on that initial day may influence favorably or unfavorably his conduct and attitude during the rest of his service.

To maintain a high level of performance from personnel, departments use the merit system. Under the merit system, all officers advance in the department on merit, ability, and accomplishments. In the appraisal of police personnel, every effort is made to correct and eliminate deficiencies and weaknesses in personnel. Individual weaknesses revealed by periodic efficiency reports can be largely overcome by modern police training.

Transportation and equipment. Next to personnel, the most expensive item in the budget for the operation of a law enforcement agency is equipment. Transportation in the form of patrol cars is the most costly single expenditure. Therefore, many city managers and police executives require a police recruit to pass the police department's own automobile-operator drivers' test before he can qualify to operate a patrol car. This test includes knowledge about the use, care, and maintenance of automotive equipment. Some departments have found that the average police recruit neither knows nor practices the fundamentals of good driving, nor does he know how to take care of a squad car. Thus, adequate training in the care and use of automotive equipment when the officer is first appointed may result in considerable savings of life and equipment. There is no room in law enforcement for the officer who is not a safe driver.

Jail. Sooner or later, every officer comes into direct contact with the jail, either by escorting a prisoner to jail or by assignment to the jail detail. Hence, the officer needs to be familiar with the rules, regulations, and procedures of jail security. Here are some vital security measures that every officer should observe:

1. When bringing a prisoner to jail, it is the responsibility of the arresting officer to search the prisoner carefully *before* taking him to the police station. Otherwise, a prisoner might be jailed with a concealed, dangerous weapon on his person.
2. All police personnel must be conversant with the constitutional and civil rights of prisoners. These rights must not be violated. No person regardless of race, color, or creed should be arrested or detained illegally.
3. All officers must cooperate to keep the jail clean and sanitary.
4. There must be continuous supervision of all prisoners of the jail inside as well as outside of detention quarters. Thus, if medical attention is required, it must be immediately available. Also, adequate diet for all prisoners must not be overlooked.
5. Juvenile court judges rightly insist that juveniles be placed in separate jail facilities. Female prisoners should be housed in quarters for females only.
6. Each officer must know what to do in case of fire, earthquake, riot, disorder, or other emergencies so that every precaution may be taken for the safety and welfare of all concerned.

Police communications. Ever since man first went to war, communications have been a vital factor in the final outcome of his battles. Primitive man's thumping on great hollow logs or drums called forth warriors to fight. The Indians' smoke signals relayed messages across hundreds of miles. Runners from Marathon told of the Greek army's victory over the Persians in 490 B.C. The Pony Express, telegraph, telephone, and finally radio and television are important steps in man's struggle for improved communications.

The police are society's army and first line of defense against criminal forces. From the beginning, law enforcement has always striven to increase the efficiency of its communications. The call light, the pull box, and Gamewell systems were attempts to secure rapid communications. None of these was entirely satisfactory.

Meanwhile, the speed of transportation increased so rapidly that a criminal could commit a crime in one city and, in a relatively short time, seek refuge in another city hundreds of miles away. Radio, television, all-points bulletins broadcast by radio or teletype, public address systems, telephones, switchboard communication, and even the communications satellite have proved to be effective ways to keep ahead of the criminal.

The most modern means of communications is worthless, however, unless men are uniformly trained to handle it effectively. Communications is like a gun. If an officer can shoot a gun accurately and knows when and how to use it, then it can be a valuable asset to him. But, if he is untrained, his gun is practically useless. The same is true with communications.

Fortunately, radio today is one means of communication totally available to the police but only available to the criminal to a limited degree. It can be of great value if properly used. Every time a police radio station goes on the air, it is broadcasting to all listeners—both police personnel and citizens within range. The impression created by these broadcasts may be good or bad. If the system is operated efficiently, the listener will conclude that the entire department is likewise efficient. Hence, the radio dispatcher plays an important role in police communications. The dispatcher is the one who sends out radio messages from a police department. No matter whether he is a radio operator, a desk sergeant, a police officer, or a clerk, the dispatcher is the voice of his department, and the effectiveness of the police radio system depends on him. It is apparent that there are certain qualifications that a good dispatcher must bring to his job. Here are some of them.

1. He must exercise extreme level-headedness and common sense and make quick but accurate decisions.
2. He should have an accurate knowledge of the entire area served by his police department.

3. His voice should be clear, calm, steady, and should inspire confidence.
4. He must cancel previous messages when subjects have been apprehended.
5. He must use precise, clean-cut procedure so that he is understood and each case can be handled promptly and efficiently.
6. At all times, he must adhere to the rules and regulations of the Federal Communications System. This means that no one can use the radio for personal matters or use foul or abusive language while broadcasting.

The police telephone, too, may make friends or enemies for the department. Hence, switchboard operators and all personnel using the telephone must appreciate and practice courtesy at all times. Often, the only contact that a taxpayer may have with the department is by telephone. All such contacts are opportunities to create favorable impressions of the department.

Records and identification. The record and identification division of a law enforcement agency is like a library. It is the central gathering point of all information concerning police business and activities. There, all the basic types of police records are maintained in a simplified system free from red tape and other obstructions so that fast, accurate service may be provided both day and night. To ensure prompt service, the fingerprint system should be an integral part of the record bureau. All fingerprints should be filed according to classification.

Many police authorities believe that all police officers should know how to classify fingerprints. Hence, the police science student should consider a course, available at most colleges and FBI police training classes, in the classification and filing of fingerprints.

Every law enforcement record and identification division has procedures for processing a prisoner taken into custody. This is called booking. When a prisoner is brought into jail, the prisoner must be identified scientifically for future reference. Identification is accomplished in several steps. The prisoner's face and head are photographed from various angles to obtain what are known as "mug" shots. Then, ink fingerprint impressions of all ten fingers are recorded on three fingerprint cards. One copy is sent to the state bureau of identification, one is filed in the local department, and one is sent to the FBI Identification Division. When photographs and fingerprints are taken, an arrest record and identification record or "booking" is prepared. The prisoner is then eligible for release on bail if the offense is a bailable offense. If the prisoner is unable to post bail, he is held for prompt court action. If arrested for another police agency, that law enforcement department is notified at once so that if warrants and legal processes are outstanding, the prisoner may be returned to that police department to answer legal charges.

In order to locate the record and fingerprint card of each suspect and prisoner, an index card is prepared. On this 3 by 5-inch or 5 by 8-inch index card is typed the first, middle, and last name (surname) of the prisoner. Also recorded are his last known address, his physical description (age, date and place of birth, height, weight, race, color of hair and eyes, complexion), and his occupation.

These index cards are filed numerically and consecutively with the fingerprint classification on the card. The date of arrest and the charge are also noted. Since the arresting officer's report is made at time of arrest, this report must be filed in chronological order according to date received. Thus a copy of all complaints, warrants, and other matters pertaining to this prisoner is located in his file. A legal-size envelope, white or colored, which contains the negative and photograph of the prisoner is also placed in this file.

From the daily log, which is a typed recording of all police activity for each eight-hour shift, a case file or daily report (DR) file is made. Each case or report is systematically assigned a DR or case number. This facilitates access to the case, the referencing of each case, and the assembly of all supplemental reports and other material related to the case. It must be reiterated that all incidents during the day or night on the log must be filed consecutively and numerically. For accuracy, an index card is made at time of entry of the incident on the log so that all information is indexed. Then, a search through the indexes later will bring all the desired information at once.

In order to provide police personnel with quick and easy access to record bureau information, a master name index with name index cards on the following categories is employed:

Arrested persons	Driver's violation and	Juveniles
Complainants	accident record	Licensees
Suspects	Missing persons	Victims
Wanted persons	Identification	Persons injured
Witnesses	Correspondence	Persons killed

Index cards relating to the above categories are filed alphabetically. With all name cards in one file, there is no possibility of placing an index card in the wrong file. Besides the arrest and identification records, the following records are also maintained:

Traffic accident records	Type of crime and location
Property records	indexes or record
Personnel records	Statistical and prosecution
Administrative records	records
Vacant house reports	Cases cleared and pending
Special service records	Store reports
Lost and stolen property	
records	

To make certain that the record and identification bureau will not have conflicting records, a procedural manual is prepared. This manual shows the correct form to be used and the correct method for completing forms.

Recovered, lost, and stolen property. To ensure that all evidence will be available for trial and that lost or stolen property will be returned to the rightful owner, a police department has a property room. Cases can be forfeited or jeopardized by misplaced or mishandled evidence. By fixing responsibility for the care, security, and accounting of property to the property room, unnecessary embarrassment can be avoided, particularly when rules for handling such property are enforced and every member of the department understands the approved procedures.

Periodic local public auctions of unclaimed, lost or recovered, and stolen property are held, and the proceeds from such auctions are transferred to the city, county, state, or Federal treasury, as the case may be.

Maintenance. Just as a person is judged by appearance, so also a law enforcement agency is judged by its visible physical condition. Consequently, a law enforcement agency cannot afford to have its premises other than neat, clean, and presentable at all times. Intelligent use of space, frequent inspection, and the cooperation of all personnel will result in good housekeeping that will have a desirable effect on both employees and the public.

The above discussion of police services was designed to present the services separately rather than collectively so that each area of service could be presented clearly and effectively. Each service has its own importance and must not be confused with the other distinct services whereby staff officers are able to provide the needed resources to the line officers working in the field.

SPECIALIZATION VERSUS ROTATION

In small law enforcement agencies, personnel must be versatile and able to handle effectively all kinds of cases, problems, and emergencies. As departments increase in size and stature, opportunities for specializing in certain fields such as traffic, fingerprinting, photography, laboratory, records, firearms, and narcotics become possible. Modern police departments exert every effort to prevent officers from becoming stereotyped, limited, and disinterested in police activities other than their own. Some departments use rotation of personnel to broaden the officers' view of the problems and goals of the department. There is a trend toward employing expert, civilian personnel in fingerprinting, photography, and laboratory areas where specialization may be needed. This frees full-time peace officers for police work in the field.

FINANCIAL ADMINISTRATION

Every police department faces a never-ending conflict between efficiency and economy. To resolve the conflict, the department must provide for constant control of the law enforcement budget and other fiscal matters. This fiscal control is exercised through procedures which all police personnel must understand. A few such typical financial controls are given below.

1. Maintaining a record of all departmental fines, recoveries of automobiles, bicycles, moneys, and jewelry.
2. Keeping a record of all police expenditures so that it can be shown exactly where police funds were used and what amounts were recovered by the police department.
3. Maintaining "watchdog" supervision over the budget. All expenditures must be scrutinized to prevent exceeding the budget limitations. Some departments strive to return a "savings" annually to the city or county treasury.
4. Using performance budgeting, that is, making budget estimates according to what each unit of service costs. To do this, the department needs accurate facts and figures.

It can be seen from the types of controls listed above that each officer can contribute to good financial administration of his department by accurate reports on his daily work.

Responsibilities of the chief of police

BASIC RESPONSIBILITIES

No discussion of police administration would be complete without including the role of the chief—the key administrative officer in law enforcement. It is quite natural for a new officer to be primarily concerned with his own immediate problems. But the complexities of modern police work require that he know something about what goes on above him in the department as well as what is going on around him.

The policies, procedures, goals, and directions established by a department have a direct bearing on the officer's work, his satisfaction, his job, and his progress in police work. It can be enlightening both to the police officer and to the police student to place themselves in the chief's position and to see how administrative matters affecting a whole department are handled.

The most pressing responsibility of the chief is the recruitment, selection, and training of superior personnel. This responsibility also includes the selection and advancement, by competitive examination, of supervisory personnel. And once personnel are placed, the chief must define the duties and the jurisdiction and limits of authority of the members of his organization in order to prevent overlapping and duplication. The chief is also responsible for departmental policy, for public relations, and for effective control of departmental costs.

Policy. The chief is responsible for establishing policy and for explaining policy to all personnel. Usually, policies are announced in departmental orders and memorandums. Before final determination, the chief consults the city manager or administrator about proposed policy for the police department. The following policy problems invariably arise, and the chief and his personnel must wrestle with them.

1. Issuing of traffic citations
2. Liquor violations
3. Enforcement of vice laws
4. Processing of traffic tickets
5. Handling of inebriates
6. Handling of drunk drivers
7. Control of juveniles
8. Investigation of business licenses and licensees

Public relations. No matter how hard the chief may endeavor to project the best possible image of his department to the public, he cannot succeed alone. While he exercises the leadership in public relations matters, he still needs the help of every man in his department. He must train and motivate all officers to render prompt, efficient service, free from favoritism, not only at headquarters but also on patrol and in all investigations. He must take precautions to ensure that his department will not become involved in politics.

Since the chief is in the position to know the progress and the direction of all investigations and matters pertaining to the police department, he supervises and controls all press releases. This is notice to the new officer that he is not at liberty to divulge facts prematurely to unauthorized persons. Doing so may interfere with the solution of a case and the proper administration of justice. By maintaining liaison with press, radio, and television, favorable reciprocal relations may be made beneficial to all—public, press, and police.

In order to avoid any duplication or conflict in correspondence, the recruit should remember that all written communications are sent over the chief's signature so that the records of the department may contain all outgoing and incoming correspondence. This prevents any officers from sidetracking vital information since all information must be guided by way of regular channels to the chief for official evaluation and action.

If a new officer wonders why he frequently sees the chief, sheriff, and other top law enforcement executives in company and conference with leaders in all walks of life, he should remember that all elements of a community must be kept advised of the policies and programs of the department. Therefore, the chief has to take advantage of every opportunity to reach the public through speeches, articles, and participation in worthwhile community civic affairs.

Throughout his career, the chief must strive to be the personification of all that he recommends for his men. He must set a good example by his own appearance, personal habits, industry, and enthusiasm.

In addition, it is the head of the law enforcement agency who must develop and maintain a forward look and professional attitude among police personnel. He keeps the department up-to-date by providing the latest facilities such as a firearms range, a police library, photographic equipment, visual aids, laboratory facilities, and scientific aids.

Normally, routine police matters are handled by duly assigned personnel. However, the chief renders personal, close supervision when major cases occur that may receive wide publicity and in which prominent people and delicate public relations are involved.

Police training. The chief and his staff must analyze their personnel development program objectively. Training should not be given at random, but should be planned to correct personnel weaknesses and to fill needs that actually exist in a department. For instance, if officers are rated low on the quality of daily reports, a report-writing school could be the answer.

All facilities and training programs of the county, state, and

Federal governments should be used to improve and assist the training within a department.

In many departments, prior to going on duty, roll-call training is a daily occurrence supervised by qualified staff officers and attended by all officers. Along with roll-call training, a police training manual provides a practical guide and reference for both new and old officers.

The following are some of the police schools that are often arranged through local, state, and Federal instructors:

1. Basic recruit school
2. Major case school (burglary, robbery, and felony investigations)
3. Patrol school—both basic and advanced
4. Firearms school—both basic and advanced, with all police weapons
5. Fingerprinting school—both classification and latent fingerprints
6. Juvenile control
7. Police photography—covering accidents, crime scenes, and physical evidence
8. Moot court and courtroom demeanor
9. Public relations, including human and race relations
10. First aid
11. Traffic control and accident investigations
12. Defensive tactics
13. Penal code
14. Laws of arrest, search, and seizure
15. Police administration for supervisors
16. Police management for chief and assistants

Personnel rating. At least once per year an annual efficiency report is written for each officer by his superior officer. In this way, an evaluation of the abilities and deficiencies of each officer may be made a matter of record. Such efficiency reports are a guide to future promotion of personnel in the department.

Personnel progress file. In order that each officer may be evaluated equitably, a personnel folder containing the application, investigation, appointment, and subsequent achievements and failures of each employee is maintained. The efficiency report of an officer is part of his personnel file. Thus, ready reference to individual progress can be made. Training should be made available to each officer to correct any failings revealed by the report. Any police school attendance records and diplomas will be filed in each officer's file to reflect the interest and enthusiasm of the employee for self-improvement in his chosen profession.

Cost consciousness. Today, more than ever before, the taxpayer is scrutinizing public expenditures with a critical eye. Any reduction in taxes is welcome, but any increase is eyed with suspicion. The police executive who can stretch the dollar and keep expenditures to a reasonable minimum is acclaimed. Hence, many police executives have copied the United States Armed Forces in instituting programs in cost consciousness. This is a systematic way of alerting employees to the necessity of conserving the resources, equipment, and property of the department. Training in the efficient use of equipment eliminates abuse. Moreover, the value of materials, the cost of operation, and the price of equipment are publicized in the department. Thus, all personnel learn to appreciate the fact that it takes a lot of money to operate a law enforcement agency efficiently, but it costs even more to operate it negligently.

Through the cooperation of all police personnel in cost-consciousness programs, tremendous savings have been realized in supplies, equipment, and materials—from expendable pencils to nonexpendable automobiles.

QUESTIONS

1. Define and explain the difference between line and staff.
2. Explain and give an example of rank in a police department.
3. Describe the value and purpose of a manual of instructions.
4. Relate the value and purpose of a manual of rules and regulations.
5. Define and draw an organization chart of a police department for a city of 15,000 people.
6. Define and draw a functional chart of a police department for a city of 15,000 people.

7. Explain span of control.
8. Define, explain, and differentiate between operations and services.
9. Describe what is meant by chain of command.
10. Relate what is meant by selective law enforcement.

9. Police morale and public policy

Internal and public aspects of police work

Law enforcement is a public service. This basic truth has been emphasized again and again in previous chapters of this book. Still there remains the problem of drawing a sharper picture of the precise relationship between law enforcement and the public it serves. This relationship has many aspects. Boiled down to its essentials, the purely public service aspects of law enforcement involve two considerations: (1) the dedicated, disciplined approach which the work of law enforcement demands of the police, and (2) the manner and method by which the law is enforced for the protection of life, property, health, safety, welfare, and morals of the public.

INTERNAL CONTROL OF POLICE PERSONNEL

The first consideration involves the police themselves—their attitudes toward the work of law enforcement, and the individual and collective initiative, determination, courage, and self-discipline which they bring to their work. These are largely internal matters which are determined by the level of morale of the personnel of a department and by the quality of the department's discipline. The officer who clearly understands the public service nature of his duties and carries his duties out willingly brings a professional approach to his work. Likewise, the officer who understands what can happen to him if he does not do his duty performs his job with wisdom and practical common sense.

"Fidelity," "courage," and "morality" are three words that carry great weight and significance in law enforcement. This is so because a law enforcement agency must be staffed with personnel who have these qualities of excellence in order for the department to accomplish its traditional goals.

Frequently, when an officer becomes involved in activities that are in violation of the manual of rules and regulations or policy manual, he has failed to observe one or more of these aspects of police work.

Fidelity. The best definition of fidelity is loyalty. This means each officer must place loyalty to his department above loyalty to the brother officer, friend, relative, or well-meaning citizen. An officer who is loyal faithfully performs his duties. He does not malinger or "goldbrick." He is never absent from work without good reason. He will do nothing to embarrass or destroy the reputation of his department. Instead, his attitude is one of cooperation to the fullest extent of his ability. As an indication of how important fidelity is considered to be, in many police departments across our land, the poem appropriately entitled "Loyalty" by Elbert Hubbard is displayed prominently.

Courage. The second word in our triumvirate is "courage." Psychologists tell us that men and women are not born courageous. Rather, courage is an environmental factor that is cultivated and developed through study, training, imitation, and personal application. Consequently, no one has a monopoly on courage, and every officer may acquire this needed law enforcement attribute by making a genuine conscious effort in this direction.

It is interesting to note that no one knows how courageous or brave he is until he is tested. In law enforcement, the test may be daily and may come in various forms. It may come in a bloody gun battle with notorious gangsters or in the apprehension of a most wanted criminal; with the calm composure needed to withstand the taunts and verbal abuse of irate citizens or with the intestinal fortitude needed to stand by convictions when the officer knows he is right. It may come with the fearless rescue of a person from a burning building or even with the courage to resist temptation and to enforce unpopular laws.

Courage does not mean being foolhardy or tempting fate. A person who plays Russian roulette with a revolver is not brave or fearless. Instead, courage is exhibited by one who has the mental capacity and quality which help him to face problems firmly, bravely, and successfully. An officer who is well trained will develop the confidence to handle hazardous tasks. His reactions and timing will be swift, sure, and correct, for he has learned to be courageous.

Morality. One of the most frequently discussed topics in our country is morality. Consequently, it deserves attention and comment in our reference to personnel problems.

Morality is defined simply as right and is distinguished from immorality, which is wrong. One of the gravest problems facing our people today is the fact that what is right and what is wrong is becoming blurred and fuzzy. There is a prevalent belief that one may do whatever he feels like doing, as long as he does not get caught. If one is caught, he is considered a jerk and a dope; however, if he gets away with it, he is described as clever.

Thus, absolute standards are being lowered; barriers are being broken; efforts are being made to justify anything wrong, such as violations of the law or deviations from the traditional normal codes and standards of civilization. Such words as "old-fashioned," "square," and "prude" have been conjured to excuse descents into avenues of immorality, including promiscuity, dishonesty, and fraud.

Any breakdown in the moral fiber of America must not take place within the ranks of law enforcement. All officers must be encouraged to maintain a high level of performance. In so doing they will always report the facts, never testify falsely, and report incidents of gangsters and vice operators who try to buy protection to circumvent the law. In this way law enforcement will always come into court with clean hands and receive a clean bill of health for moral integrity.

Another consideration is the external or public reaction to police work. Enforcing laws as they are written is not a simple matter. It requires the establishment of guidelines known as policies. These policies affect the way in which the police enforce laws and the way in which the public reacts to law enforcement. Policies are most effective when they are wisely conceived, carefully written, and widely communicated both to police and to public alike.

These two important considerations, police morale and public policy, deserve special study by the student of police science. Seeing the relationship between these two seemingly unrelated matters helps him to bring into focus the personal and public aspects of law enforcement.

Morale is a vague word that defies being reduced to a concrete definition. Philosophers and psychologists have described morale as happiness or a sense of well being. Plato, 400 years before Christ, termed happiness as the highest good. Since then, millions of words have been written about happiness and morale so that today they are considered to have the same meanings. When one is happy, he has high morale; when one is sad, he has low morale. It follows that if an officer enjoys his work, likes his associates, and is enthusiastic about his assignments, he will have high morale. On the other hand, if his work is unpleasant, if he has conflict with his brother officers, or if he dislikes his duties, low morale is inevitable.

Morale has been found to be as hard to build as a skyscraper, as fragile as an eggshell, and as slippery as mercury. It may take weeks, even years, to develop, but it can be destroyed in a fraction of a second. Organizations of all types have tried to cultivate morale by the adoption of inspiring theme songs, poems, phrases, distinctive uniforms, mottoes, and slogans. Famous regiments and ship and airplane crews have devised special names, mottoes, or symbols that unify people in the cause to which they are dedicated.

In law enforcement, morale is that mental attitude and spirit which inspire officers individually and collectively with enthusiasm, initiative, determination, and courage. To be effective, it must be shared equally by all. It manifests itself in a healthy, cooperative, and loyal department. It is that quality which makes a police department click. Without morale, a law enforcement agency cannot succeed. With it, a department can overcome fatigue, danger, and discouragement to conquer any task.

Executives have found that morale is something you cannot beg, borrow, buy, order, or even persuade into existence. It can best be cultivated and maintained by leaders and officers who have been screened, trained, and counseled, and are imbued with the high ideals and objectives of law enforcement. Morale is most easily identified by its effects.

Effects of high morale. The importance of morale cannot be overemphasized. It works in a cycle. Good morale produces police efficiency and harmony. This in turn promotes a good public image which attracts better-qualified men to the department. These high-caliber officers perform more efficient police work, and the public takes justifiable pride in the community's law enforcement.

Effects of low morale. On the other hand, low morale sets in motion an unfavorable cycle. Without high morale the department will not perform outstandingly. Thus, it will suffer loss of prestige and develop a poor public image. It will, therefore, be shunned by superior applicants and will attract only inferior personnel. The cycle is completed by the lowering of police standards and loss of efficiency.

In short, morale is the lubricant that keeps the machinery of law enforcement moving so that the department operates smoothly, effectively, and efficiently.

Developing morale. At the very core of good morale is the mental attitude of the officer who brings to his work the enthusiasm and confidence which he and his department develop. The officer with high morale has the following qualities:

1. Zeal—the enthusiasm with which he performs daily work
2. Hope—the optimism for his own future and that of his department
3. Ambition—the fervent desire to improve himself and his department
4. Receptiveness—the eagerness to learn more and more about all phases of law enforcement
5. Confidence—the freedom from fear that enables him to perform his duties, even beyond the call of duty if necessary
6. Loyalty—the quality and ability to be faithful, dependable, and devoted to the cause of law enforcement

There are many appropriate examples to illustrate the value of good morale and discipline in law enforcement. One that will bear repeating is the case of an officer who was assigned early one morning to a stakeout post to observe the movements in a criminal case preparatory to arrest. It was a freezing cold, damp day, and the officer was stationed on top of a building where he was exposed to the elements but not to the suspects. About mid-afternoon of that day, the suspects were arrested and supposedly all the officers were relieved of their assignments. Late that evening, it was discovered that the officer on top of the building had not been notified to return to headquarters. Quickly, an officer was dispatched to relieve him. Sure enough, this officer was still at his post. Despite the cold and inconveniences, he had not deserted his responsibility. For adhering to duty and exhibiting such dependable qualities, he was commended by his superiors. Asked later if he were angry because he had been allowed to remain at his post unnecessarily, this officer replied, "When you enjoy your work and are proud of your organization and your superiors, you are able to take the bitter with the better."

POLICE DISCIPLINE

It has been said that "No man is fit to command another that cannot command himself." A variation of that statement, "No man is fit to discipline another that cannot discipline himself," might also apply to the police officer. How can a police officer effectively enforce the law in public if he cannot abide by the internal rules and regulations of his department? Thus, internal police discipline and external law enforcement are distinctly related in the work of the police officer.

What is discipline? The word "discipline" comes from the Latin word *discipline* which means "instruction, teaching, training." It is also associated with the word "disciple" which means "a follower." In a law enforcement agency, discipline means knowing and following the rules and regulations of the department. The conduct of well-disciplined personnel is the result of training that has moved the officers to agree to and comply with departmental standards of behavior.

Unfortunately the word discipline is often associated with punishment. However, that is the negative side of discipline and is officially imposed as a remedy in a serious breach of conduct. The positive aspect of discipline is the mental, physical, and moral training that helps an officer accept regulations, supervisory control, and high standards of individual conduct for the welfare of his department. Positive discipline can be developed into a habit pattern. To be constructive it must be acquired willingly and with enthusiasm.

Morale factor in discipline. Morale was discussed first in this chapter because morale may be characterized as the social vaccine that eliminates the need for discipline. The higher the department's morale, the fewer disciplinary problems there are. But the lower the morale, the greater the necessity for disciplinary action.

Reason for discipline. One of the most important reasons for screening and investigating police applicants is to weed out those candidates who may lack discipline. An experienced police recruiting officer usually can detect personality traits and attitudes that are not in the best interests of law enforcement. The recruiting officer is aided considerably by various modern testing methods, including the polygraph and psychiatric examinations, which are excellent tools in this evaluation process.

A law enforcement officer must first have self-discipline—self-control over his emotions and appetites. If an officer is unable to exercise control over his own actions, it is believed that he will not be able to control others. Theoretically, the conscientiously recruited police officer should not need to be disciplined. If disciplinary action becomes necessary after employment, then perhaps the candidate should not have been appointed in the first place. Nevertheless, because of the many uncontrollable factors involved, police departments find that, no matter how carefully recruits are screened, the problem of discipline arises and must be handled judiciously.

As law enforcement agencies continue to grow in size, the purposes and objectives of the department may become more or less obscured to the individual members. Hence, large metropolitan departments cannot afford to lose control of personnel. Specific rules and regulations must be established to emphasize clearly the required personal conduct. In this way, every member of the department will know exactly what is expected of him and what is forbidden.

Acquiring self-discipline. The training and education that a police officer receives prepare him for the kind of group discipline he will encounter with the police department. Actually, his training and education began many years before he even thought of police work. Since the time of his birth, he has had to face the responsibility of conforming to rules and regulations set up by the society of which he is a part. Failure to do so usually resulted in discipline.

From teachings in the home, church, and schools, moreover, the individual has learned self-control, restraint, and respect for law and order and for the property rights of others. As he becomes older, he gradually outgrows the need for discipline by others and acquires a measure of self-discipline which permits him to live comfortably and willingly within the rules of conduct demanded by society.

Police science students should realize that discipline is not only for children, for members of the Armed Forces, and for those in religious orders. It is exercised in every walk of life. Even a person who joins a society, club, or social group has to meet established requirements and abide by certain rules and regulations. If a person wants the advantages of a club or a society, he has to give up certain freedoms in order to gain even greater privileges and pleasures that the club or group is able to confer upon him.

Since a law enforcement agency is a public service, the standards of behavior are higher than are standards for private groups. Each officer's conduct, off duty and on, must be above reproach. Strong disciplinary measures must be taken when violations occur. No one is exempt, for all must adhere to the rules, regulations, and code of ethics.

Pitfalls. A recruit with a practical understanding and appreciation of the problem of discipline will avoid the following pitfalls which necessitate disciplinary action:

1. Dishonesty
2. Absenteeism
3. Poor appearance
4. Abuse of equipment
5. Nonpayment of bills
6. Tardiness
7. Laziness
8. Acts unbecoming an officer
9. Embarrassment to the service
10. Malingering
11. Intemperance
12. Insubordination

In the long run, it is clear that the best kind of discipline is self-discipline because it is the inner force which directs an officer's own conduct, voluntarily, along paths of social acceptability. But the police student should also realize that when individual self-discipline breaks down, discipline has to be applied from outside the individual. This, above all else, should be best understood by those who hope to spend their lives opposing the lawless, undisciplined forces of crime.

Policy in law enforcement

WHAT IS POLICY?

Defining policy. Attempting to define policy, John B. Joynt makes this comment about it: "Policy may mean different things to different people. Any attempt to classify policy is like trying to classify the weather as hot, cold, mild, cool, clear—partly cloudy or cloudy represent varying degrees of temperature or atmospheric conditions, but it is a little difficult to draw a clear distinction between them."

One of the most misunderstood phases of law enforcement is the area surrounding the word "policy." An abstract word, it is easy to use in discussions but difficult to explain and pinpoint. Dictionaries endeavor to define policy as management or procedure based primarily on material interest, rather than higher principles. Also, dictionaries state that policy is prudence and wisdom in the management of affairs. Practically, policy for police work is an agreed-upon course of action that helps achieve the objectives and purposes of law enforcement.

Understanding policy. To understand policy it must be remembered that citizens delegate to their elected representatives the power to regulate certain actions of the people within a city, county, or state. Laws enacted by these elected representatives are passed with the objective of protecting the life, property, health, safety, welfare, and morals of the people. The public being served has a great effect not only on the laws adopted but on their enforcement. Both laws and the way these laws are carried out, therefore, must be palatable to the public, functional to those who must carry out their provisions, and enforceable by the agencies charged with their enforcement.

It would appear to be a simple matter just to enforce the laws as they read. However, the human element intervenes when laws, like the Bible, are subject to different interpretations. Consequently, those responsible in the government for the enforcement of the laws must establish policy or guidelines on how, when, and where the laws will be enforced. In a local government, the city council, city manager, or chief of police has the responsibility of setting forth in writing the manner and method of enforcing the laws. This essentially is law enforcement policy. Such policy provides the framework within which the efforts of a department are channeled for utmost efficiency and effectiveness. Determining policy is not an easy task, but when it has been determined, it serves as a guide for applying the law with wisdom and prudence.

There are times when circumstances call for leniency and clemency in the application of the law because to invoke the law as written would be harsh and cruel. Such policies make the law more palatable and equitable, just as seasoning flavors food.

To be official and effective, policy must must originate at the top levels of government. In a police department, this means that the chief establishes policy after advice from and consultation with the city manager, the city council, and his own staff officers. If it is to succeed, his policy must have the support of everyone involved in forming it.

When policy on many phases of law enforcement has been decided, it may become necessary to produce and issue a policy manual to all members of the department. If not actually issued, copies should be made available to officers during training sessions and should be placed in the police library for ready reference. The manual defines the policies of the department, explains them, and gives examples of how the policies are applied in specific instances. Through the manual, the policy of the department will be known to all members and will have a better chance of being uniformly administered and enforced. A policy manual clarifies public understanding of police policy and eliminates misunderstanding, inequities, favoritism, disciplinary problems, and low morale within the department.

PUTTING POLICY TO WORK

It is necessary not only to have established policy in the enforcement of the law, but also to use good judgment and tact in applying policy. Otherwise, mistakes may be made. For example, there is the case of the young officer who followed policy, but used poor technique. In this case, a member of the clergy parked his car in a red zone because there was no place else to park. He was in a hurry and intended to be gone only a few minutes. But when he returned to his car, there was the officer writing a citation. The clergyman politely tried to explain and apologize for his illegal parking, but the conscientious officer merely continued to write the ticket. The clergyman's patience began to wear thin, and finally he said to the officer, "You can't write me a citation. Don't you know who I am? I am _____ of the _____ Church." But this officer, who had been taught that no one was exempt and that he was required to enforce the law uniformly to all persons regardless of race, color, or creed, shot back with, "I don't care if you're Mickey Mouse. You're going to get this ticket." And he got it. For years afterward, the clergyman had a good story to tell about the fearless but tactless young officer.

Most police departments have a manual on policy that covers police matters of many kinds. A few examples of policy, as written into policy manuals, are given in the following sections.

Example of policy in public relations. It is the department policy that members shall strive to gain public support for and win friendly citizen cooperation in the department's programs and procedures in order to facilitate the accomplishment of departmental objectives. The attitude of each member shall be one of service and courtesy but not servility or softness. In nonrestrictive situations, the member should be pleasant and personal, and on occasions calling for regulation and control, the attitude shall be firm and impersonal, but never rude.

Example of policy in juvenile matters. It shall be the department policy, in cases involving the delinquency of juvenile offenders, to view the matter with a preventive attitude. All feasible steps shall be taken with a view to properly adjusting such cases or referring them to allied social agencies before resorting to court action.

Juveniles alleged to be delinquent shall be referred to as subjects, or, in dependency matters, as victims. It is of utmost importance that each officer's attitude, demeanor, and speech toward juveniles be civil and respectful, but at the same time firm. It is the responsibility of every member of the department to report properly any matter coming to his attention in which a juvenile is delinquent or is the victim of an offense of neglect.

Example of policy regarding vice violation. It is the department policy that officers shall make arrests in all instances wherein the officer feels reasonably certain that the suspect is guilty of the violation of any law or ordinance pertaining to vice and there is sufficient evidence to warrant the arrest. If any peace officer personally observes such violation, he should proceed as in any other crime committed in his presence.

However, where he has information or suspects that vice violations are occurring behind closed doors, he is generally in no position to secure the type of evidence necessary to convict. In such cases, he shall gather all information possible without making himself obvious to the suspects and shall make a full report on the matter to his immediate superior. If it appears that the matter requires immediate attention, he shall contact his superior immediately for instructions.

Where information is received from a complainant, victim, or informant which requires immediate attention, an oral report to his immediate superior, followed by a written report, shall be made immediately. It shall be the responsibility of every member who is given information concerning vice violations to communicate that information to his proper superior.

Example of policy governing the recruitment of employees. Because the functions of the police department involve the protection of life and property and the enforcement of the law, because fundamentally all functions of the department are in the interests of public welfare and safety, and because peace officers, by law, are endowed with authority far beyond that possessed by the ordinary civilian, the department has an obligation to the public it serves to ensure that individuals with criminal records, questionable loyalty or morals, and unstable personalities are not employed. Therefore, an investigation shall be conducted into the character and background of each candidate for such employment. Candidates with criminal records, questionable loyalty or morals, and unstable personalities shall be rejected.

Example of policy pertaining to traffic. From time to time, changing conditions will require changes in the regulations and rules which govern them. Traffic and parking problems are typical examples of present situations necessitating changes in safety controls. In order to gain public cooperation and goodwill, the announcing of policies and changes in regulations *before* enforcement is a recommended procedure. Suppose that a proposed traffic or parking regulation is planned for enforcement on the first of the new year. Press releases and radio and television announcements notifying the public and defining the new procedure should be made for at least two weeks before the designated deadline. During the two-week period of grace before the ultimate date, warning notices explaining the need for a regulation should be posted on the problem car or handed to the motorist. Hence, when the new rule does become enforceable, the public is cognizant of the change and amenable to enforcement.

Announcing new policies prior to enforcement of the following have produced a favorable reaction and public acceptance:

1. Boulevard stops
2. One-way streets
3. Double parking
4. License renewal date
5. Speed limits
6. Automotive equipment changes
7. Curfew
8. Overnight parking limitations

Example of policy regarding the use of force or firearms. When policy is defined and set forth clearly, it is easy to understand and follow. As an example, here is a policy regarding the use of force and firearms that was adopted and successfully implemented by a chief of police:

1. No one shall use firearms or force likely to produce great bodily injury upon any person who is arrested solely on a misdemeanor charge.
2. In all arrests, no one employs any more force than is absolutely necessary.
3. All arrests for a felony charge must be based on reasonable cause determined from credible or observed acts.
4. It is the full responsibility of each individual officer to use firearms only when absolutely necessary and fully justified by circumstances.
5. Firearms must be regarded as defensive weapons to be used only as a last resort.
6. Each officer involved in the shooting of a person is subject to the same type of civil action for damages as may be brought against any citizen under such circumstances.
7. Officers are not to be restricted in the lawful performance of their duty. They have a positive duty to use firearms when necessary for the protection of their own life and the lives of others.
8. Whenever any officer of this department discharges a firearm (except on range), he shall immediately write a full report describing the incident. The report shall be directed to the chief's office. The supervisory officer and all witnessing officers shall direct individual interoffice memorandums to the chief's office giving all available facts relating to said gunshot.

Policy changes. Before concluding this discussion on policy, it must be mentioned that policy is established to accomplish the enforcement of a law, rule, or regulation. When the need for a particular policy no longer exists, the policy should be rescinded or modified as the case indicates. Modification is necessary because situations demanding policy decisions change from time to time and all personnel should be given refresher courses to keep them abreast of any changes. Also, repeated training at roll call or informal sessions serve to remind even the veterans that certain standards of existing policy have not changed.

SUMMARY

Policy may be defined as a settled course of action, a procedure, or a method of handling a situation or problem. Once resolved, policy is followed by the appropriate governmental agency, institution, organization, or individual. Policy is based upon both written and case law, on customs and community desires, and on past experiences as studied and analyzed by duly constituted authorities. It is implemented by general orders which cover long-range policies and special orders which apply to particular events. Implementation may be successfully accomplished through use of a procedure manual and application of rules and regulations.

QUESTIONS

POLICE MORALE AND DISCIPLINE

1. Define morale.
2. Explain the importance of morale for a law enforcement agency.
3. Describe what happens to a law enforcement agency when low morale prevails.
4. Relate what each officer can do personally to improve morale.
5. What effect does morale have on the problem of discipline?
6. What steps may a police science student take before he becomes a member of law enforcement so that he may be amenable to discipline?
7. Enumerate the reasons for disciplinary action in an average police department.
8. If department A had a manual of rules and regulations and department B did not, which department would be most likely to have more disciplinary problems? Why?

9. Define the word "policy" as it pertains to law enforcement.
10. Give an example of how policy affects the application of the law.
11. Why should every police officer know the policy of his police department?
12. In what police activities are matters involving policy most prevalent?
13. As a matter of personal policy, would you cite your wife if she violated a traffic law? Explain your reasons pro and con.

10. The status of the police officer

Law enforcement in action

Police records are filled with examples of good police work performed in the day-to-day law enforcement activities of local police. Police work is seldom the spectacular, sensational work of the private eye glamorized by the mystery stories. More often, it involves the conscientious, careful, intelligent, day-to-day efforts of the police officers who accomplish most police work. These officers may be patrolmen, detectives, juvenile officers, traffic officers, laboratory criminalists, training officers, or identification officers. Their on-the-job activities, as described in this chapter, will help police science students to see law enforcement in action.

PATROLMAN

A most important part of the investigation of any crime is the preservation of the physical evidence. Only by protecting the crime scene can evidence be made secure. This task falls on the shoulders of the first officer to arrive at the crime scene. The patrolman is usually the officer who either discovers the crime or is first detailed to the scene. How well he keeps the crime

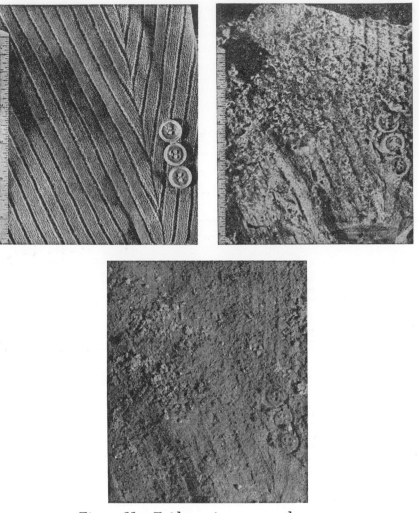

Figure 11. Evidence in rape-murder case.

scene intact may determine the success or failure of the prosecution.

For example, a three-year-old girl was raped and murdered in a lonely field near a country dance hall where her parents had gone. They had left the child in a car outside the dance hall, thinking that they would be gone "only a minute." A constable, who was also a patrol deputy sheriff, located the body and immediately protected the crime scene by roping off the entire area.

No sooner was this accomplished than curiosity seekers, attracted by the patrol car, poured into the field. The physical barriers, however, kept them from the crime scene. In the meantime, the local sheriff's office was contacted and a detective unit with its portable laboratory arrived.

Fortunately, the crime scene had been properly protected by the patrol deputy. Due to the recent rains, the soil was perfect for retaining footprints. Alongside the body, the detectives located several footprints and an imprint of a loose button on a corduroy jacket sleeve. First, photographs were taken of the entire crime scene and the physical evidence contained therein. Then, plaster casts were made and all of the evidence was preserved. Logical suspects were interrogated. Within hours, a friend of the parents was implicated. He had accompanied the parents to the dance. When he was confronted with the evidence of the photographers and the plaster casts (see Figure 11) which matched his corduroy jacket, he confessed.

This case is just one of many which emphasize the important role of the patrolman as he pursues his daily work. He is a vital member of an important team with which he works to serve the ends of justice.

The value of the patrolman is recognized in many ways. Perhaps the most notable form of recognition is the Awards for Valor programs initiated and sponsored by peace officers' associations. Only regularly appointed law enforcement officers are eligible to receive this worthy recognition of police work of unusual merit.

DETECTIVE

The modern detective does not underestimate the cunning, intelligence, and resourcefulness of criminals. Hence, the successful detective must be schooled not only in the fundamentals of modern law enforcement but also in related arts and sciences. Teamwork and cooperation with other governmental agencies are essential because investigations that start in Boston, Massachusetts, may end in Seattle, Washington.

Alertness and powers of observation are the qualities most necessary to the modern detective. A man now lodged in a Midwestern prison can testify to these detective qualities. The man became attracted to another's wife and carried on an affair with her. But soon the romance began to fade and the lover decided to break off the illicit affair. En route to a tavern, the pair parked in a lover's lane area. When he explained his plans of jilting her, the victim became furious and drew a gun from the glove compartment. In the struggle for the gun, she wounded him in the right shoulder, but she was killed. He fabricated a likely story and immediately went to the nearest police department. He explained that an unknown assailant, who resembled the victim's husband, had approached the driver's side of the car in which the victim and he were seated and had held him up at the point of a gun. Then, when he would not cooperate, the assailant shot him in the right shoulder and killed the woman.

Detectives immediately conducted a crime scene search. They checked the car and observed that the windows of the sedan were all in a closed position and the doors were locked. The windows were not broken or shattered by a bullet. Photographs of the entire car, plus positions of the windows and locks, were taken to contradict the defendant's statement of how the incident occurred. When the detective showed the photographs to the defendant, he realized that his alibi was no longer valid and confessed.

JUVENILE OFFICER

Juvenile experts estimate that each year in the United States there are about 1½ million youths who get into serious trouble with the law. Of these, at least 1 million are so expertly and judiciously handled by the police that they never again are involved in crime. This is a great tribute to the juvenile officers who work so closely and zealously with youth. At a recent law enforcement meeting, a noted police executive was praising the splendid efforts of juvenile officers in directing the pent-up energy of youths away from juvenile crime and into wholesome, character-building activities. When the police executive had concluded his remarks, one of the young officers present stood up and stated, "I'd like this audience of law enforcement officers to know that I would probably have wound up as an habitual criminal except that a juvenile officer got a hold of me when I was a boy and straightened me out before it was too late. Mostly because of him and his help, I turned to law enforcement myself. Believe me, I'll always be grateful to this juvenile officer for his guidance." The response of the police audience was thunderous applause!

This is just one of many instances of the outstanding rehabilitation work that juvenile officers are doing to help youngsters. These officers greatly help society not only by saving so many

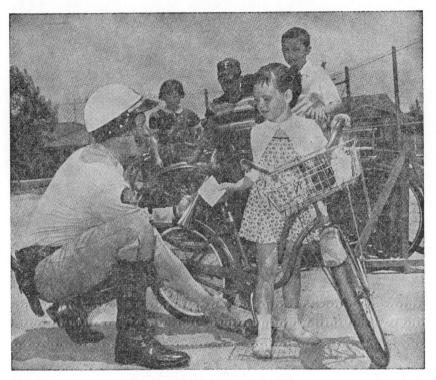

Figure 12. Crime prevention.

youngsters from a life of crime but also by reducing the cost of crime to the American public.

TRAFFIC OFFICER

Traffic officers write millions of traffic citations and millions of parking tickets each year. Traffic offenders often claim that traffic officers are on a "quota," that each officer must write a certain number of tickets each shift. But the fact is that normally an officer does not have to search for violations; they are all about him. Almost everyone is a potential traffic offender. For instance, how many motorists obey the 15-, 25-, and 35-miles-per-hour

Figure 13. Traffic officer monitoring traffic via radar.

speed-zone limitations or the numerous other traffic restrictions? In fact, a traffic officer could get writer's cramp from writing citations if he handled every violation he saw. Instead, he frequently operates under a tolerance policy of sometimes allowing a motorist to exceed the restricted-area speed limit slightly.

Besides enforcing the traffic laws, the traffic officer often performs errands of mercy. For example, highway patrol officers are called upon to rush blood plasma, vaccines, and rare medicines to save stricken people. Frequently, traffic officers arrive at accidents in time to pull occupants from burning cars, render first aid, and protect the injured until the ambulance arrives.

A typical example of how the traffic officer is always prepared to help when he is needed can be found in the letter a chief in a large Eastern city received recently. A woman driving a late-model car on a congested highway in Fourth of July traffic suddenly noticed smoke coming from the front of her car. Almost at once, a traffic officer flagged her over to the side of the road. As soon as she stopped the car, the officer raised the car hood and removed an oily, smoldering rag from the top of the motor. Apparently, the gas station attendant who had checked the car five miles back had negligently left the oily rag on the motor. The grateful motorist complimented the traffic officer for his quick thinking and action in her letter to the police chief. She admitted that with four small children in the car and not knowing what to do she would have been otherwise helpless.

The traffic officer has more face-to-face contact with the public than any other officer in law enforcement. Consequently, his conduct and attitude are most important. Here are some of the qualities of a successful traffic officer.

1. Sense of responsibility
2. Investigative ability
3. Leadership with tact and understanding
4. Technical knowledge
5. Initiative
6. Ability to think logically and clearly
7. Sense of duty to protect life and property equitably
8. Perseverance
9. Enthusiasm
10. Determination
11. Sincerity
12. Equilibrium
13. Self-control
14. Honesty

College students majoring in criminalistics today are destined to be the criminal-laboratory experts of tomorrow. Already, these college graduates are assuming positions of responsibility in police laboratories and in technical services departments of law enforcement agencies throughout our country.

The laboratory has rightly been called the bloodhound of law enforcement. Relying on science, laboratory technicians use chemistry, physics, and all aspects of science to find solutions for cases that often seem unsolvable. An illustration of the remarkable work of the police laboratory is shown in the following case.

Police officers, investigating an early morning complaint about a prowler, discovered a fire in the rear of a house. Investigation after the fire indicated arson because partly burned matches were located at the scene. A partly used book of matches was subsequently found in a suspect's car. The book of matches and all matches recovered at the scene of the fire were sent to the laboratory for examination. The laboratory expert, using the comparison microscope, reported that a partly burned match found at the scene of the arson had been torn from the matchbook found in the suspect's car. Testimony of the laboratory expert was introduced during the trial, and the suspect was found guilty of arson and sentenced to six to eight years in the state penitentiary.

This and many other cases prove that competent use of the scientific laboratory is a great asset to law enforcement. No shred of evidence is too small or insignificant to escape detection under the powerful and revealing light of scientific laboratory analysis. A student with the necessary aptitude and interest can find a useful, exciting, and interesting career in the police laboratory.

POLICE TRAINING OFFICER

For those who like to "share and give," the police profession offers splendid teaching careers in police training. Furthermore, personnel of the police training academy are often delegated the additional responsibility of finding answers and solutions to new and knotty problems. For example, among the most pressing problems are the civil rights demonstration, the teen-age riot, and the sit-in.

Sincere and dedicated police officials realize that unless these tension-packed gatherings are handled equitably and firmly, serious results can occur. The effects of these disorders can be long and lasting and hazardous to both life and property. In fact, the thoughtless, negligent act of one officer can trigger a series of almost uncontrollable events of a disastrous nature in the tense atmosphere of a demonstration.

This is the kind of police training problem with which training officers must deal because the proper handling of demonstrations depends upon how well the police are trained.

One department used an imaginative training approach to the problem. After considerable thought about, research on, and study of a number of demonstration incidents, police training instructors recommended a formula for police action described as "self-control." Instead of meeting force with force and blow with blow, police trainers advocated a program of self-control on the part of the officers. Here is how the program worked.

Twenty-two officers were selected to undergo intensive training, as a special squad, to keep the peace at sensitive public meetings and at demonstrations. In order to fix the philosophy of self-control in the minds of these 22 chosen trainees, the officers were placed under hypnosis and given lectures stressing self-control. Moreover, they were given a posthypnotic suggestion that they would practice self-control under all and any trying conditions.

The opportunity to test this new training presented itself sooner than expected. Word was received that a visiting foreign dignitary would be making a rare public-speaking appearance at one of the local hotels. The specially trained squad was dispatched to the hotel to keep the peace. In the squad was a young officer, known to be fair but firm, but who had a quick temper. For the sake of anonymity, he will be called "Joe." It was the instructor's considered opinion that if Joe could master self-control almost anyone could.

At the hotel, demonstrators had gathered and one, who appeared to be the leader, began to harass the speaker. Joe very carefully placed a police come-along hold on the agitator and proceeded to remove him from the scene. As Joe did so, the agitator kept spitting in Joe's face and on his uniform. Nevertheless, Joe escorted the demonstrator to a parked police car about a block from the scene without any violence whatsoever. Consequently, the demonstration fizzled and the demonstrators dispersed peacefully.

Later on, the instructor, who was at the scene and feared the worst when the demonstrator began to spit at Joe, questioned Joe about the incident. He asked Officer Joe how he had been able to keep his temper under control when the demonstrator was spitting at him. Joe replied that his first impulse was "to slug"

Figure 14. Firearms training program.

the demonstrator. However, in the back of his mind he could hear a voice repeating, "Self-control; have self-control; keep your temper." He kept his self-control and averted a nasty situation. A police executive who witnessed this exhibition of self-control under fire was so impressed that he wrote Joe a letter of commendation. Thus, self-control paid dividends for Joe. Moreover, the incident showed that the police training officers had devised a solution to a difficult police problem.

One phase of police training that cannot be overlooked is firearms training. Every law enforcement officer must be able to handle all firearms safely, sanely, and effectively. Hence, each officer must receive instruction in the care and use of firearms. It is also vitally important that an officer know not only *how* to use a weapon but also *when* he has the legal right to do so. For these reasons, many law enforcement agencies have established continuous, intensive firearms training programs supervised by their own expert instructor at their own firearms range.

Because the revolver is the official regulation weapon of law enforcement, particular emphasis is placed on learning to shoot the revolver in various positions and under various conditions. One of the most important skills is combat shooting, such as the hip shooting shown in Figure 14. The lives of officers and innocent bystanders are made safer by this training.

IDENTIFICATION OFFICER

One of the most fascinating and interesting phases of law enforcement is the science of fingerprints. Identification officers are engaged in the work of fingerprinting and of classifying and filing fingerprints. Law enforcement agencies in the United States and throughout the world have created an organization called the International Association for Identification. This association also has state divisions in the various states. Its members are proud of their important role in criminal identification. Fingerprint identification is one of law enforcement's most powerful methods of apprehending persons who violate the law.

Although fingerprinting is a relatively new science, the pages of history contain references to centuries-old searches for positive means of identification. Through the years, various methods such as branding, tattooing, photography, physical measurements, and personal descriptions have been used. None have proved to be so accurate as fingerprints because, to this date, no two persons have been found with identical fingerprints. It seems almost paradoxical that the fate of criminals, who in 1966 cost the American taxpayer about 27 billion dollars, often hinges on a small square of cardboard, the 8 by 8-inch fingerprint card.

A typical example of fingerprint work is one that occurred in a New England state. There, a sheriff took the right hand of a prisoner whom he was preparing to fingerprint and found, to his surprise, a $100 bill tucked in the palm. "It is all yours," the prisoner said, "if you don't take my prints." The prisoner had been arrested merely as an accessory to the unauthorized removal of $500 worth of mortgaged property—a comparatively minor offense. He looked like the poor farmer he claimed to be. However, he had the criminal's respect for the fingerprint files because he knew what his fingerprints would reveal. A telegram from the Identification Division of the FBI promptly informed the sheriff that the allegedly poor farmer was wanted under another name by California authorities in connection with a $672,000 swindle.

From the above case and many others just as interesting, it is clear that the identification officer has an extremely important place in law enforcement.

QUESTIONS

1. What simple technique did the patrolman use that materially assisted in the solution of the rape case?
2. Name the specific way in which the value of the patrolman is recognized.
3. What are some of the qualities most necessary to the modern detective?
4. How do juvenile officers help to reduce juvenile crime?
5. Explain important duties of the traffic officer other than enforcing traffic laws.
6. Enumerate 10 qualities of a successful traffic officer.
7. Explain the role of the criminalist in law enforcement.
8. Describe how an officer using self-control may avert serious crowd problems.
9. Name the various methods of identification used before fingerprinting.
10. Besides knowing *how* to use a police firearm, what other information must an officer have about police weapons in order to handle them safely, sanely, and effectively?

Train up a child in the way he should go and when he is old, he will not depart from it.
PROVERBS 22:6

11. Police training

THE KEY TO KNOWLEDGE IS TRAINING

Invariably, police executives will testify that comprehensive training develops exceptional police departments. During a lecture at a police academy before his retirement, a greatly admired and respected police training executive related that he always advised his recruits on their first day in the department that *"The key to knowledge is training."* He then proceeded to expose the recruits to a concentrated classroom and on-the-job training program. Consequently, he developed an outstanding police organization. This police executive is not alone in his accent on training. Since World War II, there has been a tremendous improvement in all aspects of training for law enforcement officers.

What do I do now?

No one appreciates the value and advantage of police training more than the officer who has had a close brush with death or serious injury. The many instances where life and property were saved because an officer knew what had to be done are recorded

221

in every law enforcement agency. Effective training perhaps shows more in cases involving arrest than it does in other phases of law enforcement because an untrained officer may consider an arrest just a routine matter, and some night he may be looking unexpectedly into the barrel of a gun. Then, too late, the crucial question may flash across his numbed mind, "What do I do now?"

This is the very same question an officer faced recently while on night patrol in a large city. He was cruising alone in a patrol car. There had been no police activity of any consequence for the previous several hours. Suddenly, his peaceful patrol was interrupted by a police radio broadcast concerning a stolen car. As the officer took down the radioed license number of the stolen car, he observed proceeding directly in front of his car a sedan bearing the same license number he had just jotted down. He noted that there were four men in this large, black sedan. The key questions popped into his mind, "What do I do now? Should I stop the car and arrest the four suspects?" He had almost decided to do this when he remembered opportunely his police instructor's stating emphatically, "Don't be a dead hero. Look before you leap. Whenever you need help, get it." So, he immediately advised his headquarters by radio that he had located the stolen car. He also gave his location, direction of travel, and a description of the car and its occupants. At once, his department flashed a radio message to all local police departments in the vicinity. In the meantime, the officer kept the stolen car and the suspects under surveillance, broadcasting his location continually. After several minutes, which seemed to him like hours, two other police patrol cars appeared on the scene. Then, with flashing red lights and sirens, the suspects were signaled to stop the stolen car. They submitted peacefully in the face of police superiority in manpower and firearms.

Later, the officer learned that the four occupants of the stolen vehicle were escapees from a state prison. They had stolen the car from a physician whom they had lured to their motel on a phony emergency call. They had overpowered, bound, gagged, and driven the doctor in his sedan to a secluded place, where they hid him in some bushes. With narcotics from the doctor's bag and the guns they already had, the escapees were en route to a robbery. However, the wife of the doctor had become alarmed when he did not return from his motel call and had phoned the police to alert them.

Thanks to his training, this officer achieved a perfect solution to a potentially dangerous arrest problem. In this instance, four convicts were captured, a stolen car with guns and narcotics was recovered, and additional crimes were prevented. As for the doctor, he was found unhurt and returned to his practice.

ESSENTIALS OF POLICE TRAINING

There are three essentials in the process of selecting and training a peace officer. The first essential involves the careful *screening* of all applicants so that only the best-qualified are employed. The second essential requires that each recruit receive realistic, *practical training* in the fundamentals of police work so that he may develop and mature into an efficient law man. The third essential dictates that all officers have the benefit of intelligent, consistent *supervision* while employed in the police service. Supervision is especially important for the recruit during his probation and formative years on the department.

Although the first two steps are recognized and followed, the third step is often overlooked. As an example, one of the major administrative problems in the police service is report writing. This subject is so important that police chiefs are constantly scheduling report-writing schools, year after year. However, no permanent solution or improvement in the report-writing problem is noticeable. At first blush, it would appear that the fault may be due to inferior instruction. However, surveys indicate that in this instance as well as in other phases of training, there must be an effective, vigorous follow-up program in supervision by sergeants, lieutenants, and captains. Where necessary, the training received must be reinforced, corrected, and implemented. Only when these three essentials are consistently utilized may the high goals of training be realized.

Objectives and advantages of police training

There are clear-cut objectives and specific advantages to be gained through police training; these benefits are important not only to police executives but, most of all, to the trainees themselves.

1. Through training and education at all levels, the police profession is being reinforced constantly by men and women with the knowledge and ability to perform increasingly better police work.
2. During periods of academic and technical training, police training officers frequently discover personnel who possess latent abilities which they are then able to develop further. As potential supervisors, administrators, specialists, and technicians are discovered, they can be groomed within the department to assume greater responsibilities.
3. Police supervisors may use the training to detect certain weaknesses in the trainees which were not evident during the process of selection. Special training can then be provided to eliminate these weaknesses.
4. Police procedure may be standardized and law enforcement made more uniform through well-rounded training programs.
5. When supervisors recognize that certain phases of police work are being performed below par, training courses may be designed to remove and correct these deficiencies. By effective suitable training, weaknesses are eliminated and strengths are emphasized.
6. An extensive training and evaluation program tends to reveal specific weaknesses in some officers who are not capable of performing certain necessary police duties such as participating in long hours of surveillance or in hazardous stakeouts, riding motorcycles, or handling firearms expertly. Inability to meet standards necessary to successful completion of such training may encourage otherwise well-qualified officers to transfer to other areas of police work where they can put their strongest talents to best use for the good of the service.
7. When a police officer receives excellent training and knows that his department is developing him in the latest scientific techniques for his safety, welfare, and improvement, he is likely to have high morale and enthusiasm for his work. Problems of discipline will also be rare because police personnel appreciate personal recognition, attention, and guided steps

toward professional advancement. Training, therefore, is one of the best methods to develop loyalty, fidelity, and longevity in the police service.

A physician may change his diagnosis or prescription; a lawyer may amend his pleadings; a judge may take days and even weeks to render a decision; but when a police officer makes a decision, it frequently must be instantaneous. As police records reflect, there are many critical cases which compel swift but correct action.

To cope with the many complex emergency duties and responsibilities that may confront an officer on his tour of duty, the peace officer cannot depend entirely upon native ability. Instead, he must be expertly trained to function effectively as an integral part of today's modern mechanized police force. Training must start immediately upon appointment and continue according to a planned program thereafter. Only by diversified and comprehensive police training can an officer keep abreast of technical advancements, social changes, scientific improvements, and recent court interpretations of the law.

Hazards of lack of training. Appropriately adorning a wall of the squad room in a modern police department is a photograph depicting the four occupational hazards of law enforcement. These are:

1. Lack of training
2. Carelessness
3. Overconfidence
4. Immaturity

The number-one hazard, of course, is the lack of training. As the chief of a metropolitan city police department puts it, "The police department is embarrassed every time a law suit is filed against the department or the city officials, and every time a citizen is offended. Investigation reveals that the officer concerned lacked the training to cope effectively with the problem involved." The same chief added, "When an officer doesn't know what to do or how to do it, he frequently throws his weight around and someone gets hurt—usually the police department." For example, an untrained officer, dispatched to handle a simple neighborhood "noise" complaint or family disturbance, through failure to act prudently may precipitate a riot requiring the presence of many officers at the scene.

Early concepts of training. While all police officials now stress the need for training, many leading police officials can verify that police training programs were not always as highly regarded as they are now. Instead, they can recall when there were no police training academies, no facilities for training, and no training programs. They can remember when training consisted of a short briefing and a cursory glance at the Penal Code. One senior chief recalled at a police conference that when he was first employed as a peace officer he was handed a badge, a loaded revolver, and a copy of the Ten Commandments. While he was being escorted to his beat, the chief told him, "If you keep the Ten Commandments and see to it that others do likewise, you won't have any trouble."

Another chief described his early training at the hands of a grizzled veteran of the force who stressed three things:

1. When you hit a suspect, hit him hard.
2. When you tell someone something, tell him only once because once is enough.
3. Do not trust anyone—not even your wife.

It must be said for the chief that he ignored this advice and never regretted it. Obviously, these outmoded police training methods are neither recommended nor taught in the modern police department of today.

"Breaking-in" methods. One of the most widely used early instructional methods employed by many police departments to train new officers when instructors and facilities were not available was to place the new officer with an older officer. The latter was delegated the duty of "breaking in" the new man. Although this procedure was convenient and normally workable, surveys revealed that the recruit sometimes picked up the older officer's bad habits along with his good ones. A good, experienced officer,

226   *Introduction to police science*

it became clear, was not necessarily the best teacher. Of course, there were exceptions, but more often than not this type of training was not the total answer to the training problem.

Step-by-step method. Success in the use of trained senior officers for on-the-job training of new officers calls for step-by-step training in the field, using a checkoff list containing the things to be taught. This procedure requires that the qualified senior officer maintain a personnel folder on each recruit to record his progress in each phase of instruction. For instance, the senior officer first demonstrates such skills as how to make an arrest, write a citation, make a search, and perform many other required police tasks. The recruit observes and then performs the same tasks under the supervision of the senior officer, who coaches the recruit until he is skilled in the required technique. As each task is mastered, this requirement is checked off, indicating the progress and efficiency of the recruit.

"Anticipation" method of training. A technique currently encouraged at all levels of law enforcement is the anticipation method of self-training. This method is not a formal type of police training, but it is a practical method which every officer can use to enforce the habit of being alert and prepared for any event. By carefully surveying his beat, an officer should be able to imagine practically every possible situation that might confront him during his tour of patrol duty. By anticipating police problems that might occur during a bank robbery, a burglary, or any of the other felonies or misdemeanors, the officer has an opportunity to decide in advance what he would do if these crimes actually were committed. In this way, he has an advantage over the criminal because he can anticipate and avoid costly mistakes, snap judgments, and carelessness. This method can also be used to advantage at roll-call training, in-service training, or informal group discussions by posing hypothetical questions.

Police training programs—Federal, state, and local

RESPONSIBILITY FOR TRAINING

Years ago, perhaps, special and continuing training may not have been as important to the police officer as it is today. But now an officer cannot do his job efficiently without training. There is no substitute for training except experience, but learning by experience is too costly in time and equipment. Progressive police management recognizes this factor and also realizes that needed training makes police work easier and more enjoyable. Because of the great number and variety of tasks an officer must perform, he must learn early and quickly the elements of his profession. For this reason, police training is carefully planned, organized, and conducted to help trainees achieve police standards as rapidly as possible.

A recruit is hired in the first place because he meets the high employment standards set by the law enforcement agency. He brings with him native intelligence and natural ability. Usually, he has little or no knowledge of his job, nor is this expected of him in the beginning. It is the responsibility of the law enforcement agency to train him in the fundamentals of law enforcement, and it is the officer's responsibility to put forth the effort which will help the recruit to benefit from the organized training.

The Judy Coplon Case. A convincing example of the importance of continual training for all law enforcement officers is the case of Judy Coplon. She was employed as an analyst in the Internal Security Division of the U.S. Department of Justice, Washington, D.C., when she allegedly became involved in espionage activities with Valentin Gubitchev, originally a member of the Soviet delegation to the United Nations and subsequently a member of the Secretariat.

In 1949, Judy Coplon and her Russian counterpart met surreptitiously on several occasions in New York City. During these clandestine meetings, FBI agents who were trained in counterespionage watched them as closely as possible in order to determine what government secrets, if any, Miss Coplon was passing illegally to Gubitchev.

As the FBI agents watched the suspicious actions of Coplon and her Russian cohort, it was their expert opinion that Coplon was slipping confidential government information to the Russian. They were convinced that Coplon and Gubitchev were violating our Federal espionage laws; so they arrested the two suspects. In the course of the arrest, a search incidental to the arrest revealed unauthorized government documents in the possession of Coplon and also in the possession of Gubitchev.

Coplon and Gubitchev were convicted in two Federal jurisdictions, New York and Washington, D.C., on charges of espionage. However, on appeal, the United States Court of Appeals in Washington, D.C., upheld the guilty verdict but also ruled that Coplon was entitled to a lower court hearing to ascertain whether her telephone had been tapped. If so, she was eligible for a new trial in Washington, D.C. The hearing was never held. Both the prosecution and the defense asked for a United States Supreme Court ruling, but this court of last resort refused to review the case.

In the New York case, the United States Circuit Court of Appeals, convening in New York, set aside her conviction. This court decided that the prosecution had failed to prove conclusively that the evidence introduced against Coplon and Gubitchev did not come from other than illegal methods. The court added that the government documents allegedly located in the handbag of Miss Coplon could not be introduced against her because the FBI agents had seized the documents without a warrant.

Here is an illustration of qualified government agents at the scene of what they believed to be the crime of espionage. They were under pressure. They had to make an instant and momentous decision. Their decision to arrest was later ruled wrong by judges who had considerable time to deliberate and to research. This case exemplifies significantly that if even the best-trained officers have their honest deliberations nullified by the courts, what possible success could untrained police officers have under similar or even less favorable circumstances, especially in a situation such as the Judy Coplon case, where the agents allegedly had reasonable cause to believe that a felony was committed and the illegal transaction executed before their very eyes? Such facts would justify an arrest if the illegal act had been a misdemeanor in a state jurisdiction.

All local, state, and Federal law enforcement agencies assume responsibility for police training. The following sections of this chapter will discuss some of the programs by which Federal, state, highway patrol, and local police departments train their personnel.

The obligation for training personnel in law enforcement was first recognized by metropolitan police departments and Federal agencies. On the Federal level, the Federal Bureau of Investigation led the way. In 1924, after he was appointed Director of the FBI, J. Edgar Hoover inaugurated extensive training programs for his carefully screened special agents. He enlisted the help of specialized police executives in training his personnel. Since then, he has sponsored countless numbers of FBI police training schools for local law enforcement in every state. These FBI police schools are geared to reach every officer from the rookie to the chief of police. To promote and ensure continual, outstanding law enforcement training, Director Hoover established the FBI National Academy in 1935. This FBI-sponsored training institution has been described as the West Point and the Annapolis of law enforcement.

During the past 30 years more than 4,800 carefully selected law enforcement officers have graduated from the FBI National Academy. A 12-week course is conducted twice each year. When the FBI National Academy associates return to their department upon the completion of this prized training, they are motivated to organize police schools and teach members of their own law enforcement agency the latest techniques in modern criminalistics. Besides investigative courses, the associates receive training in supervision and police administration so that they may qualify for positions of command and leadership in their department.

STATE TRAINING

While Federal agencies were forging ahead, the individual states were not delinquent in the field of training. Instead, many states with vocational education assistance from the Federal government developed model police training programs for recruits as well as for experienced officers. Possibly one of the oldest and most extensive peace officers' training programs operating with Federal vocational education funds was started in the 1930s. In collaboration with the training and education committee of the Peace

Officers' Association of the State of California, Inc. (many of whose members served on the advisory committee), the California State Department of Education, Bureau of Industrial Education, began a series of comprehensive peace officer training programs. The following are examples of the many types of police training programs sponsored under its capable supervision and progressive leadership:

1. Departmental training for local law enforcement
2. Zone schools for several departments in the same area
3. Preemployment educational courses in collaboration with junior colleges and state colleges
4. Technical institutes
5. Instructor training schools
6. Conference leadership training for supervisory officers

Many junior colleges in California are now teaching these police training programs in both academy and college police science programs. With the guidance and the supervision of the state department of education, valuable reference material was also developed by leading law enforcement officials and was made available to all law enforcement officers.

It should be noted that before the Commission on Peace Officers Standards and Training was created in California, there were many excellent Federal, state, county, and local police training programs in existence. However, there was no central coordination, established standards, or uniformity in titles or in course content. Now, through the efforts of the Commission on Peace Officers Standards and Training (POST), more than 48 junior colleges in California have a coordinated uniform curriculum leading to an Associate in Arts degree. Many police academies sponsored by police departments, sheriffs' offices, and junior colleges have also developed state-approved recruit training programs certified by this commission. With this outstanding and needed leadership, law enforcement has made great forward strides in the field of police education and training. POST has developed a practical, feasible police training program that is being adopted by other states.

Training for careers in the highway patrol commences immediately upon appointment and never ceases. In order that members may develop the capabilities needed to accomplish the law enforcement objectives of the highway patrol, one of the very best training programs has been perfected. Over the past several years, training concepts have been tested and changed gradually to meet refinements in traffic laws, traffic education, traffic engineering, and traffic enforcement. In most states, this development has meant increasing the initial training period from 12 to 16 weeks. The increase was necessary in order to introduce new courses and to provide more hours of practical application of instruction. Certain in-service classes which were formerly held at headquarters are now taught in the field. This practice eliminates taking needed personnel off the highways for several weeks. Specialists are trained at the highway patrol academy and then assigned to the field to conduct practical on-the-job training. In this manner, instruction in auto-theft enforcement, air-brake systems, and recent rulings regarding the Vehicle Code is conducted effectively and opportunely. Other specialized classes have also been developed. These classes include techniques of motorcycle operation, techniques of ascertaining speed from skid marks, problems of enforcing the laws pertaining to school buses, effective report writing, and problems in supervision.

LOCAL POLICE TRAINING

Types available. Let us suppose that a recruit has been appointed and reports for duty on the first day of employment. What training can he expect to receive? If he is a member of the large metropolitan police department in New York, Chicago, Los Angeles, and other cities, he will be sent to the department's police academy; or if he is a deputy sheriff, to the sheriff's academy. There he will receive from 12 to 16 weeks of intensive training, 8 hours a day, 5 days a week. These academies are staffed by experts from the various divisions in the police or sheriff's department. The rookie, as he is called, is not usually assigned to any other duty while detailed to the academy for recruit training.

When he finishes his basic training, he can anticipate continual training until he retires. This later training includes:

1. *Roll-call training* consisting of 15 to 30 minutes' briefing before each tour of duty in important field problems, often suggested by the ranks
2. *Specialized training* in such areas as traffic, vice, patrol, juvenile, surveillances, crowd control, firearms, and defensive tactics
3. *Technical training* in classification of fingerprints, developing latent fingerprints, police photography, laboratory techniques, radio, polygraph and various recording devices, and other investigative aids such as plaster casting and moulage
4. *Supervisory and administrative training* for sergeants, lieutenants, and captains, covering techniques of supervision
5. *Command schools* for chiefs of police and their deputies, in which budgets, public relations, policy, and personnel problems are stressed

Police schools. If the recruit becomes a member of a small or average-sized department, he will be enrolled immediately in a zone police school approved and certified by a state commission on peace officers' standards and training, provided the state has such an organization. Many of these police schools are under the supervision of a police science coordinator at a local junior college. However, some of the large police departments and sheriff's offices have their own academies, which are also approved and certified. Outstanding police executives from local, county, state, and Federal agencies are employed to present the rookie with the most practical basic police education. This course in a junior college academy usually lasts six weeks. It consists of about 240 hours of lecture and practical field work. The classes are scheduled for eight hours a day, five days a week, on a semimilitary disciplinary basis.

Some police academies require the rookie officer to live full-time at the academy. Others specify four hours in classes and four hours on the job at their own department. Most departments allow new officers to return home each night. Each system has advantages and allows the chief of police or the sheriff to choose the academy that best fits the needs of his department and its trainees.

When the recruit returns to his department at the conclusion of his training, he receives additional training concerning local ordinances, rules, regulations, departmental policy, procedures, and techniques unique to his department. Again, the new officer can expect continual, worthwhile police training as long as he remains in the department.

Besides his own departmental training, the new officer may plan to enroll in other law enforcement training programs that are available in his area. These include FBI police schools, police conferences, institutes, and local college police science classes. For the convenience of the police officer and preemployment students, many junior colleges and state colleges schedule police science classes so that the officer or preemployment student may attend either or both day and night classes.

Advanced courses. For the enterprising officer, there are even more advanced courses. These include:

1. *FBI National Academy,* Washington, D.C. (general and specialized law enforcement training)
2. *Northwestern Traffic Institute* at Northwestern University, Evanston, Illinois (traffic-accident investigation and control)
3. *Delinquency Control Institute* at the University of Southern California (juvenile procedure and control)
4. *Seminars, institutes,* and *conferences* scheduled at state colleges and universities throughout the United States (vice, firearms, police administration, supervision, narcotics)

So for all intents and purposes, there exists for all ambitions and talents a wealth of exciting, interesting courses to assist the officer to become as self-sufficient and versatile as his own capabilities will allow.

CONTENT OF POLICE TRAINING COURSES

Spelling, grammar, mathematics, and typing. Almost without exception, law enforcement supervisors will agree that inability to spell correctly is one of the foremost handicaps confronting a new officer. It is the consensus among police executives that the police candidate must be able to spell at the time of his appointment because the department does not have the time to teach him the fundamentals of spelling after his appointment. For example, a police chief in a modern department was very much impressed with a police applicant. He planned to hire him until he saw the written examination results on his spelling. The spelling of this candidate was so far below par that even though he passed all of the other requirements, the chief of police denied his application.

When questioned by the candidate concerning his failure, the chief of police frankly explained that the applicant's failure to spell was so great that he could not employ him. The candidate asked the chief to reconsider his application. He even volunteered to enroll in night classes to improve his spelling. The chief assented with the provision that the candidate pass the required spelling examination. Six months later, the candidate returned and submitted an almost perfect spelling examination. When queried by the chief as to how he had accomplished this miracle, the young, aspiring officer said that he was so determined to be a peace officer that he was not going to let a little obstacle like spelling stop him. So he purchased a spelling book, a dictionary, and grammar book. Every night, with the help of his wife, he spent at least an hour studying. When he took the police examination the second time he was well prepared. This is an excellent lesson for potential police candidates. Police science students who are weak in spelling, grammar, and basic mathematics should exert every effort to master these fundamentals as soon as possible. To do so will save time, energy, and embarrassment for the candidate and all concerned.

Recently, after six months on a local police department, a graduate from a popular junior college with a police science major returned to his alma mater for a visit. As soon as mutual pleasantries were exchanged, the young officer advised, "You have an excellent police science course and I recommend it for prelaw enforcement students, but I suggest that you also include typing in the police science curriculum. On one occasion, it took me five hours to type a report, which I completed at 5:00 o'clock in the morning. Unfortunately, I use the 'hunt and peck' method. So, advise your students to learn to type, and it will make their initial adjustment to law enforcement much easier and more profitable."

Peace officers' basic training school

A typical peace officers' basic training school consists of 240 hours, 6 weeks in duration, 8 hours per day, 5 days per week, is

Figure 15.   Peace officers' basic training class.

state approved, and operates on an academy basis. The following police courses are typical of the fundamental training offered to new officers by such programs.

UNIT NUMBER	DURATION IN HOURS
1. *Classroom Note-taking and Orientation*	5
Fundamental methods and tech-	

niques of taking comprehensive notes in the classroom. Instruction will be supplemented with written material and sample forms for maintaining notes in the basic police training school. Rules, regulations, and operating procedures of the basic school.

2. *Law Enforcement Ethics* 4
The definition of a profession as it applies to law enforcement. Defines and discusses ethical and unethical acts. Emphasizes the obligation of all officers to conduct themselves ethically and prevent unethical conduct.

3. *Laws of Arrest, Search and Seizure* 8
Peace officers' right and duty to make an arrest. Distinction between felony and misdemeanor. Requisites of a legal arrest as set forth in the Penal Code. Immunity from arrest and legal rights of a suspect. Legal use of force and attitudes of arresting officers.

4. *Rules of Evidence* 6
Rules of evidence and their application to proper law enforcement. The tests of admissibility applied by the courts, including direct and circumstantial evidence, hearsay, confessions, dying declarations, documentary evidence, competency of witnesses, degrading and incriminating questions, privileged and nonprivileged communications.

5. *Criminal Law (Penal Code)* (15 hours) plus exam (2 hours)   17
Covers state law relating to criminal acts with emphasis on the elements of crime, parties to crime, defenses, and those specific sections most frequently used in the Penal Code.

6. *Vehicle Code* (10 hours) and *Traffic Control* (2 hours)   12
Outline of the most frequently used sections of the Vehicle Code. Sections of the Vehicle Code will be repeated as they relate to special subjects throughout the training. Traffic law enforcement regulation and control, citations, mechanics, and psychology.

7. *Traffic-accident Investigation*   6
Method and procedure to be employed in investigating traffic accidents, such as use and care of department equipment, questioning witnesses, observation of drivers, checking vehicles involved in accidents, checking roadway, observation of signs and signals, use of photography and measurements, with special emphasis on hit-and-run. Forms required.

8. *Beat Patrol and Observation*   10
Principal purposes of beat patrol: protection, prevention, repression, identification, and apprehension. Type of patrol: fixed, auto, and foot patrol. Police hazards: recognition,

inspection, and control. Operation of police vehicles: on patrol, answering assignments, on emergencies and non-emergencies. Methods of developing powers of perception and observation of persons, places, and things.

9. *Interviews and Interrogation*   8
Routine interrogations: approach, attitude, securing complete essential information, evaluation, file checks. To prepare recruit policemen to conduct routine interrogations of complainants, witnesses, victims, suspects, suspicious persons, and citizen informants. To indicate methods and techniques employed in station and field interrogations, touching upon separation, approach, attitude of and the rights and treatment of subjects. Introduction of methods and uses of scientific aids. Statements, admissions, and confessions.

10. *Defensive Tactics*   11
To teach the fundamentals of the use of the baton, riot stick, handholds, come-alongs, and throws. Methods of disarming and protection against persons armed with dangerous and deadly weapons. Demonstration and practice in the use of the riot stick and limited number of come-alongs. Handcuffing and restraint of prisoners and mentally ill persons.

11. *Crowd and Panic Control*   4
Laws regulating crowds and/or gath-

ings. Types of crowds and gatherings. Police authority. Prevention and control of panic and riots. Causes of panic and riot.

12. *Arrest Techniques*   6
Methods of approaching a suspect on the street or in an auto, stopping autos, approaching in building, self-protection, search and frisk on arrest. Demonstration of search of prisoners. Psychological effect created by officers, including demeanor. Use of come-alongs, batons, guns, handcuffs. Protection of prisoners. Protection of evidence. Transportation of offenders to place of detention. Problems in transporting insane persons.

13. *Firearms and Their Use* plus
Legal Aspects   12
Instruction in the use and care of police firearms. Explanation of the situations warranting the use of firearms, legal provisions, and restrictions as defined by Penal Code and General Laws. Provisions concerning justifiable and excusable homicide and the law of self-defense. Policy covering use in performance of duty, safety precautions, and nomenclature. Familiarization firing of the riot gun and range practice with the service revolver.

14. *Collection, Identification, and
Preservation of Evidence,*
including *crime scene search*   10

240 *Introduction to police science*

The proper handling of each type of evidence from the time it is located until it is offered in evidence at the trial. Includes a discussion of laboratory processing of evidence and the assistance the investigator can expect to receive. Collection, preservation, identification, and recording of evidence. Developing and preserving latent fingerprints. Practical crime scene search project.

15. *Field Note-taking and Crime-scene Recording*   6
Methods of taking comprehensive notes in investigations: value, necessity of keeping, and preservation. Use of sketches, diagrams, and charts in recollecting and reproducing crime scene in court. Use of field notes in court and in writing investigation report.

16. *Report Writing and Descriptions*   12
Necessity of reports in law enforcement. Operation, requirements of good reports. Basic understanding of the types of reports, their use, value, and purpose. Reports: narrative, elements of composition, general procedure regarding forms, substances, conclusion, statistics. Emphasis on *modus operandi* reports. Development of an appreciation for accurate and complete description of persons and property.

17. *Juvenile Procedure*   6
Responsibility of law enforcement
agencies. Various juvenile agencies,
including the California Youth Authority. Procedure in handling juveniles and obtaining petitions. Discussion of most frequently used sections
of the Welfare and Institutions Code.

18. *Courtroom Demeanor and Testifying*   4
Stresses fundamentals of being most
effective as a witness in court. Includes preparation before court. Appearance, manner, and attitude in
court while waiting to testify and
while on the stand. Common pitfalls
facing the new officers in court. Use
of notebook as reference. Techniques
helpful when being cross-examined.

19. *Public Relations and Race Relations*   10
Covers the necessity for excellent conduct of officers on and off duty, appearance, loyalty to the job and organization. Emphasizes self-control,
level-headedness, courtesy, fairness,
personal appearance, neatness, and
punctuality. Stresses the importance
of off-duty conduct including temper-
ance, personal domestic relations, off-
duty activities, and integrity. The em-
ployer-employee relationships, promotion of goodwill with the general
public and other officers, interdepart-
mental relations. Attitude and procedure in those cases and offenses involving officers of other enforcement

agencies. Importance of press relations to the police services, with emphasis upon principal benefits to job
performance, departmental and individual welfare, department policies
toward the newspaper reports. Covers the racial groups that may become police problems. Dangers of
improper handling of matters having
to do with such groups. Elements of
proper relations with ethnic groups.

20. *Court Organization and Procedure*   2
General court procedure and functions including mechanics of jury selection, complaint forms, writs, subpoenas, warrants, and other allied
papers and court orders. Organization, relationships, and responsibilities of various courts.

21. *Basic Criminal Investigations and*
Procedures   61
Covers fundamental procedures in
the investigation of those complaints,
services, and reports of most frequent
occurrence. Treats the elements of
the crime, the preliminary methods
and techniques necessary to successfully investigate the cases listed below:

a. Introduction to investigation	8
b. Domestic complaints	2
c. Missing persons	2
d. Narcotics	4
e. Disorderly conduct	2
f. Sex crimes	4

g. Assaults   4

h. Prowler and disturbance reports   2

i. Petty theft and receiving stolen
   property   4

j. Auto theft   2

k. Impounded and abandoned autos   2

l. Mental illness cases   2

m. Injury and death cases   4

n. Robbery and grand-theft cases   2

o. Burglary: commercial and safe   2

p. Burglary: residence   2

q. Drunk and drunk-driving cases   2

r. Liquor-law violations   3

s. Civil problems   4

t. Dangerous drugs   2

u. Use of police radio and teletype   2

22. *First Aid*   10
The immediate and temporary care given in case of accident, illness, and emergency childbirth, with poisoning and asphyxiation cases stressed. Course qualifies students for the Standard Red Cross First Aid Certificate.

23. *Jurisdiction of Other Agencies*   2
Discusses the duties and jurisdiction of Federal, state, county, and local law enforcement agencies. Cooperation emphasized.

24. *Car Pullovers and Shakedowns*   2
Practical demonstration and practice in stopping cars involving various realistic problems will be staged. Safety precautions stressed.

UNIT NUMBER	DURATION IN HOURS
25. *Final Examination, Critique, and* *Graduation* Periodic examinations and critique of subject taught held by each instructor during the six-week school.	6

QUESTIONS

1. Name the three essentials in the process of training a peace officer.
2. Why is police training needed?
3. What are the objectives of police training?
4. What are the four hazards of law enforcement?
5. Describe a typical basic police training course for a newly appointed police officer.
6. What are the various other types of training that an officer may anticipate after basic training?
7. Explain the role of the junior college in police training.
8. Why should a police science student be proficient in basic mathematics, spelling, word association, and vocabulary?

12. Police public relations

The problem of police relations with the public

RIGHTS AND THEIR INFRINGEMENT

Above the entrance to the United States Supreme Court Building in Washington, D.C., is carved the inscription, "Equal Justice Under Law." If this phrase could be etched into the minds and hearts of the American public as the accepted image of the police, many public relations problems of law enforcement would be solved. Instead, the phrase, "A policeman's lot is not a happy one," as sung in the light opera of Gilbert and Sullivan, often describes the plight of the police force when it must, on occasion, face the court of public opinion to account for its actions.

As the law enforcement arm of government, the police must frequently regulate and, in some situations, even control the behavior of people. Even if an officer performs his clear duty in a fair, impartial, and diplomatic manner, his task is often neither pleasant nor easy. There are people who resent an officer's very presence, regardless of how dedicated his efforts may be. The justifiable concern of people for their rights as citizens often appears in conflict with what the public may regard as police infringement of those rights. Indeed, the line between citizens' rights and supposed police curbs on those rights is sometimes a very thin one. Citizens do have rights, and police must enforce the law. When these two principles clash, it is usually the police public image which suffers most.

It is for these reasons that modern police departments in recent years have begun to place heavy emphasis on their relations with the public. However, the goal of complete public cooperation and understanding, which is so necessary to outstanding police work, has yet to be achieved. But the problem is yielding to solution through modern police approaches toward improving public relations.

The problem of its relations with the public is a typically modern one for the police. At the turn of the century, there was little need and no plans for public relations programs in law enforcement. Police rarely came in contact with the public except to exchange greetings, receive complaints, and give directions. Today, the problems of traffic control, crowd control, and juvenile control have brought police into much closer personal contact with many more people. Police, unfortunately, were not always well trained in modern techniques of handling these new law enforcement responsibilities nor in coping with the new types of lawbreakers. The present fundamental change in police attitude toward the public and the increasing sensitivity of both the police and the public toward their relationship deserve further serious study.

MODERN SOLUTION TO A MODERN PROBLEM

While the police have always been adept in handling the hardened criminal, the new type of lawbreaker could include anyone from the mayor to a laborer. Too often, these minor offenders were treated the same as a criminal. Naturally, the minor traffic offender resented being considered a criminal and accorded the rough, tough treatment that accompanied that status. Thus, the police and the public grew farther and farther apart. A wide chasm of misunderstanding, fear, resentment, and general antagonism separated them.

Wise police officials soon realized that this widening gap between police and the public had to be closed. The police and the public, after all, were on the same team. Together, they were fighting crime. As long as the public and its law enforcement arm were at odds, only the criminal profited. Diagnosing the problem of relations with the public in this way, the police bent themselves to the task of organizing public relations programs. Some departments, through sincere, concerted efforts upon the part of all employees, succeeded in improving public relations. Others, through indifference, lack of training, and lack of coordination, did not fare as well.

The programs that succeeded took into account the fact that law enforcement is a public service occupation. Law enforcement officers were taught that they were employees of the public and that the public was entitled to the many rights of an employer. The public also held the purse strings. Through such programs, built around these major considerations, successful law enforcement agencies learned to embrace public relations—and to survive and to benefit from its many advantages. Thus, modern law enforcement departments have come a long way in improving the public image of police.

An experienced police executive who visits any city can soon ascertain if the relations between the police and the public are good or bad. When the city has good public relations, the police have modern facilities, planned retirements, a merit system, and many other fringe benefits. On the other hand, in the city with adverse public relations, wages are lower and there are fewer benefits. Often police headquarters are located in the basement of the city hall or in some other old building where the space and equipment are inadequate to do an efficient job.

Most law enforcement agencies have recognized that cooperation from the public greatly simplifies the work of police. Favorable public attitude means newer and better facilities, higher salaries, and many fringe benefits. All of these things have great impact on the quality of law enforcement in a community. Only by working in harmony can the police and the public fight the rising tide of crime and mutually benefit each other.

It would be good for the student of police science to obtain a clearer idea of what police public relations really is. It is much more than a vague, wished-for, disorganized approach to simply being "nice" to the public. Police public relations, like any other well-conceived police program, is carefully planned, properly organized, and competently put into operation. It has certain goals and objectives because the value of a public relations program is measured by the results it achieves in a community. If a police department plans its program well, it will involve every member of the department. Thus, a police public relations program must not only be well designed by its police planners but must be effectively carried out by each member of the police team.

Throughout the rest of this chapter, the student will have the opportunity (1) to obtain a clearer idea of what police public relations programs really are and (2) to understand the importance of the personal role of the police officer in helping the public relations program achieve its goals.

POLICE PUBLIC RELATIONS DEFINED

The following characteristics of public relations, as a departmental program, will serve to orient the student and to set the stage for later discussions in this chapter:

1. Public relations is a planned program or system designed to gain and hold the public's goodwill.
2. Police public relations aims to achieve friendliness, fairness, understanding, and service.
3. Police public relations is not negative (locked up at headquarters). It is not press-agentry, propaganda, window dressing, a quick paint job, or a deodorant to stifle a smelly police problem.
4. It may consist of both a selling job and an unselling job. There are lots of people who dislike police because of wrong impressions, false information, rumors, and gossip. Eliminating these roadblocks to good relations is part of the program.
5. Police public relations is the combined, deliberate effort of

all employees of a department to implant in the minds of the people the idea that policemen are friendly, capable, understanding, and willing to be of service to the community.

6. Police public relations fosters goodwill toward all the people, regardless of race, color, or creed.

There is no panacea for unfavorable public relations. Good police public relations is much more than a program. Large law enforcement agencies and many smaller departments do have definite public relations programs. In fact, planned programs, with responsible leadership, are recommended. It is certain, however, that public relations cannot be turned off and on like a light switch. Public relations is based on a continual effort to improve all police activities. Every member of a department must realize that public relations is not only the responsibility of the chief or his immediate assistants. It is the *individual responsibility* of every person on the department.

Police public relations has often been compared to a chain. Just as a chain is as strong as its weakest link, so also the public relations of a department is as strong as its weakest public-relations-minded officer. This means that every officer must be personally aware of the problems involved in his actions and must work continually to improve his own personal public relations. How he can achieve this goal is explained in the remainder of this chapter.

Personal appearance. Robert Burns, the Scottish poet, wrote "O wad some Power the giftie gie us/To see oursels as ithers see us!" The police officer cannot merely wish for the gift of seeing himself as others see him. He cannot take his appearance for granted. He cannot afford to assume that he creates a favorable image. His appearance must be a measure of excellence.

When an officer is appointed to a department, he is lean, clean, and in excellent condition. He had to be in order to pass all the physical exams and agility tests. If he is able to maintain this high standard of physical well-being throughout his career, he will have few problems with physical appearance. However, many things can happen. This virile, active, young police officer is invariably assigned to the midnight to 8:00 A.M. shift in either a one-man or two-man patrol car. Often the eight-hour shift expires without incident; the officer rides in the squad car for eight hours with a minimum of physical activity. After a night without exercise, he returns home to his young wife, who plies him with food. Before long, he is fighting the battle of the midriff bulge. Although he keeps loosening his belt, he finally reaches the last notch. After that, he has no alternative but to drop the paunch over the belt. He is aware of his changing silhouette but does not really mind the transition. In fact, he may even be proud of his new paunch.

Then one night he surprises a burglary, robbery, or juvenile car theft ring in action. The felons take off on foot. The officer takes off in hot pursuit but finds he is no match for the felons as he stumbles and falls exhausted. When he picks himself up, he mutters, "I guess I'm out of condition." But the public expects its police to make successful apprehensions. When an officer fails to do so, he also fails to retain the confidence of the public. This lack of physical conditioning can occur in anyone; so a word to the wise should be enough. Gene Tunney, the ex-heavyweight champion, recommends healthful diet, regular exercise, sufficient sleep, and relaxing recreation as the four ways to good health. An officer should remember that he is on parade at all times during his tour of duty. The eyes of the public are constantly upon him. They keep an eye on his movements, his appearance, and even his wearing apparel.

Appearance includes such important visible items as condition of uniform, hair, and shoes. Uniforms should fit and be neat and clean at all times. A man is often judged by his clothes. By them, he may be rated clean or sloppy, flashy or conservative, or even successful or unsuccessful. The Canadian Mounted Police has a worldwide reputation for invincibility. Much of its favorable image is due largely to the striking appearance of its officers.

Empathy. Empathy is the ability to completely understand another person's point of view. It is a great asset in police work and the basis for all good public relations. By practicing empathy, the police officer can avoid the closed mind. He must try to see all sides of any traffic accident or criminal incident. No one should be convicted before having his day in court where all of the facts are brought out. Thus, empathy eliminates bias and, instead, introduces tolerance, understanding, and sympathetic human relations.

Unfortunately, the police are exposed to the seedy and seamy side of life. After days and nights on end of such exposure, it takes forbearance and the empathy of a hardy soul not to become cynical and disillusioned when rubbing elbows with drunks, vagrants, felons, and the many other stark examples of human frailty. Consequently, it would be good for each officer to practice the old prayer of the Sioux Indians, "Great Spirit, help us never to judge another until we have walked for two weeks in his moccasins."

Speech. It is estimated that the average person has a vocabulary of about ten to twenty thousand words. Of these, about two thousand are slang words. Although slang usage is prevalent in the underworld, among teen-agers, and in business, it is not recommended in law enforcement. Too many conversations end up in the courtroom under the spotlight of judicial and public scrutiny—where slang is hardly appropriate. When one slang word can have several meanings, it is most confusing. As an example, in the field of narcotics enforcement marijuana is called "the weed," "tea," and "pot." New slang words, moreover, are coined continually to confuse the police. Unless he is careful, the police officer may adopt the underworld jargon of the criminal and thus create an unfavorable public impression.

It is estimated that 80 percent of police work each day consists in speaking to people in all walks of life. The police officer may talk to the lawyer, judge, doctor, social worker, laborer, teacher, criminal, or member of the clergy during his daily meetings. Therefore, the officer must be versatile and correct in his speech. He must be particularly careful when testifying on the witness stand to express himself intelligently and to convey his thoughts, ideas, and findings in good, plain English. In short, he must be able to communicate.

He must also remember that the day when the police officer had to look, act, and be tough is no more. Hence, swearing and cursing are absolutely prohibited under all circumstances, no matter what the provocation may be. Nothing is gained by foul language, and no police officer should stoop to it to win an argument or to emphasize a point. Obscene words spoken in haste may mean years of repentance and embarrassment, as well as financial loss to the officer and his department. Officers should enroll in English, speech, and public-speaking courses to develop the art of communication. It is just as easy to cultivate good habits of speech as bad habits.

Use of police equipment. Since the police department is an emergency organization, all equipment and facilities must be available and functional on instant notice. Every piece of equipment, especially guns, cars, ammunition, and all other tools of the police profession, must be in top working condition at all times. Equipment and facilities rank second in the budget as the greatest expense in the operation of a law enforcement agency. These must never be abused.

The police patrol car is in constant sight of the public. Its flashing red lights and screaming siren attract attention. Obviously, the police officer must use this emergency equipment judiciously. Use of the red light and the siren in violation of the state law or departmental regulations cannot be tolerated.

Police weapons also receive public attention. Favorable publicity is generated with firearm demonstrations at police schools, at exhibitions, and during open house. However, the safety and welfare of the public must be carefully considered whenever police weapons such as tear gas, machine guns, water hoses, and police dogs are used to enforce the law. Otherwise, the police department will be subject to critical public reaction. Every time a police officer uses police weapons, good public relations is at stake.

Courtesy. Courtesy has been defined as the lubricant that oils the machinery of public relations. It helps to reduce friction and promote harmony. In short, courtesy is politeness, consideration for the welfare of others, and the practice of the golden rule.

Courtesy, like kindness and cleanliness, must be cultivated. An officer must develop this trait and practice it from his first day of service. If he does, courtesy will be an asset to him throughout his career. The observant officer soon learns that courtesy helps him to handle all types of people, both individually and collectively, with efficiency and dispatch.

The kernel of courtesy is not so much *what* a person says as *how* he says it. This fact was exemplified dramatically in a western movie when Gary Cooper effectively admonished the villain, "Smile when you say that!" The villain smiled and saved his life. It should be understood that an act or word of courtesy is defeated when accompanied by a frown or a wrinkled brow. To convey courtesy expressively, an officer must be courteous wholeheartedly and without reservation. This is always accomplished best with a smile and a pleasant demeanor. Words like "please," "thank you," "pardon me," and "you're welcome" may be small words, but when accompanied with a smile, they carry a lot of weight and good will. They should become a spontaneous part of a policeman's vocabulary.

Many police departments throughout the United States have recognized the value of courtesy. "Courtesy is contagious" signs are posted in various sections of their facilities. Courtesy works, and those who practice courtesy will testify to the accuracy of this statement. Try it and experience the pleasant reaction to courtesy wherever you go.

Power of a smile. A smile is good public relations. Songwriters and poets have extolled the virtues of smiling. It has also been observed that a smile speaks every language and knows no permanent barriers. Physiologists advise that it takes only 12 facial muscles to smile. It requires many more muscles to frown. A smile costs nothing, expresses good will, and is everyone's best prescription for avoiding trouble. So smile and almost everyone will work with you. Frown and you will work harder and accomplish less.

Attitude. "Don't look now, but your slip is showing." This remark can be appropriately directed toward the conduct of a policeman who is haughty, sarcastic, officious, or flippant in his role as public servant. His attitude shows. No matter whether he wears a natty uniform or carries a late-model revolver, the public is constantly appraising the officer and his apparent attitude. The public might forgive an officer for shoddy appearance or blame his superiors for it, but an indifferent, negative, antisocial attitude is a matter that is the personal responsibility of the officer. An officer must remember that a positive attitude toward his work lightens the day's burden for all. The public is impressed with the officer who displays enthusiasm for his job. A good attitude will help to overcome almost any other handicaps the police officer might have.

Conduct off duty. The police officer has a 24-hour job. Because of the nature of his employment and the agreements made at the time of his appointment, a police officer is technically never off duty. He must abide by the rules and regulations of the department during his 8 hours on duty and expect to live by these rules and regulations the other 16 hours of a day. There are no exceptions.

When the police officer is sworn into office, he must recognize that he is leaving the ranks of plain Mr. Citizen. By accepting a police appointment, he assumes responsibilities that cannot be shirked or compromised. As a public servant, his actions and conduct are scrutinized around the clock, on or off duty. He makes many sacrifices in order to become a member of the police profession.

Many off-duty police officers devote their leisure hours to the Boy Scouts, PTA, and other worthwhile community activities. They become involved in civic affairs and government projects and give generously of their time to public welfare projects. Their leadership, even when off duty, is geared toward breaking down lawlessness and helping to make the community a better place to live.

Gratuities. One of the most revealing books ever written about law enforcement is *The Plight of the Honest Cop* by Howard Whitman. This book was the result of a nationwide tour of police departments in which the author reveals intimate details and permits glimpses of the trials, tribulations, and temptations of the average peace officer, pointing out the constant pressures under which police officers must work.

One of the problems that confronts every officer sooner or later involves gratuities, special privileges, and gifts. Many American people, especially the gangster element, ask for extra favors in an effort to get around the law. Attempts to fix traffic tickets and parking violations are particularly annoying to most law enforcement officers.

A method of operation employed by those who want to gain unusual privileges and immunity from the law is to bestow gifts ranging from money to liquor and appliances upon the unwary officer. As soon as the officer accepts a gift, he becomes obligated. He is indebted to the donor and has compromised both himself and his department. The donor may be a criminal or an unsavory, unscrupulous person who will use such a situation to the detriment of the officer, the department, and society. As an example, an officer, handling vice cases in a metropolitan area, received a case of whiskey from a person of questionable reputation. He had the presence of mind to send it back and thereby avoided a web of intrigue from which he would never have escaped.

In basic training, the police student should be cautioned, "You can't get something for nothing." He should be warned that he has to pay for what he gets. Illegitimate gifts are paid for in embarrassment, heartaches, sleepless nights, ulcers, and possibly grand jury investigation. Never let it be said as you walk down the street, "There goes the best officer that money can buy."

Recently, a farsighted chief of police who was organizing a new but large suburban police department issued a general order to prevent any offers of gratuities from demoralizing his personnel. This order, still in effect, reads, "So that no confusion exists as to the policy of this department regarding free coffee and meals, the following order is written: Officers will not accept free coffee from the proprietor or employees of any commercial business establishment, nor will they accept meals at any discount or price other than that charged civilian customers. Any officer guilty of an infraction of this policy will be subject to disciplinary action." The above order kept the problem under control.

In the earlier days of low police wages, it was accepted procedure for local businessmen to provide police families with food, clothing, and even luxuries to augment meager police salaries. After a while, the average officer began to depend upon this undesirable arrangement to meet the family's economic needs.

Similarly, the free coffee was often not the wish of the local police. More often than not, it was forced upon the officer because the restaurant owner or drive-in proprietor liked to have police on the premises. As one café owner confided, "I never have any trouble when an officer is on the premises. Police customers are excellent security for my business, and the free coffee is just a sound investment."

But the price is too high. One officer recalled how he had refused to accept free coffee for a long time, until in a weak moment, he capitulated. It was not very long before the owner presented him with a traffic ticket he had just received. When the officer explained that he was unable to fix the ticket, he fell from grace at the owner's establishment.

Problems involving all forms of gratuities have generally developed through public solicitation. An officer must maintain his independence and refuse to become involved in gratuities in order to avoid unpleasant and illegal complications. It has been found that when police salaries are below average and fringe benefits are negative, gratuities are most prevalent. On the other hand, when police incomes are representative of the national average and fringe benefits are available, the problem is at a minimum, if it exists at all. Reasonable police wage scales and attractive fringe benefits are the most practical ways to eliminate the gratuities problem which, if not eliminated, undermines the morale and effectiveness of any department.

Social outlets. The old adage, "Birds of a feather flock together," should remind police that law enforcement officers are judged by the company they keep. When the public sees its police fraternizing with hoodlums and gangsters at race tracks, late night spots, and social events, it loses faith in law enforcement. It is hard to understand how law enforcement officials can socialize with and lionize the members of the underworld when the two are at opposite ends of the law. The excuse that efforts are being made to cultivate the violator as an informant will not hold water.

Another social outlet that the public cannot understand is the subsidizing of places of ill repute. This subsidizing occurs when police meetings and conferences are held in resorts, hotels, or motels which are known to be owned or financed by gangland blood money or when police families congregate and relax at night clubs and offbeat amusement places reputed to be involved in illegal activities or just skirting the pale of the law. By frequenting such places, the police place their stamp of approval on them. As a result, the public may think that if such places are all right for the police, they must be all right for the public. Thus, according to a kind of cycle, the resort becomes popular, the owner becomes wealthy, crime receives another shot in the financial arm, and the police department helps create a bigger problem for itself.

Honesty. Honesty is a synonym of integrity. When a police officer is described as a man of integrity, he is a man with a conscience—one who is able to distinguish and choose right from wrong. Integrity is a gem of great value in an officer's life. It must be guarded zealously and is never for sale.

Diogenes, the Greek philosopher, used to look for an honest man by shining the light of a lantern into the faces of strangers. But honesty cannot be identified by physical features, nor is it an inborn trait. Honesty is a quality cultivated from cradle to grave. The training received from parents, clergy, and teachers forms our patterns of honesty. Thus, honesty is relative. Some people are more honest than others. Just as a person should know his IQ (intelligence quotient), so, too, he should learn his HQ (honesty quotient). The practice of honesty in the little things of life will help pave the way for the needed strength when the difficult decisions involving honesty must be made. Now is the time to check your HQ lest later, perhaps, the grand jury may have to do so. In the words of the poet Pope, "An honest man's the noblest work of God."

Reception at headquarters. When a citizen comes to the police station, he has problems. If he receives rude, impertinent treatment, he will never forget it and will always resent it. His experience may create his first and last impression of the police. It should be a favorable one. Police cannot afford to alienate anyone because every person can become a potential aide to the police and, in times of emergency and disaster, everyone in the community is needed as an ally.

Instead of building an invisible wall between the public and the police, good public relations demands that the lines of communication always remain open. People should be encouraged to come to the police department to receive help, advice, and counsel. When they arrive, they should be greeted warmly and made to feel welcome. The prompt handling of complaints is a key to good relations.

No citizen enjoys cooling his heels in the anteroom. He does not come to the police station to watch horseplay, flirtations, card playing, gossiping, or other forms of extracurricular activities.

The complainant has other business to attend to and does not want to be put on a merry-go-round of needless misdirection. Rather, he expects courtesy and efficiency.

HOW TO UNDERMINE PUBLIC RELATIONS

Both rookies and seasoned veterans should know the negative actions of police officers that will destroy good public relations. The following represent negative actions on the part of the police that the public particularly abhors and resents.

Overbearing attitude. It is difficult to understand how a young, pleasant, intelligent rookie can be changed from a popular all-American youth into a mean, cantankerous officer. Like the Dr. Jekyll and Mr. Hyde transformation, the change is unbelievable and intolerable.

From the very beginning, a young officer should know that he does not have to be tough, mean, and officious to handle people. Swinging the nightstick, pushing people around, or giving them a difficult time will effectively sabotage public relations. Nothing irritates a citizen more than to be made to feel insignificant, small, or silly. The irritation is especially aggravated when an officer is also issuing a citation, directing traffic, or controlling a crowd.

Unpleasant tone of voice. No one likes to have his ego deflated, but this is easily accomplished by the officer who uses his authority to harshly and unnecessarily reprimand a citizen. "What are you sitting on—your brains?" "Where are you going—to a fire?" "Why don't you buy yourself some glasses?" are examples of caustic, sarcastic queries the public receives from untrained officers. When accompanied by a haughty manner, such needless remarks spell the ruination of public relations. The public has a right to expect to be interrogated civilly and with respect.

Favoritism. In the United States, all people, regardless of race, color, or creed, have the same rights, privileges, and protection under the laws of our land. To give special favor to certain individuals or groups tears at the very foundation of our American heritage. Whether a person is rich or poor, or belongs to the same union, fraternity, civic organization, political party, or church, should not influence the officer. Rather, all persons, whether adults, old people, children, sick, or infirm, should receive pleasant, considerate treatment. The public wants neither a favoring police nor preferential treatment for those who count. Instead, there must be no favoritism of any kind at any time for anyone.

Unnecessary rough treatment. Complaints of mishandling are usually registered by prisoners, inebriates, prostitutes, older people, and children. With the intensive training in public relations received by the police of today, these complaints are reduced to a bare minimum. The rights and methods of handling all kinds of people are thoroughly stressed and demonstrated during police schools. The modern officer knows that no person should be mistreated. He understands that a drunk can be injured and bruised, that a prostitute has feelings like anyone else, that older people can become senile and helpless, and that children need guidance and understanding.

Using police cars indiscriminately. Since the police are the ones who enforce the laws, they should be the last to violate them. Traffic violations by the police are especially noticed by the public. For instance, turning around in the middle of a highway, parking in front of fire hydrants, driving below the speed limits on surface streets, and failing to use hand or turn signals are some of the common complaints of citizens about police handling of patrol cars.

In one city, a teacher complained to the chief of police that she was amazed at the poor driving habits of the local police, and she criticized the police for setting bad examples. The chief was most upset, but, realizing that her complaint was valid, he instituted a driving school for all officers. Soon the improvement was so great that the teacher returned to the police department and praised the chief for his recognition of and solution to the problem.

There is one use of the police traffic car and motorcycle that infuriates the public, the practice of parking mobile police equipment in a strategic location, out of view near a public street or highway. Then, without warning, an officer swoops down on the unsuspecting motorist who has been lulled into a false sense of security. This procedure is not approved nor taught at police academies.

Lavishing attention on women. In the course of police work, an officer frequently has the opportunity to work on matters which involve members of the opposite sex. Whenever an officer stops a female for jaywalking, a traffic violation, or some other infraction of the law, the eyes of all in the vicinity are usually observing every movement and gesture of the officer. He must use good judgment in dealing with women. To linger unduly, make passes, take her phone number, or give her special consideration by overlooking violations tarnishes the public image of the police department. Undue attention to women in public places will not enhance police public relations.

Projecting the wrong impression. During patrol duty or vice assignments, officers have occasion to visit bars, taverns, night clubs, and other places where alcoholic beverages are served. In such places, taking a drink or even sipping a Coke may be questionable conduct for a police officer, especially when he is in uniform.

Another problem arises when an officer receives money in public. A traffic officer may own a small apartment building, or he may perform some work for a neighbor. To be paid in cash in view of everyone on a street corner may cause raised eyebrows. Thoughts of payoff and corruption enter the minds of some suspecting citizens. At no time nor at any place should an officer conduct himself so as to create a public scandal or give the wrong impression.

The public—friends or enemies? In summation, the ideal requirement for building public relations is a law enforcement agency that has a good, clean record and reputation. The agency must be free of graft and corruption. Some departments depend on police bands, public speaking engagements, open-house programs, exhibits, tours, pistol teams, and other good-will methods to promote public relations. They are all very helpful. However, such programs can never take the place of those fundamental requirements which a department must possess in order to have a good public image. A favorable public image depends upon honesty, fairness, impartiality, and efficiency in law enforcement. Those police agencies developed on the sound principles of integrity, fidelity, and effective law enforcement will gain the respect and confidence of the public. When this ideal is accomplished, there will be good public relations.

Each day, every police officer is urged to take personal inventory of his progress in promoting public relations for his department. He can do this by asking himself, "Am I making friends or enemies for my department?" This question is a simple but accurate test. If he is making enemies for his department, he is sabotaging the public relations of his department. If he is making friends for his department, he is functioning as an ideal police officer who is creating good public relations. Good public relations is the necessary climate in which effective law enforcement can flourish.

QUESTIONS

1. Define "police public relations."
2. Explain how personal appearance of its police officers can enhance public relations of a police department.
3. Why is the speech of a police officer a factor to be considered in public relations?
4. How does the attitude of a police officer affect public relations?
5. Describe how use of police equipment can favorably or unfavorably influence public relations.
6. Why is the conduct of an officer when off duty so important to the correct public image of a police department?
7. Explain the problems involved when an officer succumbs to gratuities.
8. What are the hazards of law enforcement officers fraternizing with members of the underworld?
9. What is meant by honesty quotient?
10. What is meant when it is said that law enforcement is a service occupation?
11. What are some ways in which police can give the public erroneous impressions of their otherwise innocent acts?
12. Why does a department that is free of corruption and is noted for efficiency and cooperation tend to create conditions favorable to good public relations?

13. Police ethics

The meaning of police ethics

In a police science class at Pasadena City College, students were asked to pool their thoughts on a definition of police ethics. After considerable discussion, the following definition emerged: Police ethics is a set of rules and regulations devised to guide the officer in determining whether his personal conduct is right or wrong.

It was the opinion of this class that ethics in any profession develops a right conscience among its individual members and that such a conscience is helpful in law enforcement to assist the officer in doing the right thing. Other recognized professions— medicine, law, and education—have developed ethical codes to serve as clearly defined ideals and principles for their members to follow in solving the everyday problems of right and wrong that arise in their work.

Whether playing the game of football or participating in the game of life, professional standards of behavior and exemplary conduct must be recognized and observed. The opportunity to abide by such necessary standards confronts officers daily in law enforcement.

As a case in point, an officer in a West Coast city spotted the local judge's car parked illegally. The officer had just been advised in a police training school that morning before he went on duty that all laws, including traffic laws, are applicable to all people, regardless of race, color, creed, or station in life. But he hesitated because he wanted to avoid the possible embarrassment and trouble that could result from putting a ticket on the car of a VIP. Nevertheless, the lessons in the morning class were well learned and he tagged the judge's car. His decision proved to be a wise one, for the judge publicly praised the young officer's fortitude in doing the right thing. He paid the fine and admonished others to do the same in similar circumstances. He concluded, "The officer was ethical and showed good judgment."

DISTORTED CODES OF ETHICS

Unfortunately, there is a tendency in our American culture to accept certain mistaken codes of ethics. These distorted ethical concepts lead many to sympathize with the person who is "down and out," even though he may have committed a serious crime. Sympathy for the underdog, while admirable when applied to the truly unfortunate in our society, is often misplaced when it is extended to the lawbreaker. We tend to glorify the Robin Hoods and the Jesse Jameses.

The same unsound ethics appears in the ugly meanings attached to the words "fink," "stool pigeon," and "chicken." Some persons, in the belief that they are being honorable, refuse to divulge vital information to the police regarding violations of the law, even though their own personal safety or that of others may be at stake. In the same vein, the label of "chicken" has induced many to participate in criminal or reckless activities in order to retain the questionable respect of their groups.

Police science students who have been exposed to this kind of thinking must remember that such distorted codes of ethics have absolutely no place in law enforcement circles. Instead, the rules and regulations of a police department and its code of ethics take precedence over any other previous ties of friendship or relationship.

As our society changes, new and uglier words will be coined to reinforce similar mistaken codes of ethics. Problems of social discipline will increase as America reaches higher levels of affluence. To direct and guide our affluent society, realistic principles of conduct are necessary. Because of man's frailties, he must adopt and follow ideals and standards of conduct to protect himself and society. To the individual, these ideals become guidelines; to society, required rules of conduct and action.

Finally these standards of conduct become laws which people obey. As the Honorable Stanley Mosk, Justice of the California Supreme Court, stated, "Law established by the people through their elected representatives is the instrument of justice and the framework of our democratic society. It is the shield and the solid foundation of peace throughout the land."

Although every individual does not comply with every law all of the time, compliance with the law is nevertheless an ideal of our society. If voluntary compliance does not occur, outside motivation and stimuli must be exerted to enforce compliance. Thus the police and law enforcement service is created. Traditionally, in this country, the peace officer assumes the badge of authority to enforce the laws, keep the peace, and provide protection for life and property in the community. By placing this great authority and tremendous responsibility in the hands of its law enforcement agencies, the public creates a bond of trust and faith in the integrity and fidelity of the police. Law enforcement, therefore, must maintain and preserve this confidence and faith.

Professional ethics in law enforcement

Generally, the public believes that law enforcement is capable, efficient, and dedicated. So, whenever a department fails in its responsibilities and is unable to maintain lofty ethical standards, public support is soon withdrawn. With the lack of public support, a department may soon become vulnerable to subpar performance and unethical conduct. However, with high standards and a uniform strict adherence to a clear-cut code of ethics, a law enforcement agency may acquire the public support necessary to function with professional efficiency.

MARKS OF A TRUE PROFESSION

The measure of success for police in the realm of ethical behavior has been the high degree of professional status achieved by law enforcement during the past few years. Today, law enforcement has all of the accepted marks of a profession, which include the following:

1. Dedication to professional activities
2. A common bond of knowledge
3. A code of ethics to guide individual members of the profession
4. Selection and screening of personnel before admission to the profession

As representatives of a profession, the police expect and receive the recognition and public support that are needed to accomplish their sworn objectives. That this recognition actually has been achieved is made clear in an article reported in the September, 1964, issue of the FBI *Law Enforcement Bulletin,* "Law Enforcement—Truly a Profession." This article tells how two patrolmen were publicly accused in false statements made against them during the arrest and trial of a tipsy patron and a bartender. As a result, the two officers filed suits seeking damages from the tavern manager for slander. A statement made by J. Edgar Hoover, Director of the FBI, was introduced in evidence, to wit: "Law enforcement today is truly a profession." As a result, a judgment in common pleas court was rendered in favor of the two officers in the sum of $2,500 each. This recognition by the courts underscores the concept that law enforcement today is truly a profession.

A CODE OF POLICE ETHICS

There is no question that a code of ethics is essential in a profession. Without such a code, a profession could not exist. Moreover, the rules and regulations selected must reach the highest standards. There must be no opportunity for compromise. Pro-

THE FBI PLEDGE FOR LAW ENFORCEMENT OFFICERS

Humbly recognizing the responsibilities entrusted to me, I do vow that I shall always consider the high calling of law enforcement to be an honorable profession, the duties of which are recognized by me as both an art and a science. I recognize fully my responsibilities to defend the right, to protect the weak, to aid the distressed, and to uphold the law in public duty and in private living. I accept the obligation in connection with my assignments to report facts and to testify without bias or display of emotion, and to consider the information, coming to my knowledge by virtue of my position, as a sacred trust, to be used solely for official purposes. To the responsibilities entrusted to me of seeking to prevent crime, of finding the facts of law violations and of apprehending fugitives and criminals, I shall give my loyal and faithful attention and shall always be equally alert in striving to acquit the innocent and to convict the guilty. In the performance of my duties and assignments, I shall not engage in unlawful and unethical practices but shall perform the functions of my office without fear, without favor, and without prejudice. At no time shall I disclose to an unauthorized person any fact, testimony, or information in any pending matter coming to my official knowledge which may be calculated to prejudice the minds of existing or prospective judicial bodies either to favor or to disfavor any person or issue. While occupying the status of a law enforcement officer or at any other time subsequent thereto, I shall not seek to benefit personally because of my knowledge of any confidential matter which has come to my attention. I am aware of the serious responsibilities of my office and in the performance of my duties I shall, as a minister, seek to supply comfort, advice, and aid to those who may be in need of such benefits, as a soldier, I shall wage vigorous warfare against the enemies of my country, of its laws, and of its principles, and as a physician, I shall seek to eliminate the criminal parasite which preys upon our social order and to strengthen the lawful processes of our body politic. I shall strive to be both a teacher and a pupil in the art and science of law enforcement. As a lawyer, I shall acquire due knowledge of the laws of my domain and seek to preserve and maintain the majesty and dignity of the law; as a scientist, it will be my endeavor to learn all pertinent truth about accusations and complaints which come to my lawful knowledge; as an artist, I shall seek to use my skill for the purpose of making each assignment a masterpiece; as a neighbor, I shall bear an attitude of true friendship and courteous respect to all citizens; and as an officer, I shall always be loyal to my duty, my organization, and my country. I will support and defend the Constitution of the United States against all enemies, foreign and domestic; I will bear true faith and allegiance to the same, and will constantly strive to cooperate with and promote cooperation between all regularly constituted law enforcement agencies and officers in the performance of duties of mutual interest and obligation.

Figure 16. The FBI pledge for law enforcement officers. (Courtesy of J. Edgar Hoover, Director, Federal Bureau of Investigation, Washington, D.C.)

fessional ethics dictates the application of such absolutes as "always" and "never." To be effective, the code must cover all areas of endeavor, leaving no questions of right or wrong unanswered. Naturally, it is admitted that no code could, when phrased only in words, encompass every possible circumstance. However, within the confines of reason, a sensible, attainable set of rules can be formulated.

A code of police ethics must also embrace all basic objectives. The late Don L. Kooken in his book, *Ethics in Police Service,* outlined the following law enforcement objectives:

1. To elevate the standing of the profession in the public mind and to strengthen public confidence in law enforcement
2. To encourage law enforcement officers to fully appreciate the responsibilities of their office
3. To develop and maintain complete support and cooperation of the public in law enforcement
4. To ensure the effectiveness of the services by encouraging complete cooperation of its members for their mutual benefit
5. To strive for full coordination of effort in all official relationships with other governmental bodies
6. To consider police work an honorable profession, and to recognize in it an opportunity to render a worthwhile service to society

In order to achieve these high objectives, the International Association of Chiefs of Police (IACP), the Federal Bureau of Investigation, the Peace Officers' Association of the State of California, Inc., and many other law enforcement agencies have adopted a code of ethics. The FBI code appears in Figure 16. Other police codes are given in the following sections.

Law enforcement code of ethics

This code of ethics was first created and publicized by the Peace Officers' Research Association of California (PORAC). Subsequently, it was adopted by the Peace Officers' Association of the State of California, Inc., and thereafter universally promulgated by the International Association of Chiefs of Police and the National Conference of Police Associations.

Recently, the Commission on Peace Officers' Standards and Training of California, known as POST, required the following code of ethics to be read and discussed at all approved basic police schools. After discussion, each officer is presented with the following printed code of ethics for his personal use and limitation.

CODE OF ETHICS

AS A LAW ENFORCEMENT OFFICER my fundamental duty is to serve mankind; to safeguard lives and property; to protect the innocent against deception, the weak against oppression and intimidation, and the peaceful against violence and disorder; to respect the CONSTITUTIONAL rights of all men to liberty, equality and justice.

I will keep my private life unsullied as an example to all; maintain courageous calm in the face of danger, scorn or ridicule; develop self-restraint; and be constantly mindful of the welfare of others. I will be exemplary in obeying the laws of the land and the regulations of my department. Whatever I see or hear of a confidential nature, or that is confided in me in my official capacity, will be kept secret unless revelation is necessary in the performance of my duty.

I will never act officiously or permit personal feelings, prejudices, animosities or friendships to influence my decisions. With no compromise for crime and with relentless prosecution of criminals, I will enforce the law courteously and appropriately without fear or favor, malice or ill-will, never employing unnecessary force or violence and never accepting gratuities. I RECOGNIZE the badge of my office as a symbol of public faith, and I accept it as a public trust to be held so long as I am true to the ethics of the police service. I will constantly strive to achieve these objectives and ideals, dedicating myself before God to my chosen profession . . . *Law Enforcement.*

CANONS OF POLICE ETHICS

To stress the importance and explain the specific problems in police ethics, the IACP adopted the following *Canons of Ethics for Law Enforcement:*[1]

Article 1. *The primary responsibility.*
   To protect life and property and keep the peace of all people.
   To enforce the laws, equitably and fairly, regarding all persons.
Article 2. *Limitations of authority.*
   Each officer must know the bounds of his authority and never abuse his police power of arrest, search and seizure.

[1] The descriptions beneath each of the canons are the author's.

Article 3. *Duty to be familiar with the law and with the responsibilities of self and other public officials.*

Each officer should keep abreast of changes in the law; should attend law enforcement conferences and schools for improvement; and know his area of responsibility.

Article 4. *Utilization of proper means to gain proper ends.*

A law enforcement officer must be the first to obey the law and not be a bad example by flouting the law or granting special privileges to friends and relatives. Moreover, he must not use the law for personal power or gain.

Article 5. *Cooperation with public officials in the discharge of their official duties.*

This is a two-way street and an ethical officer will always cooperate legally with other departments, regardless of political or official affiliation.

Article 6. *Private conduct.*

Every police officer must remember that he is a public official 24 hours a day. Conduct on and off the job must be above reproach.

Article 7. *Conduct toward the public.*

An exemplary officer always remembers that he is a public servant. Hence, he cannot be overbearing or subservient.

Article 8. *Conduct in arresting and dealing with violators.*

Every officer must refrain from undue use of force or violation of the civil rights of the public.

Article 9. *Gifts and favors.*

No officer may accept gratuities and gifts from the public. Nothing must influence his mind or interfere with the administration of justice.

Article 10. *Presentation of evidence.*

During investigations, police must seek the facts and must obtain the truth. They must defend the innocent as well as enforce the law; and gather the evidence against the wrongdoer.

Article 11. *Attitude toward profession.*

The officer today must regard his duties as a public trust; should strive for the professional attitude; should help present a good image of police to the public; should endeavor to improve himself and his department.

UNETHICAL ACTS

In order to cover every aspect of the problems involving police ethics, the characteristics of the negative side, reflecting unethical acts to be avoided, are listed as follows:

1. Dishonesty
2. Brutality
3. Racial prejudice
4. Gratuities and chiseling
5. Conversion of prisoner's property
6. Violations of laws and regulations
7. Violations of civil rights; false arrest; illegal search and seizures
8. Discourteous conduct
9. Deliberate inefficiency
10. Failure to improve
11. Divulging confidential information
12. Malicious gossip
13. Violation of privileged communications

The most practical solution for the prevention of unethical activity on the part of law enforcement officers involves the judicious screening and selection of new personnel; the continual practical training of all officers, stressing public relations and ethical conduct; and the prompt dismissal of those officers who are not able to abide by the rules and regulations of the police profession.

QUESTIONS

1. Define "police ethics."
2. Discuss law enforcement as a profession.
3. What is meant by the phrase "code of ethics"?
4. What are the objectives of a code of ethics?
5. Name the organization that has developed a model code of ethics for adoption by police agencies in the United States.
6. Discuss the canons of ethics promulgated by the International Association of Chiefs of Police.
7. Enumerate police activities that are considered unethical.
8. What is the most practical solution to the prevention of unethical activity on the part of law enforcement officers?

Appendix A
Police science
glossary

Police science students should become familiar with the terminology used in connection with crime, courts, and criminal procedure. It is recommended that such students become conversant with the definitions and spellings of the following list of words:

Abet	To encourage, incite, or assist another to commit a crime.
Abortion	The crime of abortion is the illegal procuring of a miscarriage. Specific intent is required.
Abrogate	To annul, repeal, or cancel, such as to repeal a former law by legislative act or by usage.
Abscond	To depart from the jurisdiction of the courts; to hide, conceal, or absent oneself with the intent of avoiding legal process.
Accessory	Any person who, while not actually present, assists in a criminal act or one who aids or shelters an offender in order to defeat justice.
Acquitted	Set free, discharged, found not guilty of a crime.
Admission	A statement made by a person that can be used in evidence against him.
Adultery	The act of sexual intercourse between two

	people, at least one of whom is married to someone else.
Affidavit	A sworn statement made before a person who has the legal authority to administer an oath.
Affirmation	A solemn declaration made before an authorized magistrate by persons who conscientiously decline taking an oath. In law, it is equal to an oath.
Affray	The fighting of two or more persons in a public place, to the terror of others.
Alias	A name used instead of the real name of the person.
Alibi	An excuse in which the accused insists that he was in another place at the time an alleged crime was committed.
Alienist	A specialist in the treating of diseases of the mind.
Amend	To correct an error or deficiency.
Appeal	A complaint in a superior court of an injustice or error committed by an inferior court. The superior court above is called upon to correct or reverse the judgment or decision of the inferior court.
Arraignment	A legal procedure whereby a court informs a defendant of the charges against him, ascertains if defendant is the person wanted, advises defendant of his legal rights, and asks for his plea.
Arrest	The taking of a person into custody in a manner authorized by law.
Arson	The malicious and intentional burning of property specified in the statute.
Asportation	The carrying away of goods. This is one of the conditions required to constitute the crime of larceny.
Assault	An unlawful attempt coupled with the present ability to commit violent injury on the person of another.
Attempt	A try to commit a crime. Often, the attempt alone is punishable by law.
Attestation	The act of witnessing the signature or execution of a deed or other instrument and of sub-

274 *Introduction to police science*

	scribing the name of the witness in testimony of such fact.
Autopsy	The dissection of a dead human body by an authorized person in order to determine the cause of death.
Axiom	In logic, a self-evident truth.
Bail	Security required to guarantee appearance of a person for trial at a later date so that he can be released from prison.
Bailee	The person for whom bail is given.
Bailor	The person who originally furnishes the bail.
Ballistics	The science of projectiles. The use of guns, shells, powder marks, and bullets in tests as a means of criminal identification.
Barrister	An attorney or a lawyer admitted to practice law. In England, a common word used to describe a lawyer who can practice in any court.
Battery	The unlawful use of force by one person upon another; this includes beating, wounding, and touching, no matter how trifling, of another's person or clothes in an angry, insolent, or hostile manner. Legally the offense may be a civil wrong, a tort, or a criminal offense.
Bench warrant	A warrant issued by a court of law. A process for the arrest of the party against whom an indictment has been found. Generally issued by the judge when an individual fails to appear in answer to a court request.
Bequeath	To leave or to give personal property by will.
Bias	To foster prejudice; also the tendency to favor and support a certain point of view.
Bigamy	The act of marrying one person while married to another.
Blackmail	To extort money by threats of exposure to public accusation, censure, or disgrace; also money extorted from one by threats of exposure, force, and fear.
Bogus	False; not genuine.
Bona fide	In good faith or with good faith.
Bribery	Act of giving or taking a favor with a view to corrupting the conduct of a person in a position of trust.

$\frac{1}{6}$

Burglary	Forcible entry into any house, store, or building with intent to commit larceny or felony. The intent does not have to be executed.
Catalepsy	A seizure in which consciousness is lost and the muscles become rigid.
Circumstantial evidence	Conditions and surroundings from which the existence of the main fact may be inferred logically and reasonably.
Coercion	The act of forcing someone to commit a crime.
Collusion	A deceitful agreement or compact between two or more persons for one party to bring an action against another for some evil purpose or to defraud a third person of his rights.
Commitment	A court order that officially directs the taking of a person to a jail, prison, or institution.
Common law	Unwritten law as derived chiefly from the laws of England. The common law has been superseded by statute in most of our states.
Complaint	A charge made to a court of law that a crime has been committed.
Compounding	An act by which a person having knowledge of the actual commission of a crime takes some reward or forbears to assist in the prosecution of a criminal or allows him to escape.
Concussion	A violent shock to some part of the human body caused by a heavy blow.
Confession	A voluntary statement by an accused person acknowledging that he committed a crime.
Conspiracy	A criminal partnership wherein two or more persons agree to commit a crime. An act of preparation will suffice.
Contempt	Willful disregard of the order or process of the court. It is an act against the dignity of the court.
Contraband	Merchandise which the law forbids to be sold or purchased, imported or exported.
Contusion	A bruise on some part of the human body.
Conveyance	A carrier such as a taxi, bus, or private vehicle. Also, in law, an instrument in writing by which property or title to property is transferred from one person to another.

Conviction	A ruling by a court that a person is guilty of the crime alleged.
Coroner	An officer whose duty is to determine the cause of violent or unusual death.
Coroner's jury	A jury appointed by a coroner to determine the cause of death.
Corpus delicti	The basic facts necessary to prove the commission of a crime.
Corroboration	Additional evidence to confirm or support the testimony of a witness.
Counterfeit	To make an imitation of something genuine such as a coin without lawful authority and with intent to deceive.
Credibility	The extent of worthiness of belief.
Crime	A public offense against the state, punishable upon conviction.
Cross examination	The questioning of a previously examined witness in the same matter by the side that did not produce him as a witness.
Demurrer	A reply to an accusation. Although not a denial, the reply states that the accusation itself is defective or legally faulty.
Deposition	A written statement signed and sworn to and obtained through questions and answers.
Direct examination	The examination of a witness by the party producing the witness.
Dirk	A kind of dagger.
Disorderly conduct	Conduct offensive to and incompatible with good morals and public decency.
Docket	A book kept by the clerk of court containing a list of the cases to be tried.
Double jeopardy	The danger which a person is exposed to when being tried the second time for the same offense.
Duress	Restraint by force on a person to do something against his will.
Embezzlement	The taking by a person of money or other property entrusted to him.
Entrapment	The act by police of inducing a person to commit a crime not contemplated by him for the purpose of prosecuting him. The idea of the crime originates with the police.

(9

Evidence	All the means by which an alleged fact is established or disproved. Evidence consists of testimony of witnesses, documents, and other physical matter that can be seen. Evidence may be direct, real, and circumstantial.
Execution	The act of complying with court orders against a person or his property. Also, the death of a person by the state for a capital offense.
Ex post facto	After the fact; pertains to a law that is designed to punish acts that were committed before the passage of the law.
Extradition	The process of returning an accused or convicted person to a state in which he is wanted by another state.
False imprisonment	Any unlawful violation of the personal liberty or freedom of another.
False pretense	A deceitful and fraudulent act used to gain money or other property owned by another unlawfully.
Felony	A major crime that is punishable by death or imprisonment in a state or Federal prison.
Fence	A person who knowingly receives stolen property to aid in its disposition.
Fiduciary	One who holds property or goods in trust for another.
Fine	A money penalty for committing an unlawful act, such as a traffic violation.
Forfeiture	The loss of goods or other property as a punishment for a criminal act.
Forgery	The false making or altering of a writing, such as a check or other instrument, with intent to defraud.
Fornication	Unlawful sexual intercourse on the part of an unmarried person.
Fratricide	The act of one who murders or kills his own brother or sister.
Gaming	A contract between persons by which they gamble with dice, cards, or other contrivances.
Garnishee	A party in whose hands money or property is attached by the creditor of another and who

	has had warning of garnishment not to pay or deliver it to the defendant.
Garnishment	A warning to a person who holds the attached property or money of another not to pay or deliver it to the defendant but to appear and answer the plaintiff's suit.
Genetics	The study of origins. In biology, the study of the transmission of characteristics of organisms by heredity.
Grand jury	A body of persons sworn to inquire into crimes and bring accusations, known as indictments, against suspected criminals.
Gross negligence	Obvious failure to exercise care demanded by circumstances.
Habeas corpus	A writ commanding a person having another in his custody to produce the detained person before a court.
Habitual criminal	A person sentenced to prison for a long term or for life because of two or more previous convictions.
Hearsay	Information received indirectly such as evidence which a witness had heard from others but which did not originate with him.
Homicide	The killing of a human being by another human being.
Incest	The crime of intermarriage or sexual relations between persons related within the degrees of consanguinity in which marriage is prohibited by law.
Indictment	An indictment is a formal charge of crime based on legal testimony of witnesses and the concurring judgment of the grand jury. If approved by the grand jury, it is presented to the court as a "true bill."
Information	An accusation or complaint of a crime, presented by the district attorney to the court. The grand jury is not involved.
Inquest	A judicial inquiry by a court or coroner into the cause of sudden or unusual death.
Judgment	The sentence or final order of a court in a civil or criminal proceeding. The official declaration by a court of the result of a lawsuit.

Judicial notice	The notice a judge takes of facts of common knowledge which it is not necessary to prove, such as existence and boundaries of a city.
Kidnapping	The forcible stealing, taking, enticing, or carrying away of a human being for the purpose of extorting money or property.
Kleptomaniac	A person with an uncontrollable, morbid impulse to steal.
Larceny	The crime of intentionally taking and carrying away the property of another person against his will.
Libel	A malicious defamation expressed in writing or by signs or pictures tending to blacken the memory of a dead person or the reputation of a living person.
Lottery	A scheme or device for the distribution of prizes by chance among the buyers of the chances.
Lynching	The taking, by a mob, of any person from the lawful custody of a peace officer. (Legal def.)
Magistrate	A judge, usually of a lower court. A justice of the peace is a magistrate.
Malice	A wish to vex, annoy, or injure another. An evil state of mind leading to the intentional performance of a wrongful act.
Malicious mischief	Maliciously injuring or destroying any real or personal property.
Manslaughter	The unlawful killing of a person without malice; usually through negligence or in heat of passion.
Mayhem	The maiming of a person by maliciously and willfully depriving him of the use of a part of his body, such as putting out an eye.
Misdemeanor	Any crime not a felony is a misdemeanor. This is a lesser crime, usually punishable by county jail sentence or a money fine.
Misprision	The concealment of a crime, especially of treason or a felony.
Mittimus	An order by a judge to an officer directing him to take a person to a jail.
Modus operandi	The method of operation of a criminal.

Moulage	A plaster cast used to preserve physical evidence such as a tire track or footprint.
Murder	The unlawful killing of a human being with malice aforethought.
Nolle prosequi	A formal statement by a district attorney that he will not prosecute a criminal charge.
Nolo contendere	A plea by a defendant in a criminal action that he will not contest the accusation. It is not an admission of guilt.
Non compos mentis	Mentally unsound.
Nuisance	A condition which annoys, vexes, or interferes with the use of property by others, such as smell, noise, or a health hazard.
Obstructing justice	The crime of interfering with the activities of those who seek justice in a court or of those who have the power or duty of administering justice or enforcing the law.
Ordinance	A law, order, or decree of a municipal body such as a city or county.
Overt act	An open act from which intent to commit a crime can be implied.
Parole	The conditional release from prison of a person who has served part of his sentence in an institution.
Penal	A word pertaining to punishment for crime, e.g., penal institution or penal code.
Perjury	The willful giving of false testimony while under oath.
Petit jury	A trial jury. It is not a grand jury.
Plea	An allegation made by either party in a case. The defendant may plead guilty or not guilty.
Police power	The broad power under which the state can restrain private rights for the general welfare of the people. Authority delegated to the police by the people.
Posse	A force of men called by a sheriff to assist him in pursuing a criminal, quelling a riot, or making an arrest.
Post mortem	After death; pertains to an expert examination, called an autopsy, to determine the cause of death.

Preliminary examination	A hearing before a magistrate to decide if an accused person should be held on a criminal charge and whether or not a crime was actually committed.
Presentment	A report made by a grand jury and presented to the court concerning some wrongdoing.
Presumption	The inference of a fact. It is assumed that an act is so until proved to the contrary. The presumption of innocence is an example.
Prima facie	At first view; the evidence which, unless contradicted, is enough to establish a fact.
Principal	Any person involved in the criminal act, whether it be a felony or a misdemeanor.
Privileged communication	Conversation that may not be introduced in evidence, as communication between husband and wife or with a priest, doctor, or lawyer.
Probation	A method of permitting a convicted person to stay out of jail, instead of imprisoning him, on condition that he observe specific terms.
Process	A judicial writ or order issued by a court, such as a summons, citation, or subpoena.
Prosecution	Proceedings in court conducted by the district attorney.
Psychotic	A person who loses adequate contact with reality and must be institutionalized.
Rape	Act of sexual intercourse with a female, not the wife of the perpetrator, accomplished by force, fear, or deceit; or with a person under 18 or mentally ill.
Receiver	A person who knowingly buys or receives stolen merchandise from a thief.
Recidivist	A habitual criminal; one who has been convicted more than once of a crime, misdemeanor, or delinquency; most aptly describes a confirmed criminal such as a repeater.
Relevant	In the law of evidence, relevant means relating to the case at hand; pertinent, meaningful, and having to do with the matter before the court.
Replevin	The recovery of goods claimed to have been wrongfully seized. The owner gets the property back by a writ or court order.

Repression	The act of rechecking or keeping under restraint or control.
Reprieve	A delay in the execution of a sentence.
Repudiate	To reject; to refuse to acknowledge or to pay.
Res adjudicata	A case that has been tried in a court of law. The matter has been legally adjudicated.
Res gestae	Things done; refers to the entire transaction or event. Includes words and acts done immediately after the incident which are usually spontaneous and are considered to be part of the act or event.
Restitution	The act of restoring and returning a thing or its value to the lawful owner.
Rigor mortis	The stiffening of the muscles of the body after death.
Riot	Disturbance of the peace by two or more persons acting together and without the authority of law. More specifically, in criminal law, the violent disturbance of the peace, actually executed in a wild and turbulent manner, by *three* or more persons assembled without the authority of the law and with the intent mutually to assist each other in accomplishing a private objective.
Robbery	The felonious taking of personal property in the possession of another, from his person or immediate presence, and against his will. Accomplished by means of force and fear.
Rout	Two or more persons, assembled and acting together, making any attempt or advance toward the commission of an act which would be a riot if actually committed.
Sabotage	The willful obstruction of and interference with the normal processes of government and industry.
Search warrant	A written order by a justice or magistrate authorizing an officer of the law to search a specific area for certain unlawful goods concealed in a house, store, or other premises. The recovered personal property, if any, is brought before the court for legal disposition.
Secrete	To conceal or hide away.

Sedition	An offense against the government of a country, not capital and not amounting to treason, consisting of attempts made by meetings, speeches, or publications to disturb the tranquillity of the state or excite discontent against the government.
Squatter	One who settles on another's land without title or authority.
Statute	An act of the Legislature of a state declaring, commanding, or prohibiting something. Statute law is the express written will of the Legislature, rendered authentic by certain prescribed forms.
Subornation of perjury	The offense of willfully procuring another person to commit perjury.
Subpoena	A writ commanding the attendance or appearance of a witness or party in court, or before a judicial officer, under a penalty in case of disobedience.
Subpoena duces tecum	A writ commanding a person to produce legal papers in court.
Subrogation	The substitution of one person in the place of another as a creditor with the new creditor succeeding to the rights of the other.
Summons	A writ directed to a sheriff requiring him to summon a defendant to appear in court to answer a plaintiff's actions.
Theft	The wrongful or fradulent taking and carrying away by any person of the personal goods of another from any place, without any right to deprive the owner of his property permanently.
Tort	A civil wrong independent of a contract.
Trespass	Invasion of another person's rights or territory; also to enter unlawfully upon another person's land.
Usury	Interest in excess of a legal rate established by law.
Utter	To publish; to circulate; to express publicly.
Venue	Geographical location. The place or county in which an injury is declared to have been done.

Verdict	The finding of a jury in favor of one or the other party to an action at law.
Void	Of no force or effect; absolutely null; unable to be confirmed or made effectual.
Willfully	Describes the way in which a person purposefully and willingly commits an act or an omission. Having intent to violate the law or injure another is not required.
Writ	A judicial instrument by which a court commands some act to be done by the person to whom it is directed.

4

Appendix B
Words frequently
misspelled in
police reports

accident
acknowledge
acknowledgment
address
adjustment
administration
alcohol
alkali
ammunition
annual
antiseptic
application
arraignment
arrest
artery
artificial
assistance
authorize
auxiliary
beyond
bichloride

boulevard
boundary
bruise
bureau
business
canceled
capillary
careful
certificate
chauffeur
chief
commercial
commissioner
compensation
complaint
compress
consent
constable
conviction
coroner
damage

dazzling
delinquent
designated
device
diesel
discipline
dislocation
district
division
duplicate
embezzled
emergency
employee
equipment
evidence
felony
fiscal
foreign
forfeiture
fracture
guest

guilty	muscle	sheriff
height	narcotics	signal
hemorrhage	negligence	siren
husbandry	night	skeleton
immediately	obstructed	specify
implement	occasion	spine
imprisonment	operator	sprain
incised	passenger	statistics
infected	patrol	strength
injury	pedestrian	stripped
intersection	pelvis	supplies
intoxicated	penalty	surface
iodine	personal	suspend
judge	physician	symptom
judgment	pneumatic	temporary
jurisdiction	poison	testimony
justice	possession	tetanus
knowledge	prohibit	through
lacerated	propelled	tourniquet
liability	prosecution	traffic
license	prosecutor	transfer
liquor	reckless	valid
magistrate	registration	vehicle
maintenance	renewal	vein
Mercurochrome	report	violation
minor	residence	which
miscellaneous	resident	width
misdemeanor	respiration	wound
mobile	revocation	wreck
motorcycle	revoke	
municipal	right	

Appendix C
Common
abbreviations
useful in
police reports

Asst.	Assistant
Capt.	Captain
C.O.	City Ordinance
Co.	County
Dept.	Department
Dist.	District
D.M.V.	Department of Motor Vehicles
D.O.B.	Date of Birth
D.O.T.	Direction of Travel
D.P.O.B.	Date, Place of Birth
Hdqrs.	Headquarters
Inf.	Informant
Insp.	Inspector
Lt.	Lieutenant
M.O.	*Modus Operandi*
P.C.	Penal Code
P.O.B.	Place of Birth
P.O.E.	Point of Entry
P.O.I.	Point of Impact
P.O.R.	Point of Rest
R.P.	Reporting Person

Sgt.	Sergeant
Subj.	Subject
Susp.	Suspect
T.C.	Traffic Collision
T.O.	Traffic Officer
V., Vict.	Victim
V.C.	Vehicle Code
Viol.	Violation
W.F.A.	White Female Adult
W.F.J.	White Female Juvenile
W.M.A.	White Male Adult
W.M.J.	White Male Juvenile

Appendix D
Police training films

(Suggested film list for college police science course entitled Introduction to Law Enforcement)

A Day in the Life of a California Highway Patrolman. This is a 15-minute, 16-millimeter sound film in color. It is available from the California highway patrol at Sacramento or at its various headquarters throughout the state. Also, this film may be purchased or rented from Charles Cahill & Associates, Inc., 5746 Sunset Boulevard, Hollywood, California, 90028.

A Day with the FBI. For about 17 minutes this black-and-white 16-millimeter sound film will keep any audience interested, for it is an exciting portrayal of a day in the work of the FBI. Several actual cases and their solutions, through the use of the FBI laboratory, scientific techniques, and police cooperation, are illustrated. Reservations may be made through local FBI offices.

Badge of Protection. Although this 30-minute black-and-white 16-millimeter film is a long one, it is nevertheless well worth studying. It presents an overall view of the operations of the Los Angeles County

Sheriff's Department. Reservations may be made through the Los Angeles County Sheriff's Department.

Careers in Law Enforcement. This is an excellent 16-millimeter sound film, in color and 16 minutes in length. It depicts the role of police, deputy sheriffs, and highway patrolmen. It answers many questions concerning the duties of law enforcement officers. For information concerning career orientation in law enforcement, the film is unsurpassed. Reservations for rental or purchase may be made through the Peace Officers' Association of California, 804 Forum Building, Sacramento, California, 95814.

Public Relations. This 16-millimeter sound, black-and-white film is 17 minutes in duration. It emphasizes the importance of obtaining the public goodwill of all organizations and businesses. Reservations may be made at the Los Angeles County Sheriff's Office.

Boosting Is a Business. This is a 24-minute, 16-millimeter sound film, in color. Many of the techniques employed by successful shoplifters are shown in a training film for store personnel as well as for peace officers. This is not an attempt to suggest security measures but a practical demonstration of the wide variety of methods used by professional and amateur thieves in fleecing merchants. Reservations for rental or purchase may be made through the Peace Officers' Association of California, 804 Forum Building, Sacramento, California, 95814.

Defensive Driving Techniques. A road test from Chicago to Evanston, Illinois, between an "offensive" and a "defensive" driver proves that the seconds or minutes saved by aggressive "jack-rabbit" driving can never offset the accumulated traffic violations nor the ridiculous exposure to loss of life and property. This is a 16-millimeter, 12-minute, color film, produced in cooperation with the Chicago and Evanston Police Departments, National Safety Council, and Chicago Citizens Traffic Safety Board. It is produced and distributed by Charles Cahill & Associates, Inc., 5746 Sunset Blvd., Hollywood, California, 90028.

Two excellent films are planned by the California Peace Officers' Association for 1966. They are entitled "Public Relations" and "Using a Police Car Safely."

Appendix E
References and
bibliography

Abrahamson, David, M.D.: *The Psychology of Crime,* Columbia University Press, New York, 1960, pp. 1–13.

Alexander, Franz, M.D., and Hugo Staub: *The Criminal, the Judge, and the Public,* The Free Press of Glencoe, New York, 1956.

Barnes, Harry Elmer, and Negley K. Teeter: *New Horizons in Criminology,* Prentice-Hall, Inc., Englewood Cliffs, N.J., 1947.

Baughman, U. E.: *United States Secret Service, What It Is and What It Does,* Government Printing Office, Washington, D.C., 1958.

Bloch, Herbert A.: *Crime in America,* Philosophical Library, Inc., New York, 1961, chap. 22, pp. 315–329.

Career Opportunities, New York Life Insurance Co., New York, September, 1962.

Cavan, Ruth Shonle: *Criminology,* 2d ed., Thomas Y. Crowell Company, New York, 1958.

Chapman, Samuel G.: *The Police Heritage in England and America,* The Michigan State University Press, East Lansing, Mich., 1962.

Clift, Raymond E.: *A Guide to Modern Police Thinking,* W. H. Anderson Co., Cincinnati, 1956.

Cuthbert, C. R. M.: *Science and the Detection of Crime,* Hutchinson & Co. (Publishers), Ltd., London, 1958, p. 190.

Dulaney, Don E., Jr., Russel L. DeValois, David C. Beardslee, and Marion R. Winterbottom: *Contribution to Modern Psychology,* Oxford University Press, Fair Lawn, N.J., 1963.

Earle, Howard H.: *Contract Law Enforcement Services by the County of Los Angeles Sheriff's Department,* University of Southern California Press, Los Angeles, 1960.

Federal Career Directory, U.S. Civil Service Commission, Washington, D.C., 1963.

Findlay, Allyn Bruce, and Esther Blair Findlay: *Your Rugged Constitution,* Stanford University Press, Stanford, Calif., 1952.

Gammage, Allen Z.: *Your Future in Law Enforcement,* Richard Rosen Press, Inc., New York, 1961.

Germann, A. C., Frank D. Day, and Robert J. Gallati: *Introduction to Law Enforcement,* Charles C Thomas, Publisher, Springfield, Ill., 1962.

Gocke, B. W.: *Police Sergeants Manual,* Legal Book Store, Los Angeles, 1960.

Gourley, G. Douglas: *Public Relations and the Press,* Charles C Thomas, Publisher, Springfield, Ill., 1953.

Hibbert, Christopher: *The Roots of Evil,* Little, Brown and Company, Boston, 1963.

Holcomb, Richard L.: *The Police and the Public,* Institute of Public Affairs, State University of Iowa, Iowa City, Iowa, 1950.

Hollingsworth, Dan: *Rocks in the Roadway,* Stomberg Allen and Company, Chicago, 1954.

Hoover, J. Edgar: *The Science of Fingerprints,* Government Printing Office, Washington, D.C., 1957.

Horton, Paul B., and Gerald R. Leslie: *The Sociology of Social Problems,* Appleton-Century-Crofts, Inc., New York, 1955.

Inbau, Fred E., and John E. Reid: *Lie Detection and the Criminal Interrogation,* The Williams & Wilkins Company, Baltimore, 1953, pp. 5–8.

Kooken, Don L.: *Ethics in Police Service,* Charles C Thomas, Publisher, Springfield, Ill., 1957.

Korn, Richard R., and Lloyd W. McCorkle: *Criminology and Penology,* Holt, Rinehart and Winston, Inc., New York, 1959.

Leonard, V. A.: *The Police of the 20th Century,* The Foundation Press, Inc., Brooklyn, 1964.

Morris, Albert: *Criminology,* Longmans, Green & Co., Inc., New York, 1934, pp. 105–106.

Municipal Police Administration, The International City Manager's Association, Chicago, 1964.

Ottenberg, Miriam: *The Federal Investigators*, Pocket Books, Inc., New York, 1963.

Parker, William H.: *Parker on Police*, Charles C Thomas, Publisher, Springfield, Ill., 1957.

Peper, John P.: *A Recruit Asks Some Questions*, Charles C Thomas, Publisher, Springfield, Ill., 1954.

Reckless, Walter C.: *The Crime Problem*, Appleton-Century-Crofts, Inc., New York, 1955.

Reiwald, Paul: *Society and Its Criminals*, International Universities Press, Inc., New York, 1950.

Schmeck, Harold M., Jr.: "Gene Probe of the Amish," *Los Angeles Herald Examiner*, p. A-13, New York Times News Service, Aug. 14, 1964.

Seares, Robert S.: "The Police Cadet," *The Annals of the American Academy of Political and Social Science*, vol. 291, p. 107, January, 1954.

Smith, Bruce: *Police Systems in the United States*, Harper & Row, Publishers, Incorporated, New York, 1940, 1949.

Tappan, Paul W.: *Juvenile Delinquency*, McGraw-Hill Book Company, New York, 1949.

Tully, Andrew: *Treasury Agent*, Simon and Schuster, Inc., New York, 1958.

Uniform Crime Reports, U.S. Department of Justice, Federal Bureau of Investigation, Washington, D.C., 1960–1965.

Vedder, Clyde B., Samuel Koenig, and Robert E. Clark: *Criminology, a Book of Readings*, Holt, Rinehart and Winston, Inc., New York, 1953.

Vollmer, August: *The Criminal*, The Foundation Press, Inc., Brooklyn, 1949.

Waltz, George H., Jr.: *What Do You Want to Be*, Holt, Rinehart and Winston, Inc., New York, 1939.

Whaley, Henry F., and Tom MacPherson: *Find a Career in Law Enforcement*, G. P. Putnam's Sons, New York, 1961.

Wilson, O. W.: *Police Administration*, 2d ed., McGraw-Hill Book Company, New York, 1963.

Index

Private security forces, companies employing, 74, 75
  differences between public and private police, 75
  distinction between private patrolman and watchman, 73
  duties of, 71, 72
  history of, 69, 70
  restrictions of, 76, 77
  salaries, 73, 74
  special agents of, 71, 72
Probation, 117
  condition of, 118, 119
  definition of, 117
  presentence investigation, 117, 118
Probation officer, 67
  duties of, 67
  education and experience of, 68
  opportunities of, 65, 67, 68
  salaries, 67, 68
  women as, 66
Psychopaths, 93, 94
  criminal tendencies of, 93, 94
Psychotics, 95, 96
Public relations, 246–248
  definition of, 249
  importance of, 247, 248
  improving of, 250
    attitude, 254
    conduct off duty, 255
    courtesy, 253, 254
    empathy, 251, 252
    equipment, 253
    gratuities, 255–257
    honesty, 258

Public relations, improving of, personal appearance, 250, 251
    reception at headquarters, 258
    smile, 254
    social outlets, 257
  undermining of, 259
    favoritism, 259
    lavishing attention on women, 260, 261
    overbearing attitude, 259
    projecting wrong impression, 261
    unpleasant tone of voice, 259
    using police cars indiscriminately, 260
Pyromaniac, 94

Reckless, Walter, 91, 92
Records of police department, 183, 184
  mug shots, 183, 184
Reeve, 125, 131
Reports of police department, 184
  daily log, 184
  daily reports, 183
  recording of, 184, 185
  (*see also* Uniform crime reporting)
Reprieve, 120
Romans, law of, 123, 124
Rotation in police administration, 186
Rowan, Colonel John, 134
Runnymede, U.S.A., 128

Socio-psychological classifi-
cation of criminal types,
white-collar, 91
Specialization in police admin-
istration, 186
Speech, freedom of, 130
Spelling list of misspelled
words, 286, 287
Staff, officer of, 166
Star Chamber, 130
State highway patrols, 149, 150
State law enforcement, 37, 42
State police, authority of, 149
Statutory law, 109

Tort, 109
Traffic, control of, 175
officer of, 213–215
policy of, 205
Training of police, 236
basic, 236–245
courses for, 234, 236–238
essentials of, 223
Federal, 230
films, 290, 291
highway patrol, 232
in-service, 233
local, 232, 233
methods of, 226
need for, 225
schools for, 190, 233
state, 230, 231
types of, 232, 233
Training officer, 216–218
Transvestite, 93
Trial by ordeal, 126, 128
Truncheon (nightstick), 127,
135

Tuns, 125
Tything, 125
Tythingman, 125, 127

Uniform crime reporting, 96
classification of crimes, 96,
100–102
FBI uniform crime reports,
97, 98
history of, 96, 97
objectives of, 100
Part I offenses, 100, 101
Part II offenses, 100, 102, 103
report forms of, 103
role of police in, 103
stolen property, value in, 103
uniform crime statistics of,
10, 96
uses of, 97
U.S. Department of Agriculture, 154
U.S. Department of Defense,
153
U.S. Department of the Interior, 153
U.S. Department of Justice, 46,
152, 153, 228
Federal Bureau of Investigation, 46–48
U.S. Immigration and Naturalization Service, 48
Border Patrol, work of, 48
duties of, 48
job requirements of, 49
physical requirements of, 49
qualifications of, 49
salaries and benefits of, 49
training of, 50